The Battle of

The Battle of Maldon

*War and Peace in
Tenth-Century England*

Mark Atherton

BLOOMSBURY ACADEMIC
LONDON • NEW YORK • OXFORD • NEW DELHI • SYDNEY

BLOOMSBURY ACADEMIC
Bloomsbury Publishing Plc
50 Bedford Square, London, WC1B 3DP, UK
1385 Broadway, New York, NY 10018, USA

BLOOMSBURY, BLOOMSBURY ACADEMIC and the Diana logo are trademarks of
Bloomsbury Publishing Plc

First published in Great Britain 2021

A catalogue record for this book is available from the British Library.

Library of Congress Cataloging-in-Publication Data
Names: Atherton, Mark, author.
Title: The Battle of Maldon: war and peace in tenth-century England / Mark Atherton.
Description: London; New York: Bloomsbury Academic, 2020. |
Includes bibliographical references and index.
Identifiers: LCCN 2020033458 (print) | LCCN 2020033459 (ebook) |
ISBN 9781784537913 (hardback) | ISBN 9781350134034 (paperback) |
ISBN 9781350167490 (epub) | ISBN 9781350167483 (ebook)
Subjects: LCSH: Maldon (Anglo-Saxon poem) | War poetry, English (Old)–
History and criticism. | Maldon, Battle of, England, 991, in literature.
Classification: LCC PR1594 .A84 2020 (print) | LCC PR1594 (ebook) | DDC 829/.1–dc23
LC record available at https://lccn.loc.gov/2020033458
LC ebook record available at https://lccn.loc.gov/2020033459

ISBN: HB: 978-1-7845-3791-3
PB: 978-1-3501-3403-4
ePDF: 978-1-3501-6748-3
eBook: 978-1-3501-6749-0

Typeset by Deanta Global Publishing Services, Chennai, India
Printed and bound in Great Britain

To find out more about our authors and books visit www.bloomsbury.com
and sign up for our newsletters.

For my mother Brenda Atherton (1934–2007)
and my father Nigel Atherton (1931–2020)

Contents

Illustrations

Figures

Maps

Acknowledgements

The following friends and colleagues have read chapters or sections of this book and/or offered advice and suggestions, which have all been very gratefully received: Helen Appleton, Hannah Bailey, Stephen Baxter, Rachel Burns, Julie Dyson, Rob Ellis, Mark Griffith, Peter Grybauskas, Tony Harris, Susannah Jayes, Kazutomo Karasawa, Simon Keynes, Eric Lacey, Alex Larman, Stuart Lee, Francis Leneghan, Richard North, Andy Orchard, Rafael Pascual, Eleni Ponirakis, Lynn Robson, Lucinda Rumsey, Daniel Thomas, Julian Thompson, Erik Tonning , George Wright. All errors are mine and not theirs. Julie gave the closest support, and a camera, and she even purchased a car, which was invaluable for field work: we are grateful for hospitality from our friends Trace and Diane Horsman, and Simon and Julie Watson, who gave us board and lodging as we travelled the breadth and depth of East Anglia and Essex.

Map 1 Map of tenth-century England. © Reginald Piggott and Simon Keynes.

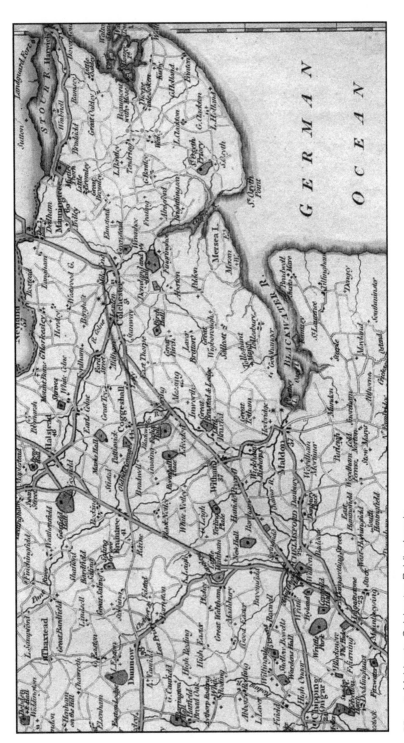

Map 2 Maldon to Colchester. Public domain.

Introduction

The importance of *The Battle of Maldon*

Feoll þa to foldan fealohilte swurd

(THE BATTLE OF MALDON, 166)¹

[It fell to the earth – the golden-hilted sword]

A rich heirloom – a nobleman's sword – lying on the ground of what the poem *The Battle of Maldon* calls 'Æthelred's kingdom' (53) is a telling image of what happened on a day in August in the year 991. The English – contemporary chroniclers identify the army as the East Saxon defence-force – lost a pitched battle against a force of Viking raiders, but many of the English fought to the end, and the wealth of England lay in the dust of the field. Indeed, the adjective 'golden-hilted', as used in the poem, is *fealo-hilte*, which is connected by alliteration and half-rhyme with *feoll*, 'fell'. And the colour-word *fealo*, though it clearly refers to the precious metal of which the hilt of the sword was made, has connotations of autumnal decline and fall. This, then, is the view of the poet in *The Battle of Maldon*, a famous poem from tenth-century England, one of the first expressions in English literature of the idea of national unity, reminiscent, perhaps, of Alfred Lord Tennyson's 'The Charge of the Light Brigade' in the Victorian period. The initial impression is heroic. The poem honours the men who died defending their land against Viking invaders, and it even glorifies the fighting. But on a second reading the reader will see other messages, suggested here in this passage by that double meaning of *fealo*. The essential background is the unification of England, a gradual process which had only relatively recently been completed under King Edgar, who ruled from 959 to 975. His sudden death plunged the country into uncertainty, and Æthelred, the king who eventually succeeded in 978, was a mere child at the time. Viking raiders, who seem to have left the country untouched for two generations, started to return. Now, in the face of Viking invasions from Denmark and Norway, and with the first line of defence shattered, the prosperity and cohesion of the new English kingdom was at stake.

The battle fought at Maldon on the coast of Essex in the year 991 is therefore important for two reasons: as a historical event and as the subject of an influential poem. First, it was a decisive event because it was a shock; it changed attitudes at the English court. It helped to introduce new policies which, at least for a time, served to halt the Viking conquest of England. The cultural renaissance that had accompanied the unification of the English kingdom and the long period of peace under Edgar was able to continue. Secondly, *The Battle of Maldon* as a poem is an important text because it is unique. It expresses very poignantly the cultural concerns and mentalities of the period, particularly of the lesser nobility and the free landowners who feature so prominently as the heroes of the action in the second half of the text. And since the rediscovery of the text in the eighteenth century, its literary value has been recognized; it has become a celebrated poem, part of the canon of English literature: an elegy, a skilfully wrought poem of action, a heroic tale of pride and piety and defiance in defeat.

As we know from the documents of the time, the veteran Byrhtnoth, the governor of the East Saxons (i.e. of Essex and the east of England) and the leading member of the English nobility, fell in the fighting. He was sorely missed. But thereafter Edgar's young son, Æthelred *Unræd*, the notoriously 'ill-advised' king, was forced to mend his wilful ways.[2] Whether he wanted to or not, he had to deal with the Danes or risk going under. And although his temporary success is not widely recognized, nevertheless for a while in the 990s things went well: he restored land that he had appropriated from the churches at Abingdon and Rochester; he appointed new ministers to his royal council; he used financial incentives to persuade the Vikings to leave; he made a treaty with the Viking leader Olaf Tryggvason, who in one chronicle is named with Swegn (Svein) as leader of the Danes at Maldon (for discussion see Chapter 10); in 994 Olaf was even baptized as a Christian, with the English king as his witness and sponsor, and he returned to Scandinavia to become King of Norway, vowing never again to return with hostile intent. Although with hindsight we know that much worse was to come later in Æthelred's reign (he died in 1016), we should not allow this knowledge to colour our judgement. In the 990s Æthelred's good reputation was still secure.[3]

The action of the poem

Since the first page of the poem *The Battle of Maldon* is lost, the reader is thrown mid-sentence into the action: a view of individual members of an English army arriving at the battlefield. The general is making arrangements for the coming battle, and is shortly named as Byrhtnoth, and later described as the grey-haired leader, the earl, King Æthelred's thegn. But here, at the beginning of the text, he rides up and down the ranks advising the men on the tactics that they will employ during the battle: it seems they will fight on foot behind a classic 'war-fence' or 'shield-wall'. As it turns out, they are the East Saxons, preparing to confront the 'ship-army', as they are called, that is, the Vikings, who have landed on the far shore of the tidal river of the Blackwater, or *Pantan stream* (the river Pant) as it is called in the poem. A 'ford' or 'bridge' (both words are used) connects the two shores at low tide. But the tide is rising and in a matter of minutes the sea covers the bridge. Soon a stretch of tidal water separates the two shores.

But now the Viking spokesman appears on the far shore (is this Olaf? we are told neither his name nor his rank). This 'messenger' (Old English *ar*) calls out across the river channel asking for payment of money and wealth, in return for which they will break off their invasion and leave in their ships. Byrhtnoth refuses, and the armies face each other off across the channel. The tide eventually recedes and the fight begins, to the detriment of the Vikings, who cannot get across the well-defended bridge. In a moment of pride, however, termed *ofermod* in the poem, Byrhtnoth allows the 'battle-wolves', that is, the Vikings, 'too much land' (the motif of *land* is significant). In a brief, dramatic speech the English leader invites the Danes to cross the water. At a suitable place, the two armies line up for formal battle.

In the ensuing mêlée, Byrhtnoth is wounded, his golden-hilted sword falls to the earth and he is killed by the Vikings. Seeing this dreadful setback, Godric and his brothers, prominent members of Byrhtnoth's retinue, flee the field, and they are followed by a large proportion of the army. The shield-wall is left incomplete and the Viking 'shipmen' take their chance. They break through the East Saxon ranks; nevertheless, some of Byrhtnoth's men remain, and move forward, but gradually, one by one, two by two, they are cut down. Though they suffer heavy losses too, the Vikings appear to be winning the battle, but the surviving text (which numbers 325 lines) is alas unfinished, for the final page was lost in transmission. The poem, as we have it, closes with these remaining members of the English forces, men from different ranks of society and even different regions of Æthelred's kingdom, each in turn making a set speech vowing to avenge their leader, then moving forward in order to fight on regardless. As this book aims to show, these men are not only East Saxons from Essex: they represent a microcosm of England in the year 991.

The disputed location

There is a very particular fascination with an occasional poem like *Maldon*, for by general consensus it is regarded as having literary value and interest, but it also engages with a real event and presents real, historically attested people. And the reader is presented with the tantalizing prospect of being able to travel to 'the very place' where the action took place. Though there are many difficulties attending such an endeavour, a similar search in the Scandinavian world for the actual places of the epic *Beowulf* and the Norse sagas had the following aim:

> To thicken . . . the reality of the northern world of medieval literature for the reader, to make it accessible to the imagination of those who actively enter into a world when they read a fiction.[4]

This quotation, by the critic and translator Marijane Osborne, is from a project with the carefully chosen title *Landscape of Desire: Partial Stories of the Medieval Scandinavian World*. Her co-author, Gillian R. Overing, writes here of the partiality involved in their task, and the inevitable negotiation required between modern and medieval perceptions of the landscape. With this in mind, but heeding the historian Cyril Hart's warnings about 'earnest speculation' and the 'need to preserve a sense of humour and balance',[5] let us now attempt to identify and locate the setting of *The Battle of Maldon*.

We have seen that the extant poem situates the action on *Pantan stream*. According to historical place-name studies, the name 'Blackwater' is not documented in the historical records until 1477, but upstream of Bocking, near Braintree in central Essex, the river is in fact still called the Pant.[6] This suggests that the older name actually was Pant (which is cognate with Welsh *pant* 'valley' and may be a pre-Roman river-name) and that it once applied to the whole of the river and the estuary. Indeed, there exists one other contemporary mention of the estuary, in a charter of 1046 granting an estate on the western half of the island of Mersea, which also refers to the Blackwater as *Pantan streame*.[7] The Anglo-Saxon Chronicle reports that a Viking invasion force made their way to Mersea in 895 and spent the winter on the island, 'which is out on the sea'; what seems to be implied is that the location at the mouth of the Blackwater made the winter camp very secure and suitable for the rapid deployment of Viking longboats. Since surviving wills demonstrate that the West Mersea estate originally belonged to Byrhtnoth's family, and since there is, even today, an ancient causeway known as 'The Strood' connecting the island to the mainland, it is tempting to consider Mersea as the site of the battle. There are, however, arguments against this, if only because Mersea is much closer to Colchester than to Maldon, which contemporary chronicles name as the location of the fight.

The nearest 'bridge' or causeway to the town of Maldon is, or was, half a mile to the north at Heybridge, the former Roman settlement.[8] At that time, before the construction in 1796 of the navigation canal and a marina at Heybridge Basin, a stretch of the river Blackwater ran in parallel to the Chelmer and so was much closer to Maldon itself – as seen on the old map of Essex of 1777.[9] In the Victorian period, the prominent historian Edward A. Freeman argued that it was here, between the rivers Blackwater and the Chelmer, that Byrhtnoth, arriving from the north, confronted the Vikings.[10]

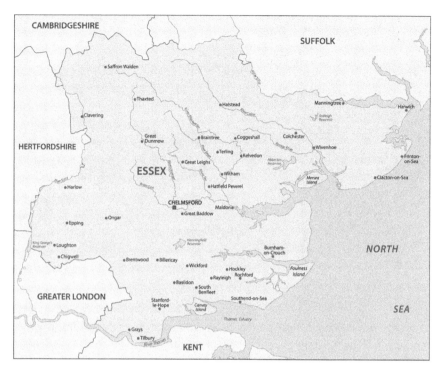

Map 3 Map of rivers of Essex showing Mersea Island. © Shutterstock/Rainer Lesniewski.

In 1992 Cyril Hart revived and adapted this theory: the Vikings left their ships in safe keeping at Mersea island and proceeded by road on the north side of the estuary via Tiptree Heath until they reached Tidwoldingtun – the Old English name of the former Roman town. The 'high bridge' of Heybridge (the thirteenth-century Middle English name being *Heahbregge*) had not yet been built; the older bridge was the *ful brycg* 'the muddy bridge' over the Blackwater and the Chelmer, which was still tidal at this point, hence the foulness from the mud.[11] (The road over the Chelmer is still known as Fullbridge Road.) Hart tentatively located the battle site not where Freeman had it (on the militarily unsuitable salt marsh between the Blackwater and the Chelmer), but closer to the old *burh* or citadel of Maldon itself – where there is firm and level ground away from the salt marshes (he perhaps means the site close to the later Beeleigh Abbey).[12] On this view Byrhtnoth had reached Maldon first, and must have been waiting for the Vikings to arrive.

Freeman's theory, for various reasons, is nowadays discredited, and Hart's reworking of it has fallen on deaf ears. Nearly all commentators in the present day agree that the most suitable location for a cross-channel confrontation between East Saxons and Vikings must be at Northey island, which is two miles to the south-east of the actual town of Maldon, and similarly connected to the

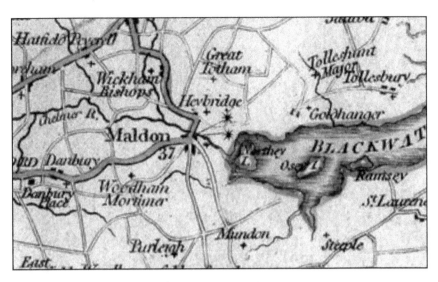

Map 4 Maldon and Heybridge. Public domain.

mainland on the Maldon side by a causeway (the channel of the Blackwater here is now known as Southey Creek).

What is more, studies of the historical topography support this theory.[13] To give credit where it is due, this identification was first made by Laborde in 1925.[14] His insight feels like a revelation, the cunning solution to a literary puzzle in which the details – the tidal setting, the woods behind the battle lines, the original tenth-century alignment of the causeway – all neatly fit. This location fixes the topography of the poem: the East Saxons are on the mainland, the Vikings with their ships are on Northey island.[15] And present-day visitors may visit the site, which is owned by the National Trust, and battle pilgrims and reenactors may cross the causeway at low tide, attempt to shout messages across the creek, or linger and wait on the (suitably safe) mainland side of the channel and watch as the tide surges in and 'the watery streams lock together' (see *Battle of Maldon*, line 66a). Nowadays only an occasional dissident voice warns readers not to take the Northey site too literally as an established fact, just in case this leads to false statements on the content of the poem or its interpretation.[16]

Critical debates

J. R. R. Tolkien's verse drama for radio, *The Homecoming of Beorhtnoth*, was first published in *Essays and Studies* in 1953 and in book form in 1964; it was broadcast on the radio on 3 December 1954. In this imaginary sequel to the Old English poem, Tolkien (who was also a distinguished professor of early medieval

Figure 1 The causeway at Northey Island. © Mark Atherton.

literature) famously presented *Maldon* as a critique of aspects of the heroic way of life; the reader may admire the bravery and loyalty of the men but decry the pride and hubris of the leader, who because of his heroic ambition grants the Vikings leave to cross the river and line up for battle.[17] Young warriors, so Tolkien argues, can afford to take heroic risks and make foolhardy gestures, but kings and leaders have responsibilities to the men they are given to lead. The example would be the hero in *Beowulf*: as a young man he can risk all in his venture against the monster Grendel; as an old man and king of a nation he should have been more cautious about fighting a dragon alone and unaided. In *Homecoming*, two men from Beorhtnoth's household not present at the battle, a young idealist and an old seasoned pragmatist, have been sent by the abbot of Ely to the field to search for the body of the slain ealdorman, the leader of the East Saxon forces. Ely, it should be added, is about seventy miles from Maldon, and perhaps the abbot is taking refuge in Maldon itself. Be that as it may, there has been a delay, and night has long since fallen. The setting therefore, in Tolkien's piece, is the dark night after the battle – there is a comparable scene at the end of his children's novel *The Hobbit*: the bleak aftermath of a battle where everyone has left the field, apart from those who have fallen. The mood is nostalgic, elegiac and ultimately tragic, Tolkien's point being that Beorhtnoth (the name is given an archaic 'Mercian' spelling) had felt constrained to follow the old heroic way of life and had died in pursuit of that goal. It seems that the two characters in *Homecoming* embody a debate over the ethos of the poem *Maldon*. On the one hand there is the young man, son of a minstrel and poet, whose conversation is full of the old legends, the stories of the life of heroes long ago; on the other hand the older man, who has seen service as a warrior, is critical, not quite cynical but certainly very suspicious of the value of such a life. It is tempting to see this debate as taking place between Tolkien's younger self, inspired by the legends of the North at the start of his writing career, and his older self, wiser but also sadder about the folly of all the heroism.[18]

In a kind of surreal dream sequence spoken by the younger man towards the end of *Homecoming* we hear in translation the much-quoted heroic lines from *The Battle of Maldon*. They are spoken there by another old warrior, Byrhtwold, named Beorhtwold in Tolkien's writings on the poem (those who may be unfamiliar with Old English should note that the letters 'þ' and 'ð' represent the same sound as modern English 'th'; so *þe* would be pronounced like a voiceless 'the'):

> Hige sceal þe heardra, heorte þe cenre,
> mod sceal þe mare, þe ure mægen lytlað.

So popular is the sentiment of determination expressed here that line 312 has been adapted from this local poem as the motto for the modern University of Essex (based at Colchester): 'thought the harder, heart the keener'. Here is the version of lines 312–13 in Tolkien's *Homecoming of Beorhtnoth*:

> Heart shall be bolder, harder be purpose,
> More proud the spirit as our power lessens![19]

These lines urge on the remaining men to summon up their courage, though their strength is fading. Tolkien clearly finds this final speech impressive, and in his essay 'On Ofermod', appended to the published version of the drama, he argues that Beorhtwold is in fact quoting from an old poem out of the distant past – it is a quotation rather than an original formulation. As he puts it (p. 124), the old retainer's words are:

> not 'original', but an ancient and honoured expression of heroic will; Beorhtwold is all the more, not the less, likely for that reason to have used them in his last hour.

In brief, then, Tolkien thought the traditional poetry was still strong in the culture of the tenth century; men were steeped in its words and themes and quoted them at suitable moments for guidance. But ultimately it seems their hopes are deluded, and Tolkien gives the final word in *Homecoming* to the monks of Ely, who sing the Christian liturgy: the light in the darkness dispelling the errors of the old way of life. In view of this, Peter Grybauskas has made the interesting suggestion that *Homecoming* serves as a kind of fictional exploration of how a young minstrel came to write the poem *Maldon* in the aftermath of the battle.[20]

Tolkien's interpretation of the poem might be termed 'heroic-tragic': it is heroic because of the courage and will, but tragic because the flaw in the hero leads to his fall. In this way the old ealdorman Beorhtnoth in *Maldon* resembles the old king Beowulf at the end of the poem *Beowulf*, or indeed the characters in Tolkien's fiction such as Thorin Oakenshield in *The Hobbit*, whose greed for gold precipitates his final tragedy, or perhaps Boromir in *The Lord of the Rings*, whose desire for the ring of power overcomes him. For Tolkien, the other key statement in *Maldon* is the narrator's comment at lines 89 and 90:

Ða se eorl ongan for his ofermode
alyfan landes to fela laþere ðeode.

My own, rather literal, translation is as follows:

Then because of his pride, the earl granted
too much land to that hostile nation.

Tolkien, with a keen sense of the implications of word and phrase, chose to interpret *to fela* more idiomatically with the concessive 'as he should not have done':

Then the earl in his overmastering pride actually yielded ground to the enemy, as he should not have done.[21]

And Tolkien links this to a comment in *Beowulf* by the heroic survivor Wiglaf, who rather critically laments the fall of his lord in the fight with the dragon with the exclamation: *oft sceall eorl monig anes willan wræc adreogan*, which Tolkien translates 'by one man's will many must woe endure'.[22] (The parallels between Byrhtnoth's fight with the Danes and Beowulf's fight with the dragon will be explored in Chapter 9.) Nevertheless, until the moment of their fall, both figures are to be seen as inspiring leaders and powerful warriors fighting in a good cause. The reader is clearly meant to find the culture from which they come admirable – the art, music, poetry, even their whole way of life – but the pride in their mental make-up is their undoing.

This kind of reading can also lead to 'anti-heroic' criticism: some readers of the poem focus on the flaw in the hero's character and see it as emblematic of the whole world portrayed in the poem. They are tempted to assert that there is 'something rotten in the state of Denmark', or, indeed, 'in the state of tenth-century England'. On this line of thought, the old ways are certainly not to be admired and the poem is rather to be seen as a piece of sociopolitical literature, a critique of the condition of England.[23] So one critic writes:

> The recurring theme of cultural production is confusion and pessimism, eschatological panic and biting social critique. English literature appears to have reached a dead end, and ideological void.[24]

Such a reading can be quite convincing, especially if it is seen in the context of the early eleventh-century writings of Wulfstan, the writer, homilist and archbishop of York. Wulfstan wrote – and no doubt when in the pulpit also spoke – like an Old Testament prophet, particularly in the years 1012–14, when he composed and preached various versions of his famous sermon *Sermo Lupi ad Anglos* ('Sermon of Wolf to the English'), which catalogues the moral failings of the English and the violent actions of the Danish invaders. In this period his message was bleak: the English were suffering for their sins at the hands of the pagans from the north (these issues will be reconsidered in detail in Chapters 5, 10 and 11). Certainly the Danes triumphed in the end, and in 1016 Cnut the Great became the first Danish ruler of England after the death first of Æthelred and, shortly after that, of his son Edmund Ironside. But this tone and atmosphere of apocalypse and conquest does not suit the culturally more vibrant period of the 990s, when *The Battle of Maldon* is likely to have been composed. King Æthelred, for instance, is treated only with worship and honour in the pages of the poem, strongly suggesting that it belongs to that earlier part of his reign.

There is another direction, however, that readings of the poem can take, and this is potentially more problematic than the anti-heroic criticism just outlined. The error is to imagine that *Maldon* expresses a pure 'Germanic' heroic ideal, akin to that of the epic *Beowulf*, but this is a *Beowulf* from which all 'Christian colouring' has been removed. It is no exaggeration to state that from this perspective both poems, *Beowulf* and *Maldon*, evoke a pre-Christian world of individualistic heroism, pagan autonomy and military glory. Tolkien did not hold such views, but it is not hard to see that he may have inspired them among some of his readers. Others may have absorbed similar ideas not from Tolkien but from the legacy of nineteenth-century neo-Romantic histories of the 'Anglo-Saxon' age. Such 'pagan-heroic' readings of *The Battle of Maldon*, if pursued further, as they later have been, without regard to the historical context, can often go astray. Writers and critics, sometimes even following in Tolkien's wake, appear to have absorbed the younger Tolkien's admiration of the heroic but ignored his later misgivings. The poem has been seen as the last expression of a 'Germanic heroic code' first observed a thousand years before *Maldon* in the *Germania* of the Roman writer Tacitus.[25] Nowadays literary critics and historians have mostly moved on from these views,[26] but similar misconceptions of the 'pagan Anglo-Saxons' have entered the popular consciousness.

As an example, one could take a radio drama from the 1970s and 1980s that was loosely based on the poem, in which Byrhtnoth's English wife is depicted as chanting prayers to Odin, as though she were a pagan Viking.[27] A review of this play in *The Listener* spoke of how the author Mr McKillop sensitively catches the ambivalence of the 'fairly recently converted' Saxons, while portraying 'the grief of a woman deprived of her hero'.[28] This is astonishingly misinformed. By no stretch of the imagination can we say that the English in 991 are 'recent converts' to Christianity. Such approaches to the poem ignore the fact that by this time the English had been part of Christendom for centuries. And Byrhtnoth's wife, whose name was Ælfflæd, left her own last will and testament in which we can hear her voice, addressing first of all the king on behalf of her lord, that is, her late husband:

> And I humbly pray you, Sire, for God's sake and for the sake of my lord's soul and for the sake of my sister's soul, that you will protect the holy foundation at Stoke in which my ancestors lie buried, and the property which they gave to it as an immune right of God for ever: which property I grant exactly as my ancestors had granted it.

It should be said that this is a Christian voice, without a trace of Nordic paganism.[29]

One corrective to this way of thinking is to engage imaginatively with the documents of the time and visit the villages and manors where these people once lived. Aesthetically and historically, of all these old villages, Chelsworth stands out as 'one of the most enchanting parishes in Suffolk, with many of its attractive features dating from the pre-Conquest period'.[30] The estate features in a separate charter, in fact the oldest charter in Suffolk (most early charters are from further west or south). In 962, King Edgar granted Chelsworth to his father's widow Æthelflæd, the older sister of Ælfflæd (Byhrtnoth's wife), and it is by this route that the property came to be held by the ealdorman. The bounds of the estate involve various still recognizable landscape features: a walk from Caford (Crow Ford), *andlang cwyrnburnan*, literally 'along the quern-stone brook', that is, the mill-stream, then along the boundaries of the neighbours, named as the man Manna's boundary and the woman Asa's boundary, through a dene or U-shaped valley, through the 'hollow fen' of Culphen Meadow, past the boundaries of the properties of Oswyth and Eadwold, along a paved road (OE *stræt*) and the Lavenham Brook back to the Mill Stream and Caford. If we cannot gain access to any of Byrhtnoth's halls and homes, with their accompanying churches and chapels, built mostly in wood and all long since gone, we can at least walk the paths that surrounded a property that he owned, in a landscape that still bears traces of its older shape and contour.

In view of the contemporary social conditions, therefore, it is more appropriate to regard the poem as the expression of the ideals of the tenth-century warrior

Figure 2 Present-day Chelsworth, Suffolk. © Mark Atherton.

aristocracy rather than that of an arcane thousand-year-old heritage. But the misreadings persist, at least in popular views of the poem, and indeed, for those who work in education, they have been found in some student essays that reflect these views. The East Saxons are seen as somehow embodying a 'pagan' ideal, despite the fact that Byrhtnoth as portrayed in the poem dies with a prayer on his lips, and despite the fact that in real life he was a patron of the church and a defender of the monastic ideal, who was buried at Ely Abbey in East Anglia. I am inclined to explain these pagan readings of the poem as misplaced nostalgia on the part of certain readers.[31] But the tenth century is interesting in its own right, and its poems are not the same as those of the eighth century, and they most certainly differ from the lost poetry of pre-seventh-century 'Dark Age' Europe. And there is another factor: because the poem *Maldon* is written in a traditional heroic style, it seems much older than it really is.

Maldon in context

The purpose of this book is to present and explore the texts associated with the tenth-century Maldon campaign and the poem that came out of it. I will cover new ground, for there are not many monographs on *Maldon*, and few have attempted a book-length synthesis of literary and historical approaches to the poem.[32] On the literary side, I will offer close readings of *The Battle of Maldon*, as well as analysing the other accounts of the battle and the sources that may have been used by the poet to compose his great poem. But the aim also is to situate *The Battle of Maldon* within the religious, cultural and political history of the period, considering the living conditions, social situation, education, the contemporary practices of lordship and power, the ranks of society, cultural institutions, the role of men and women, as well as the art and literature current at the time. The assumption will be that in order to interpret a poem that engages with a political event of the late tenth century, the details of the everyday life and culture of that period need to be made clear, as far as they are recoverable. And so to appreciate an Old English poem written in a traditional poetic style, some awareness is necessary of the other medium of English at the time: the literary and administrative prose which, though it has its own patterns of style and expression, differs in its vocabulary and grammar from the language of poetry (and often seems closer to the language of the present day). Reading the prose helps to highlight what is special about the poetry.

The structure of the book is broadly as follows. Part I provides readings of successive parts of the poem in historical context; the aim here is not to revisit all the critical issues about *Maldon* but to provide an overview of the poem, and at the same time present new approaches: the relevance of the name 'Maldon' to the choice of battlefield, the symbolism of horse and hawk, the meaning of 'home' and 'land' in a tenth-century context, the patterns of stasis and dynamic movement that are characteristic of this narrative poem. Byrhtnoth's lordship and authority and his Benedictine spirituality will feature, but also the kinship, friendship and companionship of the thegns who feature so prominently in the second half of the poem. Part II, 'After the battle', completes the wider picture and concludes the story, looking at the other, probably later, witnesses to what had happened at Maldon and their differing interpretations of its significance. This is not intended to be a full-scale history of the period but a selective look at the context of *Maldon*. Throughout the book illustrations will appear from early medieval manuscripts, along with photographs of original locations *as they now appear* in the present-day English countryside. These, I hope, will serve to promote the negotiation between the past and the present which inevitably accompanies a reading of this poem.

The starting point will be the assumption, certainly arguable though difficult to prove, that the poem is early rather than late, that it constitutes a fairly immediate response to the events of August 991. Other than the Anglo-Saxon Chronicle, the texts that do describe the battle are associated with East Anglia, with Ramsey and especially Ely. It is possible that the author of *The Book of Ely* and Byrhtferth of Ramsey, who wrote *The Life of St Oswald*, both knew the poem. This would explain the parallels that can be found between the poem and their writings, which in our discussion will be treated not only as accounts of the political event itself but also as responses to the poem. Above all, I will propose (*contra* Tolkien and others) that *The Battle of Maldon* is a product of the contemporary cult of Byrhtnoth, rather than a critique of his failings. *Maldon* is a nostalgic poem which harks back to earlier classics like *Beowulf*, while also betraying the influence of the contemporary Benedictine Reform – a hugely important movement in the politics and culture of the period – in order to present the ealdorman as a Christian hero worthy of emulation at a time of national crisis.

A note on the text and language of *The Battle of Maldon*

According to a recent catalogue, a grand total of 1,291 manuscripts survive from early medieval England up to the year 1100.[33] For a period covering five centuries, this is not a huge number of books, but the population at any given time was relatively small (up to three million), and the majority could not read and so had to enjoy their 'literature' by hearing it read. We assume also that many more books were written but did not survive intact. Fire and flood, wear and tear: these can wreak their destruction. In the case of the poem *The Battle of Maldon*, such factors certainly played a role in the fragmentary and incomplete survival of the text. Worst of all was the fire. The sole manuscript containing the original copy of the poem was destroyed in the blaze that swept through the famous Cotton library collection in 1731. Fortunately, a transcription of the text had been made before the fire took place, but this is incomplete, suggesting that by then some text had been lost. Well before the modern owner acquired the manuscript, it was already damaged. Probably the poem circulated in a separate booklet or pamphlet, unprotected by hard covers, and like the battered, well-used paperbacks of the modern world it eventually lost its two outer leaves. The damage of wear and tear means that the poem lacks a beginning and an end. There was also deliberate damage, or at least a lack of respect for the presentation of the manuscript. The owner of the original text in early modern times, Sir Robert Cotton, is well known to have pulled apart and re-assembled ancient books in order to construct personal anthologies according to his own likes and dislikes. Before the fire, *The Battle of Maldon* appeared in one such Cottonian collection, bound together with originally separate texts such as *The Life of King Alfred* by Bishop Asser, and various *lives* of saints. One theory is that Sir Robert was compiling an anthology of stories about brave men and women in passive or active resistance against Viking or other invaders.

The text that we actually have now is a later transcript of a medieval copy, but there are reasons to believe that the man who transcribed the text in the eighteenth century – this is now thought to be David Casley – was skilled and practised at his task.[34] He made a conscious effort to reproduce the look and layout of the early medieval text, despite a few mistakes that scholars have identified, and he seems to have reproduced the capital letters of the manuscript he was copying. If we are right to trust him, as E. V. Gordon did in his edition, then it is fair to conclude that these capital letters mark the sections of the original medieval copy of the poem, and that these sections are evidence for the structure of the poem as it was copied by the contemporary scribe.

I think it is important that readers of an Old English poem should be aware of the original language in which it was written: this is the optimal way to appreciate its sound, texture and rhythm, as well as its meaning, connotations and rhetorical structure. An edition with a facing-page version in modern English is strongly recommended.[35] It is not expected that all readers of this book will know Old English or Latin; the meanings and nuances of individual verses will therefore be explained where necessary, and translations will always be provided. In general, the following conventions will be used: 'Maldon' in inverted commas will refer to the events of the battle, while *Maldon* in italics will refer more precisely to the text of the poem *The Battle of Maldon*. Occasionally the abbreviation OE will be used to refer to the language 'Old English'.

As for Old English metre, this followed elaborate rules.[36] But the basics are straightforward: there were four 'lifts' or beats in a line, of which two or three began with the same alliterating sound. If we consider once again the famous lines from Byrhtwold's speech, we can mark the lifts by adding an oblique slash like an acute accent above the stressed words in the line:

/   /   /   /
Hige sceal þe heardra,   heorte þe cenre,
/   /   /   /
mod sceal þe mare,   þe ure mægen lytlað.

Accordingly, in line 312, there is the double alliteration of the 'h' in *Hige . . . heardra* of the first half-line (the on-verse), followed by the 'h' of *heorte* in the off-verse. In the next line (313) the alliteration occurs on three 'm' sounds. Usually, as here, the alliterating lifts were nouns or adjectives, but sometimes also infinitives. With this basic knowledge of where the stresses fall, the line becomes rhythmical, something to hear and feel. I would encourage readers to sound out the words and phrases of the Old English, and indeed the Latin, quotations. As a broad guide to pronunciation you could use the 'continental' values of the vowels. The Old English vowel 'æ' should sound like the open 'a' vowel of 'cat', as spoken in southern British English or General American.

In Old English pronunciation the two letters 'þ' ('thorn') and 'ð' ('eth') sound like the voiceless 'th' in present-day English 'bath', or they are voiced between

Figure 3 The Blackwater estuary near Maldon. © Mark Atherton.

vowels as in the 'th' sound of 'bathing'. The consonants 'f' and 's' are pronounced as in modern English, for example, the numerals *feower, fif, siex* 'four, five, six', but between vowels they are voiced to a 'v' or 'z' sound, as in *lufu* 'love' or *gafol* 'tribute', pronounced more like 'gavol'. The 'c' is pronounced 'k' except before 'e' or 'i' when it becomes the 'ch' of 'church', so that *ceorl* meaning 'farmer' is pronounced 'cheorl' (and indeed it eventually became 'churl' in later English). Similarly, hard 'g', as in *gold* 'gold' or *gafol* 'tribute', is softened to a palatal 'y' sound before an 'e' or an 'i', as in *gear* 'year' or *gif* 'if'. As for the 'h' in Byrhtnoth, the name of the famous ealdorman of Essex, this has a fricative sound similar to the initial 'h' of the name 'Hugh'.

PART I

Approaches to *The Battle of Maldon*

Chapter 1

The grounds of Maldon

Het þa bord beran   beornas gangan
þæt hi on þam easteðe ealle stodon
ne mihte þær for wætere,   werod to þam oðrum
þær com flowende   flod æfter ebban
lucon lagustreamas   to lang hit him þuhte
hwænne hi togædere   garas beron.

THE BATTLE OF MALDON (62–7)

[He ordered shields to be carried, men to advance,
until they all stood on the riverbank.
Because of the water the one army could not reach the other.
Then came flowing the flood-tide after the ebb,
ocean-streams locked together. Too long, it seemed to them,
before they would bear their spears together.]

Maldon the port

The long stretch of the coastline of south-eastern England, from the corner of Kent up to Suffolk, is remarkable for a number of similarly situated large river estuaries, all basically flowing down parallel lines from west to east, and all providing suitable sites for sheltered ports and trading stations. In the south of this area is the Medway, with the town of Rochester at its head, and then the Thames, by far the largest of these tidal estuaries and the reason for the growth and importance of the port of London – a process that probably began in the Roman period. In the north of this area, and already in East Anglia, you will find a confluence of three rivers where the estuaries of the Stour and the Orwell and then the narrow winding inlet of the Deben all reach the sea near present-day Harwich and Felixstowe. At the head of the Deben is Woodbridge, possibly the

Figure 4 The Orwell estuary. © Mark Atherton.

place where long ago in the seventh century the East Angles beached a sailing ship and dragged it uphill and overland to Sutton Hoo, to make it the centre of a magnificent showpiece royal ship burial.[1] At the head of the Orwell is the town of Ipswich, an important trading centre throughout the early medieval period.

In the middle of this stretch of coastline between the Thames and the Stour is the large estuary of the Blackwater, and at its head stands the town and port of Maldon, between the former administrative districts of Chelmsford Hundred and Wibertherne Hundred, now called the Dengie Peninsula. The original settlement of Maldon looks down from the hilltop over the Blackwater estuary and the surrounding territory. To the north, as we have seen, there is a crossing of the rivers Chelmer and Blackwater at Heybridge. To the west and south are three villages aptly named Woodham, in each case with a by-name derived from later Norman families who owned them: Woodham Walter, Woodham Mortimer, Woodham Farrers. The woodland implied in these place-names still survives in patches. In his literary travelogue *The Wild Places* the writer Robert Macfarlane begins a walk through a strip of ancient woodland near Woodham Walter then east along the Chelmer river to Maldon, and east of Maldon the Dengie:

> The Dengie is a blunt-nosed peninsula in eastern Essex, just under a hundred square miles in area and bordered on three sides by water – the Blackwater

estuary to its north, the North Sea to its east, the Crouch estuary to its south. Most of it is reclaimed land, below sea-level, saved from the tides by a network of sea-walls: grassed-over linear earthworks, fifteen feet high or more. It is provisional land, borrowed land. Stepping onto it you are stepping into a ghost of water.[2]

This is a mysterious, fog-bound world, celebrated by recent writers for its unpredictable salt-marsh terrain, which draws individuals on quests for a rare wild bird in the 'beyond-world' of *The Peregrine*, for the 'beast in the Blackwater' of *The Essex Serpent*.[3] The low-lying Dengie is liable to flooding, and has been for centuries, as Macfarlane points out. The last great flood was in January 1953, but an entry for the year 1099 in the Peterborough manuscript of the Anglo-Saxon Chronicle describes a similar 'great sea-flood' (OE *swiðe sæflod*) on the east coast, which *swa mycel to hearme gedyde swa nan man ne gemunet þet hit æfre æror dyde* 'did so much damage as no one remembers that it ever did before'.[4]

Historical records point to the existence of a number of prominent churches in the region. As the Northumbrian historian Bede reported in his *Ecclesiastical History of the English Nation* (completed in the year 731), the missionary and first bishop of the East Saxons was a man called Cedd (pronounced, strictly speaking, like 'chedd' in *cheddar*). Sent in the year 654 to the region by Oswy, king of the Northumbrians, to assist Sigbert, king of Essex, Cedd set about preaching to the East Saxons (*Eccelesiastical History*, bk III, ch. 22). According to Bede, Cedd built churches 'in various places', including especially *in civitate quae lingua Saxonum Ythancaestir appellatur*, 'in the city called *Ythancaestir* in the Saxon tongue'.[5] There are grounds for thinking that *Ythancaestir* is the location of the ancient chapel of St Peter-on-the-Wall, today a place of pilgrimage for Christians inspired by the so-called Celtic past, at a striking location at the end of the Dengie near Bradwell-on-Sea. With a touch of symmetry there is another early church dedicated to St Peter on the opposite side of the Blackwater estuary on the island of Mersea, as though together the two churches of St Peter would guard the mouth of the estuary.[6]

Maldon is basically a port. Before the characteristic Dengie landscape sets in, immediately to the east of Maldon itself is the harbour of Hythe Quay (*hythe*, Old English *hyð*, 'landing-place'), to which small ships that have sailed up the channel of the Blackwater estuary can dock securely. There is a church on this site, dedicated to St Mary, which has been a place of Christian worship for about 1,400 years. One might also speculate that Cedd built this church of St Mary at Hythe too, amid the old ruins of a Roman temple or sanctuary, although this cannot be proved. By the tenth century, a wooden church stood next to the *hythe*, serving the needs of sailors and traders who berthed there. Over the centuries, it became the 'Fishermen's Church'. The oldest part of the present

Figure 5 The harbour at the Hythe, Maldon. © Dreamstime/Dianamower.

building is from the Norman period, but it has been rebuilt and augmented over the centuries. In early modern times, its famous lantern served as a landmark and aid to navigation, and the present building contains memorabilia of its location and function as a mariners' church over many centuries.

Because of its location, then, the town of Maldon can be seen as one of several gateways into southern England, as part of a pattern of important trading ports each situated at the head of a long estuary and providing a safe haven for ships. Like London or Colchester, which are both walled Roman cities, Maldon is defensible, situated as it is on the site of a hill fort, and this was necessary, for not all would-be users of this landing site have had friendly intentions. The point is well illustrated by an incident during the eighteenth-century hostilities with France, a relatively recent example by the chronology of this book. In 1744, in the run-up to the 1745 Jacobite rebellion under Bonnie Prince Charlie, England was on the alert for French invasions. With good reason, for there was in fact a planned invasion by the French, whose king, Louis XV, had recently declared war, and there were rumours of support from English Jacobite sympathizers.[7]

History was repeating itself: the fear of treachery at home – from Anglo-Danish families in the Danelaw – lies behind the account of *The Battle of Maldon* too.[8] For their part, the French were aware of the potential Jacobite support for their planned invasion. A large army was assembled under Marshall Saxe, and a fleet of transports gathered, all at Dunkirk. Apparently, Maldon was the chosen destination for this D-day landing in reverse, for it was seen as the inroad to London, only forty-two miles away.[9] But the winter weather proved treacherous, at least for the French. As Norman Longmate tells the story in his book *Island Fortress*, Vice-Admiral Jacques de Roquefeuil sailed out of the Breton harbour of Brest in February 1744, with orders to cover the invasion out of Dunkirk and lure away the English fleet towards the Isle of Wight. Finding the Isle of Wight empty of English ships, Roquefeuil sent messages to Saxe to begin the invasion from Dunkirk. But meanwhile, as Roquefeuil sailed along the coast of Kent towards Essex, he ran into the superior English fleet under Admiral John Norris at Dungeness, off Romney Marsh. It seemed inevitable that a sea-battle would take place, but the French ships slipped away as night fell. At around midnight, a great northeast gale blew up and vented all its fury on the retreating French warfleet; the ships fled before it, hurrying back to safety in Britanny. Meanwhile, the French transports had begun to set out, but twelve were sunk by the storm, and the rest retreated to Dunkirk. On this occasion, unlike their tenth-century Viking precursors, the invaders never reached Maldon.

Maldon the fortified town

For over 2,000 years the hill of Maldon has been a place of refuge in times of invasion. Long before it gained its Old English name *Mældun*, there was a fortress there in the Iron Age, which fell into ruin but was rebuilt in Roman times, as archaeological finds suggest. It is a defendable position. In the early Anglo-Saxon period, it was probably a royal vill,[10] with its economy supported by the local fishing industry, which used long, complex fence-like traps to catch fish as the tide retreated in the estuary.[11] Early in the tenth century, however, with renewed wars against the Danes, this quiet settlement was transformed in size and importance.

During the campaigns of Edward the Elder, king of greater Wessex from 899 to 924 and son of Alfred the Great (871–99), the site again took on strategic importance, in his concerted efforts to recover territory conquered and settled by the Vikings during the early reign of his father. About halfway through Edward's reign, we find the first mention of the name Maldon, preserved for posterity in the records of the Anglo-Saxon Chronicle. The records for the reign of Edward and his father Alfred belong mostly to what is known as the 'common core' of the Anglo-Saxon Chronicle: despite the existence of six different versions in separate manuscripts (labelled A to F) the text is broadly the same. Only in the so-called Mercian Register, in manuscript B, and only later in the tenth century, as we shall see, do the records start to diverge noticeably and tell different stories. In the common core annal for the year 912, then, we find the king in a temporary encampment at Maldon, while his men are building fortresses – the word used is Old English *burh* (with an irregular plural *byrig*) a noun meaning literally 'a protected place' or 'fortress', that is, 'a fortified town', from the verb *beorgan* 'to protect'; the term survives in place-names as *borough*, *burgh* or *bury*). The one *burh*, so the annal reports say, was 6 miles to the north at Witham, the other, 36 miles to the west at Hertford (note again that the abbreviation '7' means *and*):

> Her on þys geare ymb Martines mæssan het Eadweard cyning atimbran þa norðran burg æt Heorotforda betweox Memeran 7 Beneficcan 7 Lygean; 7 þa æfter þam þæs on sumera. betweox gangdagum 7 middum sumera, þa for Eadweard cyning mid sumum his fultume on Eastseaxe to Mældune. 7 wicode þær þa hwile þe man þa burg worhte 7 getimbrede æt Witham; 7 him beag god dæl þæs folces to þe ær under Deniscra manna anwalde wæron, 7 sum his fultum worhte þa burg þa hwile æt Heorotforda on suþhealfe Lygean.

> [Here in this year, around Martinmas, King Edward ordered the northern fortress to be built at Hertford between the Mimram, the Beane and the Lea; and then after this, in the summer, between Rogationtide and Midsummer, King Edward travelled with part of his forces to Maldon in Essex. And he was encamped there while the *burh* was being built and constructed at Witham; and a good number of the people who had been under the rule of the Danes submitted to him. And in the meantime part of his forces constructed the *burh* at Hertford south of the Lea.]

As a year-by-year chronology of historical events, the Chronicle is usually noted for its brevity and concision, but here the geographical detail is given prominently: the writer knows of the confluence of the three rivers at Hertford, and his emphasis on the river Lea is probably significant, for this is a navigable river flowing down to Bow, on the Thames at London. Witham is another geographically important location, guarding the old Roman highway about halfway between London and Colchester. In his brief plain style, the writer is naming the strategically important sites that King Edward was seeking to secure.

Evidently, Edward's policy was to build a network of defensive places across the southern part of the Danelaw in order to control the region.[12] That policy was successful, and the mixed population – not only of East Angles and East Saxons but also of Danes, that is, descendants of Viking settlers from way back in the 870s – was slowly but surely submitting to him and acknowledging him as king. It is interesting to see Edward's choice of the securely guarded hill at Maldon as the location for his temporary encampment. The site was evidently well suited, for what at first was temporary soon became permanent. As the Chronicle briefly notes for the year 916, Maldon too was rebuilt as a fortress:

> Her on þys gere foran to middum sumera for Eadweard cyning to Mældune 7 getimbrede þa burg 7 gestaðolode ær he þonon fore.

[Here in this year, at Midsummer, King Edward went to Maldon, and built and established the fortress before he departed from there.]

The site of this *burh* is reflected in the pattern of streets in the modern town; the fortress with its earthen ramparts and reinforced palisade stood at the western end of what is now the High Street. The new walls were an effective deterrent, as events of the following year were soon to prove.

The year 917 was Edward's annus mirabilis: a number of sieges and battles took place that year, confirming the West Saxon king's control and possession of the new fortified towns in Mercia and the Danelaw, and everywhere Edward's forces seem to have emerged victorious.[13] In his entry for that year, the chronicler describes, in more detail than was his usual custom, these various engagements and their outcomes. The year began, so he tells us, with the rebuilding of the fortifications at Towcester, a timely action that allowed the citizens to repel a Danish attack. Similar successes were enjoyed at Bedford and Wigmore: the Danes were unable to take the two towns because of their renewed defences. At Bedford, the English defenders appear to have chosen their moment to sortie out of the town and defeat their attackers; while at Wigmore, the besiegers could make no headway and eventually departed. From now on the English were on the offensive, and it turned out that the Danes were unable to hold towns that they had earlier seized and occupied. In the summer a battle at Tempsford was won by an English army that had been mustered from various *byrig*, and the Danish leaders, including their king and two of his earls, were killed. The same happened in the autumn at Colchester, the old Roman settlement and principal town of the Essex region to the north-east of Maldon: an English army from Kent, Surrey and Essex took the town, killing its Danish defenders 'apart from those who escaped over the walls'. With these words, the chronicler, in his objective style, neither condemns nor condones the brutality, but he does point out that the Danes remembered this day and now wanted their revenge.

The brunt of their anger was directed at Maldon. Later in that same autumn of 917, a battle was fought at Maldon in which the English gained a decisive victory, undoubtedly because the new *burh* proved its mettle:

Þa æfter þam þa giet þæs ilcan hærfestes gegadorode micel here hine of Eastenglum ægþer ge þæs landheres ge þara wicinga þe hie him to fultume aspanen hæfdon 7 þohton þæt hie sceoldon gewrecan hira teonun 7 foron to Mældune 7 ymbsæton þa burg 7 fuhton þæron oþ þam burgwarum com mara fultum to utan to helpe, 7 forlet se here þa burg 7 for fram; 7 þa foron þa men æfter ut of þære byrig 7 eac þa þe him utan comon to fultume 7 gefliemdon þone here 7 ofslogon hira monig hund ægþer ge æscmanna ge oþerra.

[Then yet again afterwards that same autumn, a great host [*here*] gathered from East Anglia, both from the land-army [*landhere*] and from the Vikings that they had enticed to assist them; and they thought that they would avenge their wrongs. They went to Maldon and besieged the city [*burh*] and fought against it until more help came to the citizens [*þam burgwarum*] from outside. And the host left the city and departed, whereupon the men came out of the city in pursuit, along with those who had come to help them from outside. And they put the host to flight and slew many hundreds of them, both the shipmen [*æscmanna*] and the others.]

The passage indicates that East Anglia at the time was still very strongly Danish or Anglo-Danish in its affiliation. The first point to note in reading this short narrative is the use of the two-syllable noun *he-re* meaning 'raiding-army' (*here* being associated with the idea of raiding and plundering). The same expression was used in the Chronicle for the original 'great heathen army' that appeared in England in the year 865 and settled for the winter in East Anglia, returning there in 870 to conquer the whole region (we will have occasion to refer again to a key battle in that campaign: see Chapter 10). Two generations later, in the annal for 917, the chronicler refers to this army as the *landhere* 'the land host'; no doubt this army was composed of some veterans of the old wars, fortified now with the support of younger men, many of whom must have been born in East Anglia. These are the Danes of the Danelaw, Anglo-Danish by birth, but still very firmly Danish by identity. But the chronicler distinguishes them from another kind of Dane, for the East Anglian Danes are ready and willing to recruit – the verb suggestively used is 'to entice' – a much worse enemy, namely, an army of *wicinga*, 'Vikings'. These men are referred to rather pointedly and figuratively as *æscmanna*, 'shipmen', Vikings or pirates, *æsc* here meaning not 'ashwood' (the native Old English word) but a near-sounding synonym borrowed into English from the Old Norse *askr* which denoted a 'ship'. A similar expression, *æschere*, is used to characterize the Viking enemy as the 'ship-army' in the poem *The Battle of Maldon* (69).

The chronicler here deals in polarities and binary oppositions, the relevant pairs being: 'ship versus fortress', 'country versus city', perhaps even 'nature versus civilization'. Opposed to the pirates are the *burhwara*, the dwellers of the *burh*, in other words, 'the citizens'. And, with a little help from their friends, they employ the time-honoured tactic of sallying forth suddenly from the gates of their *burh* in order to inflict great damage on their enemies and defeat them. This narrative of the first battle at Maldon is a very short, short story. But it illustrates the point that, overall, Edward's *burh*-building policy had been a great success.

And with that success, Maldon fades from the records for three generations and plays no prominent role in the momentous changes of the middle years of the tenth century: the unification of the kingdom of England under Edward's son Æthelstan (925–39) and his grandson Edgar (959–75), the beginnings of urbanization, the founding of new monasteries and the rise of the Benedictine reformers to political power and influence. In all this time, the small *burh* at Maldon remained invisible: there are no further mentions of it in the Chronicle until the year of the battle there in 991 (see Chapter 10). The evidence of charters and administrative documents is also lacking for 'Maldon'. However, the fourteenth-century archive of Bury St Edmunds contains copies of a number of wills from the middle of the tenth century: for the years between 946 and 951 we have the will of Ælfgar, ealdorman of Essex and father-in-law of Byrhtnoth – it is here in fact that Byrhtnoth is mentioned for the first time in the historical record. Ælfgar's two daughters – one a royal widow, the other married to Byrhtnoth – also wrote their wills, which were deposited for safekeeping at Bury.[14] From these documents we know that – among lands and estates near Colchester, Bury and Cambridge – Byrhtnoth and his wife's family had estates near Maldon, including at one time Heybridge (Tidwoldingtun), which we saw was a possible location of the battle, and nearby Totham and its woodland, which lay north of the town; to the south there were Rettendon and Woodham, and his wife's will mentions Lawling – near Latchingdon in the Dengie peninsula. Maldon was certainly part of the home territory, which brings us back to the situation in August 991.

A pressing issue, given the strength of the *burh* and its reputation as a stronghold in the days of Edward the Elder, is why Byrhtnoth in 991 did not follow similar tactics to those used by Edward in 917. He knew, presumably, that these Viking invaders had sailed up the Orwell estuary and attacked Ipswich, which they had then overrun. Perhaps the *burh* at Maldon was more formidable than the defences of the old trading port of Ipswich, but the Vikings reportedly had ninety-three ships and presumably enough manpower to attack the fortress. If they could take Ipswich, then it is likely they would try to take Maldon too. But as was discussed in the Introduction, it is possible that Byrhtnoth mustered his men at Maldon itself. Conceivably, he could have waited for the Vikings to surround the town, after which, like his predecessor seventy-four years before, he could have made a sudden sortie and taken the besiegers by surprise.

But the Byrhtnoth of the poem is not that kind of hero, as we have already seen, for he likes magnanimous gestures and prefers in the end to fight a pitched battle. And this may reflect the decisions and attitudes of the historical person. No one kept diaries or memoirs in this period, nor are there any written despatches to help us follow closely the events of that day. Accordingly, we cannot know for certain Byrhtnoth's thoughts and motives. Arguably, he may have had some sense of heroic propriety that prevented any return to tactics of lurking in ambush within the walls of the *burh*. The historian Ryan Lavelle has written that the decision to fight before the walls of the town was based on heroic bravado inspired by a knowledge of history.[15] A text that was known and studied in tenth-century schools was the Old English *Orosius*, a paraphrase and rewriting of the Roman historian Orosius's Latin *History against the Pagans*. This textbook presents a parallel situation: the Romans make their decision to venture forth from the city to fight in a pitched battle against the invading Carthaginians under Hannibal. And they do this, so the Old English *Orosius* declares, in order to demonstrate their courage.[16] Thomas J. T. Williams accepts Lavelle's suggestion, and adds that a similar model is found in the battle scene narrative of *Judith*, a poem which was probably composed in the tenth century and later added to the *Beowulf* manuscript. Williams also compares the account in the poem *The Battle of Brunanburh* of the great battle in 937 during the reign of Æthelstan (924–39) which effectively confirmed that king as ruler of all England. This was a pitched battle *ymbe Brunnanburh* 'near Brunanburh', at what must have been an ancient landmark and fortress, Bruna's *burh*, which nevertheless did not play any role in the actual fighting.[17] To fight the battle outside the *burh* was the honourable option, and this, so the various documents imply, is the option that Bryhtnoth chose to pursue.

'Crosshill': Reflections on the name *Maldon*

Evidence recently discussed by scholars would suggest that early medieval battle sites were 'highly symbolic points in the landscape' which were in fact deliberately chosen for their auspicious or appropriate settings.[18] The landscape was seen as tied up with local myths, legends, narratives and events, and the existing name – or indeed the re-naming of the place where a significant event took place – was felt to be relevant or appropriate.[19] So, in Bede's well-known *Ecclesiastical History*, as we will see further, there is the case of the pious King Oswald who fought a decisive battle at a site that Bede calls *Heavenfield*, a renamed place with an obvious spiritual application to this particular king, who eventually became the first royal saint of Anglo-Saxon England. In the case of a pre-existing place-name, it is possible that the combatants chose the location for its symbolism. Alternatively, it is also possible that a chronicler attached the event or the battle to the nearest significant name in the locality. Whatever the reason, the name is endowed with more than usual significance. In a series of reflections on the naming of battlefields, Philip Morgan has argued that 'battle sites and battle names remain visible because they embody a system of symbols and codes which evoke meaning'.[20] The military historian Guy Halsall, for instance, has studied Anglo-Saxon historical sources from the years 600 to 850 and observed a frequent association between battlefields and water crossings or ancient monuments.[21] There is some applicability of this idea to Maldon, which is a port on a river, and as discussed earlier there are, at various points from Heybridge to Mersea, bridges or causeways crossing the channels of the tidal rivers and the estuary.

As we have seen, Maldon, or in Old English *Mæl-dun*, is situated on high ground at the head of the Blackwater estuary. The most likely interpretation of the name is 'the hill marked with a cross', but *mæl* is an unusual word, with a range of meanings covering 'mark, landmark, monument'; its meaning is broader than the synonym *rōd* (pronounced with a long 'o' vowel) which denotes very specifically a 'rood' or 'cross'. Given that the noun *mæl* has several further connotations, a few further remarks are in order on the interpretation of this name *Mældun*.[22] Fortunately, a rich wealth of comparative evidence for the place-name etymologist is provided by Anglo-Saxon charters recording gifts and transactions of land, of which many hundreds survive in the archives of cathedrals and minsters. As a grant of land, the charter is naturally filled with references to place-names and features of the landscape. In early medieval Western Europe, the land charter was recorded in Latin, which was in general use as the language of written record. But in England, for a variety of historical reasons, the vernacular mother tongue was also used in writing, for both literary and more everyday administrative purposes. In charters, therefore, since the dimensions of the land needed to be clear to all interested parties, the practice of writing vernacular bounds developed, as was noted earlier. In the Anglo-Saxon charter, or royal diploma as it is also called, the main text is in Latin but the bounds of the relevant property or estate are recorded in the mother tongue. The two parties involved would gather for a meeting, and the agreement would be read out formally; often the people affected by the transaction would perambulate the bounds of the estate, with other local dignitaries and their tenant farmers and workers in tow, for the express purpose of fixing the shape of the land and its boundaries in the collective memory: in brief, people had to memorize the landmarks. It is in the 'charter bounds', then, that we find many landscape features named and described in everyday language.[23]

A relevant example is a royal diploma or land charter from the generation before the Maldon campaign, beginning with the words *Altitrono in eternum regnante* 'To the Lord reigning in eternity', which is number 714 in Peter Sawyer's catalogue of Anglo-Saxon charters.[24] The document records a gift of land by King Æthelred's father, the great King Edgar (reigned 959–75), which he bestowed upon Æthelwold, the powerful bishop of Winchester and one of the foremost churchmen and politicians of his age. With great ceremony, expressed in the formal style of the Church Latin of the tenth century, Edgar grants the estate – located at a place called Washington in Surrey – to his bishop; and switching to Old English for the boundary clause, he describes the land as follows:

Ðis sind þa land gemæra to Wasingatuna. Ærst of horninga dene to bennan beorges, þonon ealdan cristesmæle, of þam cristes mæle to blacan pole, of þam pole to dunnan heafde, þonon to hunnes cnolle to geoc burnan, þonon to dunham lea.

[These are the boundaries of the estate at Washington. First from Horning Dene to Bennan Hill, thence to the old Christ's Cross, from the Christ's Cross to Bright Pool, from the pool to Hillhead, thence to Hun's Knoll to Cuckoo Burn, thence to Dunham Lea]

Following such directions, the men and women involved in this transaction could ride or walk the bounds of the estate. And the landscape features (which also serve as the names) of barrow, hill, cross, pool, peak and knoll were perhaps read out loud by the scribe or cleric who accompanied the rider and/or walkers on their perambulation. Some of these features are natural, some the products of human activity, but all are long-standing features, landmarks such as the early burial mounds probably going back to Anglo-Saxon pagan times or even earlier.[25] For our purposes it is the description of the standing cross in the landscape that will occupy our attention. It is described as 'the Christ's cross', or perhaps this was perceived as a name, Christ's Cross. In either interpretation, *mæl* clearly means 'cross' rather than more generally a 'landmark' or 'monument', and it is identified as old, already old, that is, by the time King Edgar and Bishop Æthelwold came to view it in the tenth century.

In this respect another charter boundary clause is relevant, a gift of land at Newnham Murren in Oxfordshire by King Edgar to his kinswoman Ælfgifu, whose name, incidentally, had been centre-stage in the dynastic politics of the previous king's brief reign.[26] The transaction took place in the year 966:[27]

Þis sint þa gemæru to niwanhamme Cattan ege into niwanham of þam hæþnan birigelsan up andlang dic innan mær wege up andlang mær wege þæt up on wearddune þær þæt cristelmæl stod of þan up on þa readan slo oþ þære ealdan byrig of þære readan slo on þæt crundel þær se haga utligeþ.

[These are the bounds of Newnham from Catta's island to Newnham: from the heathen burials up along the ditch to the boundary way, up along the boundary way to the guardian-hill where the cross stood, from there up to the red slough as far as the old fortification, from the red slough to the quarry, outside of which the park lies.][28]

The key phrasing here is *wearddune þær þæt cristelmæl stod* which means literally 'the guardian-hill where the Christ's cross stood'. Here the term for Christ's cross is written and pronounced as *cristelmæl*, rather than *cristes mæl*, evidence that this is a well-established name that has been assimilated into the speech patterns of the population rather simply being a topographical description. What both these boundary descriptions suggest, then, is that the word *mæl* in place-names of the period meant 'cross', that crosses of this kind were often regarded as 'old', that they were sometimes placed on hills, and that their location became enshrined in the collective memory.

The cross at Maldon – perhaps made of perishable wood, perhaps of stone in the familiar shape of the so-called Celtic cross, with a circle joining its four corners – has long since gone. It may have existed for only a few generations, which was enough time, however, to fix its presence in the place-name Maldon itself. Perhaps the cross had been placed there in the 650s during the successful mission of the Northumbrian bishop Cedd to the pagan East Saxons in the 650s. These events are narrated in Bede's *Ecclesiastical History* (completed 731) by the great Northumbrian monk and writer Bede, whose ideas were highly influential in the later Anglo-Saxon period, particularly when, in the years around 900, Bede's Latin *History* was translated into Old English. That translation has considerable cultural–historical interest: it shows how Bede's Latin concepts were transformed when they were turned into the vernacular. And as in the charters, there are a number of passages where the Latin word *crux*, 'cross', is rendered with the Old English *mæl* as well as the more unambiguous noun *rōd* ('rood' or 'cross').

In Book III of the Old English *Bede*, for example, there is a description of Oswald, the pious Christian king of Northumbria who died in 642, working even with his own hands as he personally helps to construct a cross, called specifically 'a Christ's cross', and to set it in the ground:

Is þæt sægd, þæt he þæt Cristæs mæl hraðe weorce geworhte ond seað adulfe, in þæm hit stondan scolde. Ond he se cyning seolf wæs wallende in his geleafan; and þæt Cristes mæl genom and in þone seað sette ond mid his hondum bæm hit heold and hæfde, oð þæt his þegnas mid moldan hit bestryðed hæfdon ond gefæstnadan.[29]

Figure 6 'Cross Hill'. © Shutterstock/Agatha Kadar.

[It is said that he constructed the Christ's cross quickly and dug out the pit in which it was to stand. And the king himself was fervent in his faith; he picked up the Christ's cross and set it in the pit and held it and had it in his two hands while his thegns covered it with earth and fixed it there.]

Unlike this cross in Northumbria, we cannot know who placed the cross in the ground on the hill at Maldon, but the name must have been appropriate to the location, and it must have constituted a prominent feature in the Essex landscape. Here was a presence (or, at least, a ghost or memory of a presence) of a significant landmark, the *mæl* or cross on the hill at the top of the walled town, not far from the site of the battle. By 991, the church on that site was visible, no doubt, from longships plying the channel of the Blackwater estuary. If the place of conflict was known as 'the Battle of Crosshill', this would reinforce a religious interpretation of the battle, and there are even possibilities of symbolism: the place of the cross, where the great and pious lord of the East Saxons fell in defence of the nation. This, it may be argued, was how the battle was perceived and understood in the minds and memories of men and women at the time.

Chapter 2

Horse and hawk

Het þa hyssa hwæne   hors forlætan,
feor afysan,   and forð gangan,
hicgan to handum   and to hige godum.

THE BATTLE OF MALDON (2–4)

[Then he commanded each of his men to release their horses,
drive them far away, and go forth,
to think on the work at hand and on their firm resolve.]

A number of very particular, concrete images feature in the opening section of *The Battle of Maldon*. These include the horse that the English leader Byrhtnoth rides and the hawk that the young man releases to the *holt* or woodland. The mentions are brief and minimalist, but they are evocative, and each image represents a real object in the world of the poem. The horse and the hawk are domestic animals or, to qualify that slightly, they are at least 'tamed' animals, broken in for riding in the case of the horse, or trained for falconry in the case of the hawk, all part of the world of the aristocratic and land-owning classes of tenth-century England. As well as having a literal value, these *realia* take on symbolic significance: the horse, the hawk, the woodland – in various ways they suggest or even symbolize mindfulness, loyalty, affection, home and commitment, which are major themes of the poem. And invariably the poet returns to these images later in the text, imbuing them with further symbolic import.

'Direct your thoughts'

In his first speech in *The Battle of Maldon*, Byrhtnoth orders the men to abandon all the horses and drive them away and then move forward, for they must *hicgan to handum and to hige godum*, literally 'direct their thoughts to hands and good courage' (lines 2–4). The point is that the horses are a distraction, to be removed; they prevent the men from 'directing their thoughts'. This practice of mindfulness is expressed in Old English by the verb *hicgan*, found often in poetry, and by the closely related verb *hogian*, as found very often in prose writings. The verb implies focus, concentration and intention, with detachment from other concerns.[1] The Old English *Boethius*, for example, a philosophical treatise based on the Latin *Consolation of Philosophy* by the late Roman philosopher Boethius, warns the reader not to 'direct their thoughts' (the verb used is *hogian*) unduly towards the gaining of political power, for that kind of power pursues a person, whether they want it or not.[2] Alternatively, in a more positive example, there is desire for, and focus on, heaven expressed by the verb *higode* in the life of Honoratus in the Old English version of Gregory's *Dialogues*.[3]

The Old English biblical epic *Exodus* (215–20) provides an appropriate military parallel to the poem *The Battle of Maldon*. Here, in the process of translation, the text is domesticated and modernized: the biblical person comes to resemble a contemporary figure. In this reworking of the story, Moses is cast as an Anglo-Saxon war-leader as he leads his people out of captivity in Egypt. And as the Egyptians pursue them, he issues his orders for the army to be mustered. The situation is broadly similar to the one Byrhtnoth has to face in *Maldon*; the day breaks, the army gathers by the shore, the leader makes a speech of encouragement:

>   oð Moyses bebead
> eorlas on uhttid   ærnum bemum
> folc somnigean,   frecan arisan,
> habban heora hlencan,   *hycgan on ellen*,
> beran beorht searo,   beacnum cigean
> sweot sande near.[4]

> [until Moses gave instruction
> for noblemen with their brass trumpets in the early morning
> to summon the people, for warriors to rise,
> put on their mail-coats, *direct their thoughts to courage*,
> take up their bright war-equipment, and by these signals call up
> the army close by the shore.]

Whereas in *Exodus* the men should direct their thoughts to 'courage' (*hycgan on ellen*), in *Maldon* the object of their attention should be, Byrhtnoth asserts, their 'hands' (*hicgan to handum*). In *Maldon*, hands serve to hold shield and sword (lines 15 and 20) or to release a spear in flight (lines 108 and 150). In other words, 'hands' is a metonym that implies action, skill, training.

In *Maldon*, the practice of 'directing one's thoughts' seems to be exclusively associated with Byrhtnoth and his speeches and actions. Accordingly, after his opening exhortation he returns to the idea in mid-battle, shortly before his final fight. The relevant passage, in fact his ninth speech, covers lines 122–9, and it will be seen that there is a cluster of three different instances of the verb *hicgan / hogian* (highlighted in italics):

Swa stemnetton   stið*hicgend*e
hysas æt hilde,   *hogodon* georne
hwa þær mid orde   ærost mihte
on fægean men   feorh gewinnan,
wigan mid wæpnum;   wæl feol on eorðan.
Stodon stædefæste;   stihte hi Byrhtnoð,
bæd þæt hyssa gehwylc   *hogode* to wige
þe on Denon wolde   dom gefeohtan.

[So they prevailed, *sternly determined*,
the men in battle, they *directed their thoughts* eagerly
as to who first at weapon point
would win a life from fated warriors,
men at arms; the dead fell to the earth.
Steadfast they stood, Byrhtnoth encouraged them,
commanded that all his men *direct their thoughts to* the fight
if they wished to gain glory against the Danes.]

At this point in the narrative it may be confidently stated that the men are focussed and *determined*, literally the 'stern-thinking ones' (122), and naturally they continue to 'direct their thoughts' to fighting with their spears (123–5) and to gaining glory against the Danes (128–9). But a sudden reversal is about to take place. Shortly after this passage, there comes the long fight sequence in which Byrhtnoth is killed and his horse is stolen by one of the traitors. Thereafter, the verb *hicgan / hogian* disappears from the poem, as though all this leader-centred mindfulness evaporates once Byrhtnoth and his horse are out of the story. The men who remain will have to *re*think, to find their own way of dealing with the crisis.

Horse

From the evidence of the poem, and also from the study of records such as the Anglo-Saxon Chronicle, it looks like most of the East Saxon army will have ridden on horseback to the battlefield and then dismounted to fight.[5] Although chivalry as a concept was still in its infancy on the Continent and cavalry were not in very regular military use in Britain at this time, it is clear that fine horses were nevertheless a status symbol among the Anglo-Saxon elite. Contemporary art, especially the illustrations of late-tenth-century manuscripts, indicates the elaborate trappings with which horses were equipped in this period.[6]

In this respect, three illustrations in manuscripts of the Preface of Prudentius's *Psychomachia* are particularly appropriate, for example, in a tenth-century manuscript of this textbook poem associated with the school and scriptorium of Christ Church Cathedral in Canterbury.[7] Here the Preface retells – and the colourful pen-and-ink drawings illustrate – the story of Genesis 14, in which five kings attack the city of Sodom where Abram's kinsman Lot lives, and take him captive. In a second picture, Abram (at this stage his name has not been changed to Abraham) mounts an expedition to rescue Lot, and a mounted guide assists them in their quest.

On the next page (folio 5v) the illustration shows Abram and his men riding back victorious, with Lot and his wife now released. One noticeable

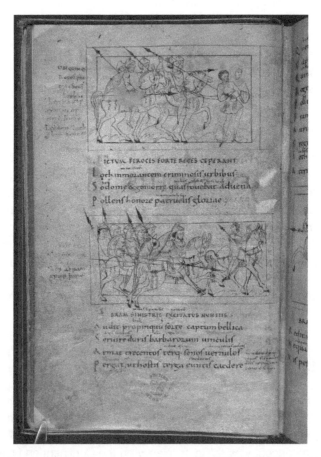

Figure 7 Abram rides out to rescue Lot, from Prudentius, *Psychomachia*. London, British Library, Cotton Cleopatra C. VIII, folio 4v. © The British Library.

aspect of these pictures is that all the characters are armed with spears, and it has been shown that spears are the usual weapon in the poem *Maldon*.[8] Some prominence is attached to the central figure of Abram: he has stirrups, whereas the five kings and other horsemen ride without stirrups. Abram's horse is bigger and finer: there is a sheepskin (or other animal skin) cover on the saddle, and the breeching and girth straps which hold the saddle in place appear to have little metal roundels attached to them, from which decorative tassels flutter in the wind as Abram's horse surges forward. Abram himself sits upright in the saddle: he is dressed in a short tunic, with a large cloak fixed at the right shoulder by a circular brooch. He wears flat black shoes on his feet and a kind of crested helmet on his head. Some of this detail may represent a real tenth-century ealdorman's dress and horse-trappings, while some individual features may be more 'semiotic'. Acquaintance with other manuscript illustrations, however, does show that the image of Abram conforms to the general 'look' of mounted thegns and ealdormen in the pictures of the period.[9] Wealth, power and status are represented in the elaborate saddles, the straps with their hanging pendants, the stirrups – the latter being a relatively recent innovation that was introduced, it is thought, by invading Vikings earlier in the tenth century.[10] Archaeology supports these conclusions. Excavations have uncovered many finds such as stirrups and spurs; there are also metal loops interpreted as decorative pendants intended to embellish horse reins, buckles for belts, and strap ends.[11]

It should be remembered that Old English poetry was rich in poetic diction, in its celebrated 'word-hoard', that is to say, the repertoire of words and phrases which include many synonyms used mostly in verse but generally avoided in prose. The ealdorman's horse in the poem *The Battle of Maldon* is referred to several times, but always with a poetic expression; the nouns used are *mearh* (188 and 239), *eoh* (189), *wicg* (240), all signifying 'horse'. These are hard to translate, for the resources of present-day English are hard-pressed to deliver suitable general synonyms for *horse* (*steed* and *mount* come to mind as still acceptable, but *destrier* is archaic and probably fails the test). The only time the poet mentions the other men's horses is of course in the opening scene, and there the humble prosaic word *hors* is all he needs (line 2). Consciously or not, the poet highlights the ealdorman's high-status horse through his choice of word. A similarly impressive warhorse is mentioned in *Beowulf* (1035–42), as one of the gifts that Hrothgar, king of the Danes, bestows on the hero Beowulf after his successful fight against Grendel. This particular horse stands out for its *sadol searwum fah, since gewurþad*, 'a saddle [. . .] made resplendent by cunning artistry, enhanced by rich adornments'.[12] If a recent amendment to the text of *Beowulf* is to be accepted, then this horse is also referred to by the poetic term *wicg*.[13]

In the opening scene of *Maldon*, it is up to the wary reader to notice that while all the horses have been driven away, Byrhtnoth stays mounted in order to inspect the men, and he only later dismounts among his personal retinue. This horse remains unmentioned until we hear how Godric, the son of Odda, was one of those who 'turned from the battle because they did not want to be there' (185). This is an ironic understatement if ever there was one, and it takes up the theme of intention and will, of directing one's thoughts, but here in its negative form. Just as the earl 'did not wish' to tolerate cowardice, so these men 'did not wish' to remain on the field. The horse that Godric steals (189–90) is defined by its high status as 'the horse that his lord had owned' and is given prominence in the passage 'with its harness and trappings' (OE *on þam geræedum*):

> he gehleop þone eoh þe ahte his hlaford,
> on þam geræedum þe hit riht ne wæs.
>
> [he mounted the steed that his lord had owned,
> with all its harness and trappings, though it was not a just action.]

The dramatic irony is in the situation, since this is the only horse left on the battlefield – at least officially – though if one is permitted to think 'outside the text', one may wonder whether Godric's brothers escape on horses cunningly concealed. Piling up the irony, the poet tells us that Byrhtnoth is Godric's lord and that this relationship had involved the giving of gifts (called *geearnunga*, 'favours', at lines 196–7); such generous, lordly gifts had included horses (187–8):

> Godric fram guþe,   and þone godan forlet
> þe him mænigne oft   mear gesealde.
>
> [Godric [fled] from the battle and abandoned the good prince
> who had often given him many a horse.]

Lordship as a relationship involved payment in kind: this is certainly true of the death-duty known as the heriot (OE *heregeatu*), by which a member of the tenth-century nobility paid back in kind to his lord (usually this lord was the king) the gift of horses, horse-trappings and swords and spears that he was held to have received when he took up service with him. A later Old English example illustrates this well. In the mid-eleventh century, a man called Ketel, who seems to have lived in Essex or East Anglia, decided to go on a pilgrimage to Rome, a dangerous journey that invariably meant an arduous crossing through the high passes of the Alps. In his will, Ketel refers to the possibility that he may not return, and so he bequeathes his heriot – including his horse and horse-trappings – to his lord, who in this case happens to be the archbishop:

> And ic an þat lond at Herlinge Stigand Archebisscop mine louerd so it stant buten þo men ben alle fre. and ten acres ic an into þe kirke. and gif ic ongein

ne cume; þan an ic him to min *heregete* an helm and a brenie. and *hors*. and *gereade*. and sverd and spere. and ic wille after þe forwarde þat ic and Eadwine. and Wlfric after mine time fon to alkere þinge þe min ower is þer on tune buten so mikel so ic an into þe kirke.

[And I grant to Archbishop Stigand, my lord, the estate at Harling just as it stands, except that the men shall all be free, and that I grant ten acres to the church. And if I do not come back again, I grant to him as my *heriot* a helmet and a coat of mail and a *horse* with *harness* and a sword and a spear. And I desire that in accordance with the agreement Edwin and Wulfric shall after my time succeed to everything which is mine everywhere in the village, except so much as I grant to the church.][14]

As we will see in Chapter 4, Byrhtnoth makes ironic allusion to a heriot in his speech to the Viking messenger. But here, at this later point in the narrative of *Maldon*, Godric as it were repudiates any such debt when he steals his own lord's horse in order to escape the battle. The verb used is *forlet*: Godric 'abandoned' his good prince; and precisely this verb, *forlætan*, was used by Byrhtnoth at the beginning of the battle preparations (*Maldon*, 2) when he ordered his men 'to abandon' their horses and drive them away. Is the echo deliberate? Old English poetry is noted for ironic textures, repetitions and significant word order: certainly many critics have observed such features in *Beowulf*.[15] Moreover, the poem *Beowulf*, as we shall see in Chapter 9, has close links to *Maldon* and may have been used as a source or model by the poet.

The second mention of the ealdorman's *horse* in the poem appears in the speech of the nobleman Offa (237–42), another account of Godric's betrayal, this time given by a character in the poem rather than by the all-seeing narrator. Rather than name Godric as 'cowardly' (OE *earh* or *earg*) the narrator prefers to leave this accusation to be made by Offa, who uses the adjective at line 238, the only instance of it in the whole poem:

> [. . .] 'Us Godric hæfð,
> earh Oddan bearn,   ealle beswicene.

> ['Godric,
> cowardly son of Odda, has betrayed us all.]

In general, cowardice is implied rather than stated in *Maldon*, yet numerous critics of this poem write about Godric and his brothers as 'the cowards', as if the poet uses this term freely and regularly. In fact the men who flee are seen as fugitives rather than cowards. Cowardice is conspicuous by its absence: the young falconer at lines 5–6 infers from the abandonment of the horses that Byrhtnoth will not tolerate 'cowardice' (OE *yrhðo*, a derivative of the adjective *earh*). The narrator tells us that 'uncowardly men' (206a: *unearge men*) hastened forward on hearing of the death of Byrhtnoth and the flight of the brothers. Presumably, Godric and his brothers are by contrast to be regarded as *earge*, 'cowards', as well as being fugitives, but the narrator does not state this as such.

By contrast, the *unearge men* are the brave men, also described by the poetic device of variation as *wlance þegenas*, 'proud thegns' (205b), *wlanc* being a generally positive adjective, with connotations of pride and splendour (rather than of pride as vice or sin, as with the celebrated noun *ofermod*). In the context of Offa's speech, one further feature to note is that Byrhtnoth's horse is also deemed to be *wlanc*, 'proud and splendid' (240a) 'when he [Godric] rode off on the horse, on the proud steed' (*þa he on meare rad, / on wlancan þam wicge*). Such a description of the general's horse is very reminiscent of Abram's horse in the *Psychomachia* illustrations, and it is not unreasonable to suggest that a well-educated tenth-century poet would have known such manuscripts, for Prudentius's *Psychomachia* was a widely used schoolbook in the monastic and cathedral schools. It seems that a number of symbolic associations hover around *Maldon*'s unique horse, which becomes the focus for the tension between bravery and cowardice in the middle section of the poem.

Hawk

If in the opening scene the sending away of the horses, is, by implication, an act of courage, a similar dramatic gesture follows immediately. It centres on the figure of a hawk (or falcon) and a young falconer. The person involved is a *cniht* – that is, a young member of the nobility with riding duties – and also a *mæg*, or kinsman to the thegn Offa, who, as we have intimated, functions as the second-in-command of the English forces. As Offa's kinsman, this young man is therefore important, and this cameo appearance obviously serves a purpose. Following the abandonment of the horses, the young kinsman responds as follows (lines 5–9):

> Þa þæt Offan mæg   ærest onfunde
> þæt se eorl nolde   yrhðo geþolian,
> he let him þa of handon   leofne fleogan
> hafoc wið þæs holtes,   and to þære hilde stop.

> [So when Offa's kinsman first realized
> that the earl would not tolerate any cowardice,
> he let his favourite fly from his hands
> – his falcon to the forest – and stepped forward to the fight.]

In this passage, word order plays a meaningful role.[16] At the line 'he let his favourite fly from his hands' the information is delayed, since, as a listening audience, we do not know who the favourite is – who literally the 'dear one' is – that the young man is allowing to fly. The masculine noun to which the adjective *leof* refers ('the dear, beloved one') is not made clear until the next line, when we learn that it is the *hawk*. And by then the emotional wrench is over, for already the hawk is on his escape flight to the woodland as the young man steps forward to the battle. Why is the hawk loved so dearly? At first sight, the affection towards the hawk may be surprising, particularly as the other uses of *leof* in the poem refer to Byrhtnoth, and the affection with which he is held by his men at lines 23, 208 and 319 (for more discussion see Chapter 8). Clearly, the implications of the beloved hawk require further exploration.

I am aware of only one other scene in tenth-century writing in which a hawk is released to the woods, and this hawk is not particularly a well-loved bird. Ælfric of Eynsham's *Colloquy on the Occupations* is an innovative text used from the 990s for the teaching of Latin in the monastic schools, its originality (though based ultimately on Greek models) lying in its use of role-play to teach and practise Latin speaking and listening, grammar and vocabulary. Each pupil is allocated a role to play as ploughman, shepherd, oxherd, hunter, fisherman, fowler, merchant, shoemaker, salter, baker, cook, monk, smith and counsellor. The *magister*, 'teacher', then asks *what* and *why* questions in Latin to each pupil in turn, who answers in role, using language as appropriate to his occupation. The dialogue is lively, with opportunities for disagreement, humour and repartee; hence it is memorable and conducive to learning. And all the language thus practised is relevant to the rural society of tenth-century England but also, at the same time, appropriate to a monastic community that engaged in farming and other occupations. The text itself is in Latin with a continuous interlinear gloss in Old English to explain the Latin words, useful for both teacher and learner.

The role of fowler in the *Colloquy* follows this model. He is a member of the peasantry rather than the nobility. He is practical and pragmatic rather than courtly, for he uses all possible methods for catching his birds, from nets to traps, from lime to hawks, both large (perhaps a goshawk) and small (perhaps a sparrowhawk). He is willing to exchange his hawk for a hound and has no emotional attachment to the bird he has trained. The *magister* asks him how he keeps his hawks, and the fowler replies that he tames them and uses them in winter for catching birds to eat, then releases them to the woods in the spring so that he does not have to feed them in the summer:

Latin text: Ipsi pascunt se et me in hieme, et in uere dimitto eos auolare ad siluam, et capio mihi pullos in autumno, et domito eos.

Old English gloss: Hig fedaþ hig sylfe and me on wintra, and on lencgten ic læte hig ætwindan to wuda, and genyme me briddas on hærfæste, and temige hig.

[They feed themselves and me in winter, and in the spring I let them escape to the woods, and capture new birds in the autumn, and tame them.]

This is the pragmatist's approach: it is all about saving money and keeping down the costs.[17]

Nothing could be further from the courtly art of falconry as practised by members of the early medieval (and indeed later medieval) nobility.

Mentions in the various wills of the thegnly class suggest that hawks were highly valued; for example, among the rich gifts that the Kentish nobleman Brihtric left to his royal lord (this must be either King Edgar or King Æthelred) are *twegen hafocas and ealle his headorhundas*, 'two hawks and all his stag-hounds'.[18] A hawk was for life, not for a season, and the nobleman seems to have developed close ties with his birds. Members of the nobility, with their characteristic cloaks and shoulder brooches, are seen hunting with hawks in

Figure 8 Hunting with hawks, from the Julius Calendar. London, British Library, Cotton Julius A.VI, folio 7v. © The British Library.

Figure 9 The falcon in the Julius Calendar. © The British Library.

the illustrated Julius Calendar depicting the Occupations of the Months.[19] And to take a later example, the Bayeux Tapestry shows the powerful earl Harold Godwineson (later King Harold II) riding a proud stallion into the woods, with his hounds coursing hares in the trees in front of him, and his retainers on lesser horses bringing up the rear. Held by its foot-straps or jesses, a suitably proud falcon sits up high, its eyes staring ahead.[20] The image is reminiscent of the falcon illustrated in the Julius Calendar.

In general, the figure of the hawk had many associations. In the Old English lexicon, different species are identified by size and function as *mushafoc*, 'kestrel' (for catching mice), or *spearhafoc*, the self-explanatory 'sparrowhawk', and *goshafoc*, 'goshawk' (for catching geese); or by origin as in the case of the *wealhhafoc*, which like the *wealh-hnutu*, the 'walnut' or 'foreign nut', denoted the special bird supposedly 'from abroad', the peregrine falcon. Though there is no extant falconry treatise from this period, some passages in Old English poems from the famous Exeter Book evoke the noble art of hawking implied by these terms. The best example is *The Fortunes of Men*, with its brief scenes from the lives of the nobility. Like a small miniature, lines 80–4 evoke the music of the plucked harp string in a princely hall; by contrast, lines 93–8 conclude the poem with a religious message of thanks to the ordaining Lord who has shaped and guided the destinies of every man and woman upon the earth. Between these two passages comes the following cameo, a poetic epitome of the falconer's art (lines 85–92):

> Sum sceal wildne fugel   wloncne atemian,
> heafoc on honda,   oþþæt seo heoroswealwe
> wynsum weorþeð;   deþ he wyrplas on,
> fedeþ swa on feterum   fiþrum dealne,
> lepeþ lyftswiftne   lytlum gieflum,
> oþþæt se wælisca   wædum ond dædum
> his ætgiefan   eaðmod weorþeð
> ond to hagostealdes   honda gelæred.[21]

S. A. J. Bradley translates as follows (I have slightly adjusted the punctuation):

> One shall train the proud wild bird, the hawk to his hand, until the savage bird becomes a thing of delight. He puts jesses upon it and thus feeds it – whose pride is in its wings – in fetters, and [he] gives the swift flier little scraps to eat until the unfriendly bird becomes subservient to his provider in livery and in actions, and accustomed to the young man's hand.[22]

The alliterating attributes of this hawk are *wlonc*, 'proud and splendid', just like Byrhtnoth's horse as we noted earlier, and *wynsum*, 'beautiful', an adjective derived from *wynn*, 'joy', hence Bradley's elegant translation, 'a thing of delight'. But to achieve this goal the falconer invests hours of patient training so that *se wælisca* is tamed. The latter expression *se wælisca* has various associations. It could mean 'servile' or perhaps even 'unfriendly'. But since the primary meaning of *wælisc* is connected with *wealh*, 'foreigner' (cf. *wealas*, literally 'the foreigners', to denote *y Cymry*, i.e. 'the Welsh'), one may quibble over the rendering 'the unfriendly bird'. Is this phrase rather to be rendered 'peregrine falcon'?

There is an oppressive tone to this description of the taming and humbling of the foreign, the Welsh, the unfriendly bird, until it has become *eaðmod*, 'humble' and 'subservient'. The same tension is felt in other, much more recent accounts of the training of a hawk. In her autobiographical *H is for Hawk* (2014) Helen Macdonald takes to task the writer T. H. White for his account of hawking in his *The Goshawk* (1951), since she argues that White intermittently treated and then maltreated the bird in his charge.[23] If Macdonald is right, White overfed his hawk and failed to achieve the balance, what the Old English poet would have called 'giving the swift flier little scraps to eat until the unfriendly bird becomes subservient to his provider'. The enormity of that task is well expressed by Macdonald as she contemplates her own goshawk:

> Here's one thing I know from years of training hawks: one of the things you must learn to do is become invisible. It's what you do when a fresh hawk sits on your left fist with food beneath her feet, in a state of savage, defensive fear. Hawks aren't social animals like dogs or horses; they understand neither coercion nor punishment. The only way to tame them is through positive reinforcement with gifts of food. You want the hawk to eat the food you hold – it's the first step in reclaiming her that will end with you being hunting partners.[24]

The hunting partnership becomes, in Old English terms, the fulfilment of the falconer's art, or *cræft* as it was called. It is this that allows the falconer to become what another Old English poem terms *hafeces cræftig*, that is, 'skilled with the hawk', or perhaps rather, 'skilled in the art of the hawk'.[25]

The other side of the coin is the sheer admiration of the *lyft-swiftne*, 'the air-swift one'. That admiration is present in the adjectives *wild* and *wlonc* and *wynsum* in *The Fortunes of Men*, or in the proverbial saying *Hafuc sceal on glofe wilde gewunian* ('Hawk must dwell wild on the glove') in the poem *Maxims II*, where the hawk is tame on the glove and yet at the same time remains wild. And the joy is felt in the sense of movement, here in a passage from the epic poem *Beowulf*, lines 2262–5:

> Næs hearpan wyn,
> gomen gleobeames,   ne god hafoc
> geond sæl swingeð,   ne se swifta mearh
> burhstede beateð.

> [The pleasure of the harp is no more, the joyous sound of the singing wood, nor does the noble hawk sweep though the hall, nor does the swift horse gallop through the township.][26]

Again, albeit in an elegiac passage, the joy and delight of the harp and the swiftness of a horse are associated with the noble hawk, winging its way through the airy space beneath the roofbeam in the high hall of a royal lord.

Such are the associations, then, of the *leof hafoc*, 'the beloved hawk' of *The Battle of Maldon*. Though the passage in which it appears is short, the background behind it is wide and, I think, necessary to know for a confident reading of the poem. The blend of joy and admiration achieved by hours of training explains the affection that the young *cniht*, Offa's kinsman, feels for his hawk. But why does he release it? The poem's narrator offers this explanation at lines 9–10:

> be þam man mihte oncnawan   þæt se cniht nolde
> wacian æt þam wige,   þa he to wæpnum feng.

> [by this it could be seen that the young man
> would not weaken in the battle, when he took up his weapons.]

There is a homiletic effect in the expression *be þam*, 'by this', that introduces the moral comment. Numerous parallels in Old English sermons, homilies and religious treatises could be adduced for this kind of language; here are two instances, the first again taken from the philosophical work known as the Old English *Boethius*, the second from a homily by the later writer Archbishop Wulfstan. The *Boethius* passage is as follows:

> Be þam is swiðe sweotol ðætte God æghwæs wealt mid þæm helman & mid ðæm stioroðre his goodnesse.[27]

> [By this it is very clear that God rules in every way with the helmet and the rudder of his goodness.]

Wulfstan in his homily is concerned with the 'very great symbolism' (*swiðe micel getacnunge*) involved in the ceremony of christening and baptism, in which every action of the priest during the ritual is explained symbolically. Wulfstan goes on to emphasize the social levelling that is implied in the *Paternoster*, that is, the 'Our Father' or Lord's Prayer, for all Christians pray the same prayer, whatever their social status, whether they are a lord or a servant, a lady or a maid:

> Be þam we magon ongitan and oncnawan þæt we synd ealle gebroðra and eac geswustra þonne we ealle to anum heofenlicum fæder swa oft clypiað swa we ure pater noster singað.[28]

> [By this we may understand and see that we are all brothers and sisters when we all call upon the one heavenly Father as often as we sing our Paternoster.]

If we take *be þam* in *Maldon* in the same way, the whole of the preceding narrative of the *cniht* releasing his beloved hawk becomes an exemplum, an illustrative moralizing story; it is a sign or symbol of the young man's renunciation of leisure pursuits and falconry, his refusal to weaken in the fight to come, and his resolve to honour his obligations.

'Beasts of battle'

Unlike the horse, the hawk does not reappear later in the poem. However, there are a number of moments where the absence of the hawk is felt, or where the poet at least offers hints or reminders of the hawk's actions earlier in the poem. One such moment is at the start of the main hostilities, after the Vikings – here called *wælwulfas* 'wolves of battle' – have been allowed by Byrhtnoth to cross the causeway (line 96–9) and the poet has stated that the 'time had come when fated men must fall' (lines 104–5). Picking up on the mention of wolves, the poet then gives his variant on the classic motif of the beasts of battle – usually wolves, carrion eagle and ravens – that appear in Old English epics, religious or secular, whenever battle is afoot (106–7):

Þær wearð hream ahafen,   hremmas wundon,
earn æses georn;   wæs on eorþan cyrm.

[A clamour was raised, ravens circled,
eagle ready for carrion; on earth there was noise.]

In a classic 'envelope pattern', as found in *Beowulf* and other poems, in which a passage begins and ends with the same idea, the *Maldon* poet emphasizes the sound and the fury of the opening engagement. Again some parallels serve to illustrate the connotations. *Hream*, the word that begins the envelope, is associated by alliteration and rhyme with the word for ravens, *hremmas*, as Richard Dance points out.[29] It is also the noise of shouting, heard for instance from the 'ploughman' in Ælfric's *Colloquy*:

Latin text: Habeo quendam puerum minantem boues cum stimulo, qui etiam modo raucus est pre frigore et clamatione.

Old English gloss: ic hæbbe sumne cnapan þywende oxan mid gadisene, þe eac swilce nu has ys for cylde and hreame.

[I have a boy driving the oxen with a goad, who is hoarse now from the cold and the shouting.]

Similarly, *cyrm* is a loud noise, one that rises in the air, associated sometimes with the noise of an army shouting, as in the following from the poem *Andreas* (1155–6):

Þa wæs wop hæfen   in wera burgum,
hlud heriges cyrm.

[Then lamentation was raised up in the cities of men,
the loud noise of an army.]

But the word is also used of the beast-like devils that attack the saint in the Guthlac stories set in the East Anglian fens. In both the prose and the poetic versions, the hermit-saint is at his vigils and prayers in the night when the attack comes:

> þa on þære nihte stilnesse gelamp semninga, þæt þær com micel mænego þara werigra gasta. (5.107) And hie eal þæt hus mid heora *cyrme* gefyldon; and him on ælce healfe inguton, ufan and neoþan and æghwænon. (5.111) Wæron hie on syne egeslice.[30]

> [Then suddenly in the middle of the night there came a great crowd of the accursed spirits. And they filled all the house with their *noise*, and they found their way in everywhere from above and below. And the sight of them was terrible.]

In the poetic version (*Guthlac B*, 907–12), the related verb *cirman* is used:

> Hwilum wedende   swa wilde deor
> *cirmdon* on corðre,   hwilum cyrdon eft
> minne mansceaþan   on mennisc hiw
> breahtma mæste,   hwilum brugdon eft
> awyrgde wærlogan   on wyrmes bleo,
> earme adloman   attre spiowdon.

> [Sometimes raging like wild beasts, they would *clamour* in chorus, sometimes the evil and wicked ravagers would turn back into human form with the utmost din, sometimes the damned faith-breakers would be transformed again into the shape of a dragon and the fire-crippled wretches would spew forth venom.][31]

As a verb, *cyrman* is also associated with the loud cries of animals and birds.[32] In *Maldon*, these meanings are all present: the noise of the birds rises in the air just as the clamour of the warriors breaks out on the earth. At this point in the poem, human and nonhuman noises meet and mingle.[33]

The 'beasts of battle' scene in *Maldon* may be compared and contrasted with the use of the same motif as written some sixty years before in *The Battle of Brunanburh*, the Chronicle poem of 937. This poem, inserted into the Anglo-Saxon Chronicle, celebrates the victory of King Æthelstan over the Scots and the Dublin Vikings, after which Æthelstan was able to consolidate his position as first king of England. At the end of the poem, the poet takes up the theme of homecoming: the Scots and the Vikings return to their respective lands mourning their losses (lines 37–44, 53–6), whereas Æthelstan and his brother Edmund go home to Wessex in militaristic triumph (57–65):

> Swilce þa gebroþer   begen ætsamne,
> cyning and æþeling,   cyþþe sohton,

Wesseaxena land,   wiges hremige.
Letan him behindan   hræw bryttian
saluwigpadan,   þone sweartan hræfn,
hyrnednebban,   and þane hasewan padan,
earn æftan hwit,   æses brucan,
grædigne guðhafoc   and þæt græge deor,
wulf on wealde.[34]

[Likewise those brothers, the two together, king and prince, headed for home, the land of the West Saxons, vaunting their valour. Behind them they left sharing out the corpses the dark-plumaged, horny-beaked black raven, and the dun-plumaged white-tailed eagle enjoying the carrion, the greedy war-hawk and that grey beast, the wolf of the forest.][35]

In this variant on the theme, the creatures are characterized by their colour and visual appearance, as the black raven and the grey wolf, while the eagle is described by various attributes, including the idea that it is a *grædigne guðhafoc*, literally 'a greedy war-hawk', reminiscent of *Maldon* poet's *earn æses georn*, 'the eagle eager for carrion'. In *Maldon* the beloved hawk, the bird of peacetime and leisure pursuits, flies to the woods at the outset, but once the battle starts, it is replaced by the far more threatening, and clamorous, birds of war.

Finally, one other reminder of the release of the hawk is the recurring motif of the hand that releases and lets fly the missile. For example, the 'beasts of battle' theme at the beginning of the hostilities is followed by a passage on the hurling of spears (108–9):

Hi leton þa of folman   feolhearde speru,
gegrundene garas fleogan.

[They let fly from their hands the file-hardened spears,
the sharpened javelins.]

At first sight it might be thought that this passage has no connection with the release of the hawk earlier in the poem. But as a quick glance will show, the syntax is very similar:

he let his favourite fly from his hands
– his falcon to the forest – and stepped forward to the fight.

There are similar 'let . . . fly' syntactic constructions denoting the release of spears at lines 149–50, 156, 321–2. This makes for an intriguing parallel, with a faint suggestion that hawks and spears, once they are released from the hand, have a life of their own, beyond the control of the warrior who wields them.

The Old English verbs *fleon* 'to flee' and *fleogan* 'to fly' both have a past tense plural form *flugon*. This again creates internal echoes within the poem, for just as the hawk flew *wið þæs holtes* 'to the holt' (8a), the definite article making *the* woodland definite and specific, so the brothers Godwine and Godwig sought out *þone wudu* and saved their lives (192–4):

> Godwine and Godwig,   guþe ne gymdon,
> ac wendon fram þam wige   and þone wudu sohton,
> flugon on þæt fæsten   and hyra feore burgon.

> [Godwine and Godwig, who did not care for battle
> but turned from the war and sought the woods,
> flew to safety and protected their lives.]

The woods of early medieval England were mostly woodland pasture, with pollards and deer enclosures; it was quite possible to ride a horse through it unimpeded.[36] The woodland at the rear of the English lines thus becomes the place of refuge, as it does also, probably in a very different kind of woodland setting, in the epic poem *Beowulf* (2596–9) when the Geatish companions take flight *on holt* 'to the woods' during Beowulf's fight with the dragon, prompting Wiglaf (a kind of model for Ælfwine in *Maldon*) to make his speech of do-or-die (see Chapter 9 for more discussion). In brief, the woodland is the symbolic location, to which birds, horses and humans fly, within the topography of the poem.

Chapter 3

Hearth and home

Þa he hæfde þæt folc   fægere getrymmed,
he lihte þa mid leodon   þær him leofost wæs,
þær he his heorðwerod   holdost wiste.

THE BATTLE OF MALDON (22–4)

[When he had deployed the people appropriately,
he dismounted among the men, where it was dearest to him,
where he knew his hearth-troop to be most loyal.]

In the early Middle Ages, war was generally seasonal; a campaign began in the summer when the roads were dry and passable and the weather was clement; in the winter hostilities ceased, and Viking armies, if they remained in the country, laid low and waited for spring. People were called to war, they went on campaign, then they returned to their towns and villages when the battle was over. It is this theme of departure from home and return home that will be explored in this chapter, and we begin with the figure of authority, the king's representative, the ealdorman.

Fyrd and *folc*

In the scene of preparations at the beginning of *The Battle of Maldon*, Ealdorman Byrhtnoth rides up and down the ranks to complete his arrangements for the coming battle (17–24). In doing so, he is fulfilling one of his major duties, to lead the men of the region in military defence; this is his role as *þæs folces ealdor* (202b), the prince or 'leader of the people', as the poem puts it.[1] The men in the ranks, called poetically the *beornas*, 'warriors', in line 17b, are clearly the ordinary soldiers, the land-owning freemen (farmers and the like) who owe their military service to the king or his representative, the ealdorman.

Such men make up the *fyrd*: in other words, these are the levies or militia, so named because they form an 'expedition', a 'travelling forth', for the noun *fyrd* is connected with the verb *faran* or *feran* 'to travel', and it is the usual term for such a defensive expeditionary force in the various versions of the Anglo-Saxon Chronicle. As the poem shows, Byrhtnoth invests a great deal of time speaking to these men; he rides along the ranks advising men how to stand and hold their position, insisting that they hold their shields firmly in their hands and 'not be afraid' (17–21).

Though some commentators have doubted it, this passage describes a seasoned general speaking to an untrained *fyrd* made up of farmers and others who need precise instructions on how to form the shield-wall correctly. These are not seasoned warriors but ordinary men, who need encouragement to stand their ground and not be afraid. The traditional shield-wall, or 'battle-wall' as it is called later in the poem, was made up of two ranks of men, the front rank holding their shields at chest height, the rear rank raising their shields above the heads of the front rank to create the effect of a defensive 'wall'.[2] This formation would need some practice, and it seems that Byrhtnoth is still training the men. A key line in the original text makes this clear (line 18); its rhythm, which certainly contributes to its overall effect, may be appreciated by reading or chanting the line out loud:

rad and rædde   rincum tæhte

[literally: he rode and gave counsel, and showed to the men . . .]

The phrase *rad and rædde* sums up the East Saxon ealdorman's actions. Meaning literally 'he rode and advised', the verse has a falling rhythm or 'Sievers type A' verse: the same falling rhythm ('dum-di, dum-di') is also used for the off-verse, or second half-line, *rincum tæhte*, literally 'to-warriors showed'. There is the common double alliteration of the 'r' in *rad and rædde* of the first half-line (the on-verse), followed by the 'r' of *rincum* in the off-verse. Since the alliterating lifts were normally nouns, adjectives or infinitives, it is unusual to place past tense verbs in prominent positions in the line, and even more unusual to find assonance and half-rhyme on the two verbs of exhortation *rædde* and *tæhte*. The poet is here departing from the norms of the traditional metre. But style closely matches content here: the theme is movement and exhortation at this point in the story, and the poet has chosen his verbs, and his rhymes, appropriately. Moreover, there are political echoes, perhaps deliberate, such as the motif of *ræd* meaning 'counsel, advice': this will be the major preoccupation of Chronicle C, as will be discussed in Chapter 10. The implication is that Byrhtnoth – unlike some of his compatriots – is better placed to give 'good counsel' as he exhorts and encourages the *fyrd*.

Figure 10 A shield-wall in action. © Shutterstock/D. Pimborough.

The use of *folc* in the poem is suggestive: it makes the *fyrd* representative of 'the people', adding a patriotic element to the description. Similarly, Chronicle C also uses the noun *folc* on a number of occasions with the double meanings of both 'people' and 'defence-force'.[3] In the annal for 1001, to cite a particular example, Chronicle C reports as follows:

> Þa gesomnede man þær ormæte fyrde Defenisces folces 7 Sumersætisces folces, 7 hi ða tosomne comon æt Peonnho, 7 sona swa hi togædere coman, þa beah þæt folc, 7 hi ðær mycel wæll ofslogan 7 ridon þa ofer þæt land, 7 wæs æfre heora æftra siþ wyrsa þonne se æra, 7 mid him ða micle herehuðe to scipon brohton.[4]

> [Then an enormous defence-force was assembled – of the Devon people and the Somerset people – and they came together (i.e. in battle) then at Pinhoe, and as soon as they they had come together the *folc* fled, and they (the Vikings) made a great slaughter and rode over the countryside, and their second sortie was worse than their first, and took great plunder with them to their ships.]

This is clearly an example of where the local *folc* 'people' are formed into a militia, untrained and ill-equipped, who flee the field at the very first moment of trouble with the enemy. And that is precisely Byrhtnoth's concern in the account given in *Maldon*: as a seasoned general, Byrhtnoth is seeking to strengthen the morale of the defence-force.

The other risk, of course, is that the general himself will desert the battlefield, causing his untrained troops to flee with him; which is what happened in Wiltshire in the year 1003, according to the C Chronicle:

Þa sceolde se ealdorman Ælfric lædan þa fyrde, ac he teah ða forð his ealdan wrencas. Sona swa hi wæron swa gehende þæt ægðer here on oþerne hawede, þa gebræd he hine seocne 7 ongan hine brecan to spiwenne 7 cwæð þæt he gesicled wære, 7 swa þæt folc becyrde þæt he lædan sceolde, swa hit gecweden ys, þonne se heretoga wacað, þonne bið eall se here swiðe gehindrad. Þa Swegen geseah þæt hi anræde næron 7 þæt hi ealle toforan, þa lædde he his here into Wiltune, 7 hi þa buruh geheregodon 7 forbærndon, 7 eode him þa to Searbyrig 7 þanone eft to sæ ferde þær he wiste his yðhengestas.

[then Ealdorman Ælfric should have led the army, but he took to his old tricks: as soon as they were close at hand that each of them looked on the other, then he pretended to be ill, and began to retch so as to vomit, and said that he was taken ill, and thus betrayed the people that he should have led. As the saying goes: 'When the commander weakens then the whole army is greatly hindered.' Then when Swein saw that they were not resolute, and all dispersed, he led his raiding-army into Wilton and raided and burned down the town, and then went to Salisbury and from there back to the sea, travelled to where he knew his 'wave-stallions' were.][5]

Again we have the *fyrd* presented as equivalent to the *folc*. Moreover, the fact that this ealdorman 'betrayed' the people, his *folc*, at the moment when battle was joined, is reminiscent of the betrayal of Godric and his brothers in *Maldon*.[6] There is also the adjective *anræd* 'of one counsel' that is, 'resolute', which is used to describe Byrhtnoth in *The Battle of Maldon*. By contrast, this passage from the Chronicle describes the absence of unity in the English – the fact they are decidedly not *anræd* or 'of one counsel', which allows the Viking leader Swegn the opportunity to plunder and burn and then escape to his ships. All this is underlined by the chronicler's poetic style seen and heard in his striking use of a sturdy rhythm and alliteration, with even an alliterative proverb to underline his point:[7]

þonne se **h**eretoga wacað, þonne bið eall se **h**ere swiðe ge**h**indrad.

[When the commander weakens then the whole army is greatly hindered.]

In the final cadence of annal, there is the kenning or poetic compound *yðhengestas*, in which *yð* means 'wave' and *hengest* 'horse'. The 'sea-stallion' is of course a poetic image for a ship or longboat, and it is found in the variant form *sæ-hengest* in the poem *Andreas* (line 488),[8] and *sundhengest* in *Christ II* (line 852) by the poet Cynewulf.[9] Here, as in *The Battle of Maldon*, the poetic language is being used by the writer to underline his rhetoric and his urgent political message, namely that the country needs to be *of one counsel* if it is to repel the Danish threat to its shores.

Hearth-troop

In *The Battle of Maldon*, after the arrangement and encouragement of the *fyrd*, the poem moves on, as also does Byrhtnoth, for he chooses not to remain with the defence-force. An apparently minor use of the possessive pronoun *his* in the passage cited at the beginning of this chapter further demonstrates that these men of the *fyrd* are not his own men as such, for the poet tells us that Byrhtnoth now dismounts from his horse at an appropriately separate location (22–4):

> When he had deployed the people appropriately,
> he dismounted among the men, where it was dearest to him,
> where he knew his hearth-troop to be most loyal.

A distinction is drawn here between 'the people' (*þæt folc*), that is, the ordinary people who make up the nation as represented in the *fyrd*, and '*his* hearth-troop' (*his heorðwerod*). The personal pronoun suggests that this is Byrhtnoth's own household, and the context supports it: the two superlatives *leofost*, 'dearest', and *holdost*, 'most loyal', emphasize the emotional bonds, the mutual affection and loyalty that bind these men together.

The language of loyalty employed here is also what the historian F. W. Maitland called 'the personal bond' of lordship in the pre-Conquest period,[10] and it suggests that at least some of these warriors are not only Byrhtnoth's household retainers but also his 'commended men'. The term is very specific: these are people who perhaps held land or fulfilled duties elsewhere, but had specifically sought out this ealdorman to be their patron and representative, the act of 'commendation' involving ceremonial oaths of loyalty and dependency.[11] The actual oath that was used is recorded in *Swerian*, a legal text of the tenth century (though the practice may well be older than this date); it should be noted that this oath is thoroughly Christian, and is taken in the presence of holy relics, perhaps with the man's hand on the altar or casket containing the relics:[12]

> Hu se man sceal swerie. On ðone Drihten, þe ðes haligdom is fore halig, ic wille beon N. hold and getriwe and eal lufian ðæt he lufað and eal ascunian ðæt he ascunað, æfter Godes rihte and æfter woroldgerysnum, and næfre

willes ne gewealdes, wordes ne weorces owiht don ðæs him laðre bið, wið þam ðe he me healde, swa ic earnian wille, and eall þæt læste, þæt uncer formæl wæs, þa ic to him gebeah and his willan geceas.[13]

[How the man must swear an oath. By the Lord, before whom these relics are holy, I will be loyal and true to N., and love all that he loves, and hate all that he hates, in accordance with God's rights and secular obligations; and never, willingly and intentionally, in word or deed, do anything that is harmful to him; on condition that he keeps me as I shall deserve, and carry out all that was our agreement, when I subjected myself to him [to him gebeah] and chose his favour.][14]

A passage in the Exeter Book poem *The Wanderer* (41–4) seems to picture such a ceremony, where the commended man kneels before his chosen lord in an act of submission:

þinceð him on mode   þæt he his mondryhten
clyppe ond cysse,   ond on cneo lecge
honda ond heafod, swa he hwilum ær
in geardagum   giefstolas breac.

[It seems to him in his mind that he embraces and kisses
his lord and lays on his knee
hands and head, as he at times before
in days of old enjoyed the gift seats.][15]

The practice of bowing before the liege lord is captured in the idiom of the verb *bugan*, which normally means 'to bow, bend', but can also signify in certain contexts, 'to submit to someone, to accept someone as one's spiritual or secular authority', as in the following passages from versions of the Chronicle:[16]

Chronicle C 901: hi hine underfengon hym to cinge 7 him to bugon.
[They received him as their king and submitted to him.]

Chronicle E 1085: 7 ealle hi bugon to him 7 weron his menn 7 him holdaðas sworon þet hi woldon ongean ealle oðre men him holde beon.
[And they all submitted to him and were his men and swore loyal oaths to him that they would be loyal to him against all other men.]

Other passages in the corpus of Old English point to the existence of commendation as a form of lordship, the Old English term being *manræden*. Perhaps the clearest example is post-Conquest, from Version E of the Chronicle for the year 1115:

Her wæs se cyng Henri to Natiuiteð on Normandig; 7 onmang þam þe he þær wæs, he dyde þet ealle þa heafodmæn on Normandig *dydon manræden* 7 holdaðas his sunu Willelme þe he be his cwæne hæfde, 7 æfter þan syððan innon Iulies monðe hider into lande com.

[Here King Henry was in Normandy over Christmas; and during the time he was there he arranged that all the chief men in Normandy *were commended* and swore oaths of loyalty to his son William whom he had with his queen, and after that he returned here to this country in the month of July.]

Why in *Maldon* does the poet refer to Byrhtnoth's retainers and commended men as a *hearth-troop*? The poetic term is traditional and because of its association with a hearth or fireplace in Old English poetry, it immediately evokes the image of a hall, the traditional seat of an Anglo-Saxon prince in older poems such as *Beowulf*, or in early historical writings of the period such as Bede's eighth-century *Ecclesiastical History of the English Nation*. In a traditional hall, the hearth was placed in the centre (there was a louvre or smoke-hole in the roof), and the lord's retainers sat around the hearth at their trestles and boards, at their mead-benches.

The mead hall is the kind of residence depicted in various poems, and whether they are biblical epic, elegy or riddle, they all partake in this kind of discourse when describing similar halls and residences. But this was not only an image from the distant past. In the tenth century, the hall was also still very much a part of everyday living for the nobleman, his wife and their family. As recent research shows, the large hall was even revived as a focus of settlements in the tenth century, and its style seems to have changed with passing trends and architectural fashions; in his *Building Anglo-Saxon England*, the historian John Blair writes as follows:

Three successive stages can now be distinguished: an increase in length and internal subdivision – giving the 'hall' a clear focal identity – associated with a new popularity for the angle-sided plan; a larger, more complex and more sophisticated elaboration of this form (the 'long range'); and finally a fashion for aisled halls, with chambers and services that were sometimes integral but sometimes detached. It seems possible that the last of these should be interpreted as a reversion to more traditional norms.[17]

Blair's argument is nicely summed up in his chapter heading: 'Free Farmers and Emergent Lords: Towards the Manorial Landscape', for this was the trajectory of thegnly living.[18] The new style of the 'long range' hall, which was in fashion in the period 950–80, is evident from excavations in the East Midlands at such sites as Raunds, Goltho, West Cotton, Sulgrave and Faccombe. Possibly influenced by

Figure 11 Building in the West Stow Anglo-Saxon village. © Wikimedia Commons (public domain).

monastic architecture, which had received a great deal of investment in the mid-century Benedictine Reform, the 'long range' is characterized by an elaboration of rooms, which, Blair shows, map well onto the parts of a building as described by Ælfric of Cerne Abbas in the 990s in his other teaching manual, the *Glossary*: *heall* 'hall', *heddern* 'storeroom', *bur* 'bower', that is, a private chamber, *upflor* 'upper chamber', *gang* 'latrine'. Accordingly, a typical long range might consist of a long narrow building divided into consecutive rooms as follows, from left to right: *heddern* – *heall* – *bur* – *bur* – *bur* – *bur*. The larger main communal hall is on the left, but what this arrangement offers is a marked increase in private accommodation in the various chambers to the right of the hall. And situated above the chamber on the far right was that new technical innovation, the *upflor* with its built-on *gang*: as Blair cheerfully points out, this marks the invention of 'en suite facilities' in mid-tenth-century England.

It is thought that the kind of people who lived in such buildings are the lesser nobility of later Anglo-Saxon England, not necessarily the high-ranking witnesses of the royal charters but the people responsible for the 'proliferating vernacular documents of the late tenth century',[19] the kind of people who furnished their houses with tapestries and wall-hangings and detailed their rich domestic possessions in their wills (the kind of men, who feature, as we will see in Chapter 7, in the second half of the poem *The Battle of Maldon*). Their living arrangements may have been partly gendered, with the communal hall oriented to the masculine culture, while the private chambers were the domain of the important ladies of the household. In this respect, mention should be made here of a certain Wynflæd, remarkable not only because her will survives but also because one of her landed properties (and in fact also her 'morning-gift' from her husband on the occasion of their wedding), which was located at Faccombe Netherton in Hampshire, has been excavated and its wider history traced.[20] The account in her will of the rich textiles she owned is likewise of great interest.[21] I have in mind again the will of Ælfflæd, Byrhtnoth's widow, who owned many properties, including also her 'morning-gift' at Rettendon, to the south of Maldon. Another document, which concerns a house and an estate inherited by the lady Leofwaru at nearby Purleigh, between Rettendon and Maldon, was written in the later 990s (see Appendix 4).

After only a short period, about two generations, the long range went out of fashion. Thereafter, the trajectory for the development in living space of this tenth-century social class was towards architectural complexes that resemble later medieval manors. Here a vernacular document provides insights that find remarkable support in the work of historians and archaeologists. The short treatise *Geþyncðo*, sometimes known as the 'Promotion Law' or 'Concerning Wergilds and Dignities', is another document attributable to the prolific Archbishop Wulfstan. Its interest lies in how it records the new social mobility that is visible in the second half of the tenth century:

Hit wæs hwilum on Engla lagum þæt leod and lagu for be geþincðum; and þa wæron leodwitan weorðscipes wyrðe ælc be his mæðe, eorl and ceorl, þegen and þeoden. And gif ceorl geþeah þæt he hæfde fullice fif hida agenes landes, cirican and kycenan, bellhus and burhgeat, setl and sundernote on cynges healle, þonne wæs he þanon forð þegenrihtes weorðe.

[Once it was in the laws of the English that people and law proceeded by rank; and at that time counsellors were worthy of honour each according to his degree: earl and *ceorl*, thegn and *theoden* (prince). And if a freeman flourished so that he had five hides of his own land, a church and kitchen, a bell-house and a castle-gate, a seat and special office in the king's hall, then he was thenceforth worthy of thegnly legal status.]

The point of this treatise is that thegnly status had become achievable: it was based on career experience at the king's court, certain possessions and certain living conditions.[22] As well as his hall, the typical thegn's property included a private church or chapel, a bell-tower, a separate kitchen building; his manor was enclosed by an earthen wall and a ditch and it had an elaborate gate-house known as a *burh-geat*.[23] Such information provides new perspectives on the status of the thegns who were members of what the poem calls the 'hearth-troop', and on the concept of 'home' as presented in *The Battle of Maldon*.

Riding home

As noted in the section '*Fyrd* and *folc*', the primary virtue of Byrhtnoth in the poem *Maldon* is his ability to be *anræd*, a quality that implies being resolute, and single-minded, keeping 'to one counsel' – and according to Chronicle C it was the lack of this very quality (of being *anræd*) that led to the defeat of the English by Swegn in 1003. One of the messages conveyed by the final scenes of *The Battle of Maldon* is exactly this: with their leader gone, the remainers are nevertheless able to achieve the virtue of being 'of one counsel', and encourage each other in their resolve.

The immediate response to the death of Byrhtnoth, however, is the division of the whole army. Some decide to stay, while others flee, and it would be tempting to argue that it is the *folc* who flees while the loyal hearth-troop remains. This may be generally true, but there are other considerations which indicate that the situation is rather more complex. We may begin by considering the leavers, the first instigators of the flight. Godric and his brothers are clearly Byrhtnoth's men, yet the narrator says that they flee the field even despite the gifts of horses that they had received from Byrhtnoth their lord. This is of course a betrayal of trust, as Offa points out later (lines 237–43), and it has unleashed a panic: the flight of members of the hearth-troop only encourages others to flee, especially as they suppose that the man riding the splendid horse must be Byrhtnoth himself. The members of the *folc*, the main body of the army, do not recognize the fleeing rider – obviously they do not know Byrhtnoth well enough to identify a helmeted rider in the heat and confusion of the battle. Similar confusions of identity are known to have occurred in other medieval battles.[24] As Offa then says, the *folc*, that is, the defence-force, was *totwæmed*, 'divided', and the shield-wall broken, and this caused them to flee.

In direct contrast is the response of the retinue, of the hearth-troop itself, to the dire situation following the flight of Godric and his brothers (lines 202–6). The passage declares that the men 'hastened eagerly' (226). Byrhtnoth's role is here determined as 'leader of the *folc* (the people)', in other words, he is the general in charge of the defence-force, as well as being 'Æthelred's earl', that is, the representative of the king himself (for more discussion of the term *earl* see Chapter 4). But now the 'hearth-companions', that is, the members of the retinue *ealle gesawon*, 'have all seen' that their lord lies dead on the field (lines 203–4). As his personal retainers and commended men, they know Byrhtnoth well, they instantly recognize him and realize what has happened. They are *þegenas* 'thegns' (205), the poet says, which, as we have seen, in tenth-century terms is a rank of society rather than simply a word for a warrior, and they are *wlance* to boot: 'proud and splendid thegns', and moreover, as we saw in the discussion of the horse earlier, they are 'uncowardly', undaunted men. Their immediate response is to move forward, an action that characterizes their inner resolve. This emphasis on action is a defining feature of the poem: we will consider such actions and reactions as standing or moving forward in more detail in the next chapter.

But as an interim conclusion to the themes of this chapter, let us return once again to the horse, Byrhtnoth's horse, which forms the principal subject of Chapter 2. By implication, the horse features one more time in the poem. The context is the death of Offa, Byrhtnoth's loyal thegn and right-hand man, whose function, it seems also, is to remind the audience of what has happened on previous occasions earlier in the story of *Maldon*. Accordingly, as Offa falls to the ground, in the same long breathless sentence with its 'envelope' structure, the narrator reminds us of another of Offa's speeches, a vow made to Byrhtnoth earlier in the day, perhaps at the *methelstede* when the troops were mustered. Here Offa had vowed that the two of them would either ride safely home together to the *burh* or die in the battle (287–94):

And ðær Gaddes mæg   grund gesohte:
raðe wearð æt hilde   Offa forheawen;
he hæfde ðeah geforþod   þæt he his frean gehet,
swa he beotode ær   wið his beahgifan
þæt hi sceoldon begen   on burh ridan,
hale to hame,   oððe on here crincgan,
on wælstowe   wundum sweltan;
he læg ðegenlice   ðeodne gehende.

[And there Gadd's kinsman went to ground:
quickly in the battle Offa was cut down;
nevertheless he had accomplished what he had promised his lord,

what he had vowed to his ring-giver:
that they would both either ride back to the *burh*,
safe to their home, or fall in the conflict
on the battlefield and die of their wounds;
he lay there in a thegnly manner close to his *theoden*.]

It is clear in this passage that *thegn* is a technical term for a social rank in the poem, and not simply a general term for a nobleman or a warrior. The crucial sentence is the last quoted, with its alliterative echoes of the 'Promotion Law' cited earlier:

he læg ðegenlice ðeodne gehende.

[he lay there in a thegnly manner close to his *theoden*.]

'Thegnly' in this passage has the same implications as does the later word 'chivalric'. *The Battle of Maldon* is a story of lord and thegnly retainer as a form of companionship. In a hypothetical daydream in which victory is achieved, the two friends ride home safely. The *burh* here mentioned is perhaps not to be identified with Maldon itself.[25] Of course this cannot be ruled out, since Maldon was the nearest *burh*, in the sense of a fortified town, to the battlefield itself. But in the late tenth century, *burh* was also a synonym for 'home' in a rather different sense. 'Home' for Byrhtnoth must have been one of the many estates that he owned in Essex or East Anglia[26] and 'home' for Offa must also have entailed a thegnly manor and estate not unlike those mentioned in the discussion earlier.

   One of the lesser warriors in the poem, Leofsunu of Sturmer, makes a similar declaration to that of Offa when he also rejects the idea of going home, in his case repudiating the very idea of returning home 'lordless'. As the laws of the period demonstrate, the 'lordless' state was unthinkable, and prohibited:

Ond we cwædon be þam *hlafordleasan* mannum, ðe mon nan ryht ætbegytan ne mæg, þæt <mon> beode ðære mægþe, ðæt hi hine to folcryhte gehamette ond him hlaford finden on folcgemote. Ond gif hi hine ðonne begytan nyllen oððe ne mægen to þam andagan, ðonne beo he syþþan flyma, ond hine lecge for ðeof se þe him tocume.[27]

With regard to *lordless* men from whom no [legal] satisfaction can be obtained, we have declared that their relatives shall be commanded to settle them in a fixed residence where they will become amenable to public law, and find them a lord at a public meeting. If, however, on the appointed day they [the relatives of such a man] will not or cannot, he shall be henceforth an outlaw, and he who encounters him may assume him to be a thief and kill him.[28]

A lordless man needed to rectify the situation at the earliest possible opportunity. Here is the passage in question from *Maldon* (lines 249–53):

> Ne þurfon me embe Sturmere   stedefæste hælæð
> wordum ætwitan,   nu min wine gecranc,
> þæt ic *hlafordleas*   ham siðie,
> wende fram wige,   ac me sceal wæpen niman,
> ord and iren.

> [The steadfast warriors of Sturmer will not be able
> to utter accusing words, now that my friend has fallen,
> that I would return home *lordless*, desert the battle;
> instead weapon must take me,
> point and iron.]

The *stedefæste hælæð* ('steadfast warriors') to whose opinion Leofsunu so poetically defers must be the local men of the vill of Sturmer, which, as its name suggests (*Sturmer*, or *stur-mere*, i.e. 'Stour-mere' or 'Stour Pond') lies on the river Stour, in the river valley that forms the border between Essex and Suffolk, not so far from many of Byrhtnoth's own family properties, and conveniently placed, some have thought, on the route from the north which the historical Byrhtnoth may have taken in August 991 as he moved southwards from Northumbria to meet the threat of a Viking fleet on the Essex coast.

What was Leofsunu's Sturmer like at the time? It seems there was a church, a small lake, a mill, a manor. The eleventh-century church is still in use, the fabric of which is partly Anglo-Saxon and partly Norman or later. The pond or small lake also still exists, situated at Sturmer Hall, now a country hotel, on the site of what was once an early medieval moated manor house with a water-mill and mill race nearby.[29]

One further text provides a few insights. In the Norman census of *Domesday Book* of 1086, the vill is mentioned as shared between two minor landholders, and there is a substantial inventory of their resources. Here is the text, from the earlier 'Little Domesday' entries for Essex, folios 82r and 82v (note that TRE is a Latin abbreviation meaning 'in the time of King Edward'):

> Tihel [the Breton] holds Sturmer in demesne, which a free woman held TRE as a manor and 1½ hides and 15 acres. Then as now [there were] 2 ploughs in demesne and the men [had] 1 plough and [there were] 2 villans [and] 3 bordars. Then and later [there was] 1 slave; now 2. [There are] 16 acres of meadow. [There were] then [. . .] cows and 2 horses and 60 pigs and 3 hives of bees. [There are] now 4 head of cattle and 1 horse and 1 colt and 44 pigs and 72 sheep and 3 hives of bees. It was then worth 40s.: now 60.

Figure 12 St Mary's Church at Sturmer. © Wikimedia Commons (public domain).

> Tihel holds Sturmer in demesne, which a free man held TRE as a manor and as [. . .] 1½ hides. Then as now [there were] 2 ploughs in demesne and 1 villan and 6 slaves. [There are] 20 acres, 1 mill. [There were] then 6 head of cattle and 1 horse and 12 pigs and 60 sheep. [There are] now 12 head of cattle and 30 pigs and 100 sheep less 2 and 1 horse and 3 colts. Then and later it was worth 40s.: now 60.[30]

It is possible that many of these agricultural features were in place in the year 991: this may well be what 'home' signified to Leofsunu of Sturmer. 'Stour Pond', then, was a real place, alluded to in the text, and the motif of 'going home' hints at a current of domesticity that runs through *The Battle of Maldon*, beneath the surface, as it were, of the discourse of lordship and heroism.

Chapter 4

'Here stands an earl'

Brimmanna boda   abeod eft ongean
sege þinum leodum   miccle laþre spell
þæt her stynt unforcuð   eorl mid his werode
þe wile gealgean   eþel þysne
Æþelredes eard   ealdres mines
folc and foldan

THE BATTLE OF MALDON (LINES 49–54A)

[Viking messenger, take back this response
deliver to your men a much more pointed reply,
that here stands undiminished an earl with his troop:
one who intends to defend this homeland,
my lord King Æthelred's country,
land and people.]

With the defiant 'here stands an earl' as a starting point, this chapter will examine aspects of Byrhtnoth's power and authority, as presented in *Maldon*. The implications of the word *eorl* will be teased out, along with the connotations of the term *ceorl* and the more lowly social status of the Vikings. We will explore how the poet skilfully weaves formal patterns around the verb *standan* 'to stand', which is also linked to the frequently recurring theme of land in the poem.

The 'heriot': Byrhtnoth's response to the messenger

A notable feature of Byrhtnoth's longest speech in *The Battle of Maldon* (lines 42–61) is his ironic references to the legal language of the will, a vernacular document which had begun to proliferate in tenth-century England.[1] The context,

Figure 13 Statue of Byrhtnoth. © Wikimedia Commons / Oxyman (public domain).

as we have seen, is the exchange between the Viking messenger and Byrhtnoth before the fighting starts: first the messenger demands tribute, a payment of a large sum of money in return for which the Vikings, or 'seamen', as they are often called in the poem, will leave in their ships; no battle will take place, no one will be hurt, the Vikings will provide protection and cease their plundering of the countryside (lines 25–41).

In his defiant rejection of this offer, Byrhtnoth replies as follows to the messenger. First, Byrhtnoth addresses the messenger with the singular *þu* meaning literally 'thou', that is, 'you-singular' (*gehyrst þu sælida*?) then, switching to *eow*, the 'you-plural', he formulates the message that this man should take back to his fellow-Vikings. This is the rhetoric he now uses to counter the Viking messenger's earlier attempts to persuade; Byrhtnoth becomes the spokesman of the *fyrd*, who are equivalent, as we have seen, to the *folc*, the ordinary people of the region (lines 45–9):

Gehyrst þu sælida   hwæt þis folc segeð?
hi willað eow to gafole   garas syllan,
ættrynne ord   and ealde swurd,
þa heregeatu   þe eow æt hilde ne deah.

[Listen, seaman, do you hear what this people is saying?
They will give you all spears as tribute,
deadly spear-point and heirloom sword,
the heriot that will not aid you in the battle!]

In brief, Byrhtnoth declares that the only tribute the Vikings are going to receive is weapons, and these will be weapons in use. In a warrior society (and to a certain extent tenth-century English society still fits that description), the custom of giving weapons as part of a gift exchange is referred to here; and it should be remembered that weapons were undoubtedly valuable objects. In addition, there are allusions here to 'heirloom swords' and 'war-equipment', both of which refer to the practice of making wills.

First, there is talk of *ealde swurd*, literally to be translated as 'old swords', although the word-for-word rendering in modern English does not express the full connotations of the term. 'Old swords' are heirloom swords: objects which have both a monetary value, because swords were crafted artefacts that needed time and skill to make, sometimes also decorated with gold and silver, and also a cultural value, because swords belonging to respected ancestors or to famous historic figures were frequently bequeathed to later generations. In *Beowulf*, taken as an example of the kind of old heroic poetry that nourished the minds and imaginations of the tenth-century nobility, there is the sword named Hrunting, an *ealdgestreon*, 'ancient treasure' (line 1458), which Unlaf gives to Beowulf when he departs to fight Grendel's mother, the she-troll in the mere. Before the actual battle there is a long sequence in which Beowulf arms himself for the fight, pulling on a cunningly wrought mailcoat to protect his body, and a white helmet for his head decorated with boar-images, made *fyrndagum*, 'in days of old', by a skilled weapon-smith.[2] And shortly before he plunges into the lake, Beowulf takes up the sword, which he calls *ealde laf*, 'an ancient heirloom' (1488b) and vows to achieve fame with it, or else death will take him (lines 1490b–91). Such a sword recalls the sword held by Byrhtnoth at the scene of his death in the poem *Maldon* (see discussion further). Heirloom swords were not, however, the reserve of the old heroic poems. A very clear example of a contemporary bequest of numerous 'old swords' is the will composed in 1012 by Æthelstan, one of the sons of Æthelred the Unready, who leaves the individual swords of his collection to various members of his household and family.[3] In particular he speaks of the 'silver-hilted sword which belonged to Ulfketel', a local hero in the Anglo-Danish wars in the two decades after Maldon, which Æthelstan bequeathes to his father Æthelred. Then there is the 'sword which belonged to King Offa' – Offa being the great Mercian king of the eighth century whose sword must have been by then at least 200 years old. Closer to home, another example of a valued sword comes from the will of Byrhtnoth's father-in-law, Ælfgar, who had served as ealdorman under King Edmund (939–46) until the latter's untimely death:

> And Bishop Theodred and Ealdorman Eadric told me, when I gave to my lord the sword which King Edmund gave to me, which was worth a hundred and twenty mancuses of gold and had four pounds of silver on the sheath, that I might have the right to make my will; and God is my witness that I have never done wrong against my lord that I may not have this right.[4]

Ælfgar is now old, and he needs to gain the new king's support by a gift of a valuable sword as he negotiates royal support for the terms and conditions of his will.

The second allusion to a will in Byrhtnoth's first speech in *Maldon* is his defiant riposte that the only tribute the people will pay is '*war-gear* that will not aid you in the battle!' The key term is *here-geatu*, a compound of two words that means literally 'war-gear', which of course fits the context of Byrhtnoth's angry rejection of the messenger's demand. But in the tenth-century wills, a *heregeatu* or 'heriot' also has a very specific technical meaning, defined by Richard Abels as 'a death-due that originated in the return of the weapons with which a lord had outfitted his man'.[5] Accordingly, in nearly every Old English will, the testator begins by promising to pay his lord (mostly this is the king) a certain sum, calculated not as a sum of money but as payment in kind, specifically in weapons, military equipment and warhorses. This is the heriot payment, a system that continued until the Norman Conquest, indicating, in the opinion of Richard Abels, 'the persistence of the military ethos among the Anglo-Saxon aristocracy'. Here, for example, is the beginning of a will from the 970s:

> Here in this document it is declared how the ealdorman Ælfheah has declared his will with his royal lord's permission.[6]

The ealdorman named here belongs to a rich and powerful Mercian family, and the heriot which he then grants to his king is valuable, consisting of land, gold bullion and silver objects, as well as the usual military equipment:

> And he grants to his royal lord [. . .] three hundred mancuses of gold and a dish of three pounds and a drinking cup [*soppcuppan*] of three pounds and a short sword [*handsex*]; and on the scabbard [*lecge*] there are eighty mancuses of gold; and six swords and six horses with trappings and as many spears and shields.

This last will and testament happens to be that of Ealdorman Ælfheah, one of the uncles of the young Mercian nobleman Ælfwine (whose speech in *The Battle of Maldon* we will examine in Chapters 6 and 9). Evidently a 'heriot' was not only a token of rank but also an index of power and status within tenth-century society.

All this adds further layers of irony to Byrhtnoth's rejection of the Viking's peace offer in the passage in *Maldon*. The Viking messenger is not identified, and is probably not a man of royal rank such as Swegn or Olaf. As we will see later in this chapter, the 'seamen' of the poem are basically lordless, and certainly at first (until Byrhtnoth's proud and fateful decision to grant them too much land) they are also landless. And throughout the narrative they are presented as low-ranking men (we will see that *ceorl* and *dreng* are the only two terms of rank used). Byrhtnoth would have no business paying a heriot to the likes of such men: his response to the Viking messenger at lines 46–8 is essentially a threat, for he implies that the Danish spokesman is most assuredly not his royal lord and that the payment of heriot will most certainly not be to his benefit.

The 'earl' and the 'churl': Byrhtnoth's last fight

Strikingly, and perhaps rather puzzlingly, in both these passages in which Ealdorman Byrhtnoth is called *anræd*, the poet refers to him not as 'the ealdorman' but as 'the earl'. The choice of word requires an explanation. In *Beowulf* and other traditional poems, *eorl* means 'nobleman' or 'warrior', but in ninth-century prose it came to denote a high-ranking Danish leader because it was similar to the Old Norse cognate *jarl*.[7] After the Danish conqueror King Cnut came to the throne in 1016, he made the term 'official': all new provincial governors were given the Danish-Norse inspired title of *eorl*, while *ealdorman* was reserved for any men appointed before 1016 who were still in power. In *Maldon*, Byrhtnoth is termed *eorl* consistently, no less than ten times in all, in the course of the poem, and on six of these occasions he is *se eorl*, with the definite

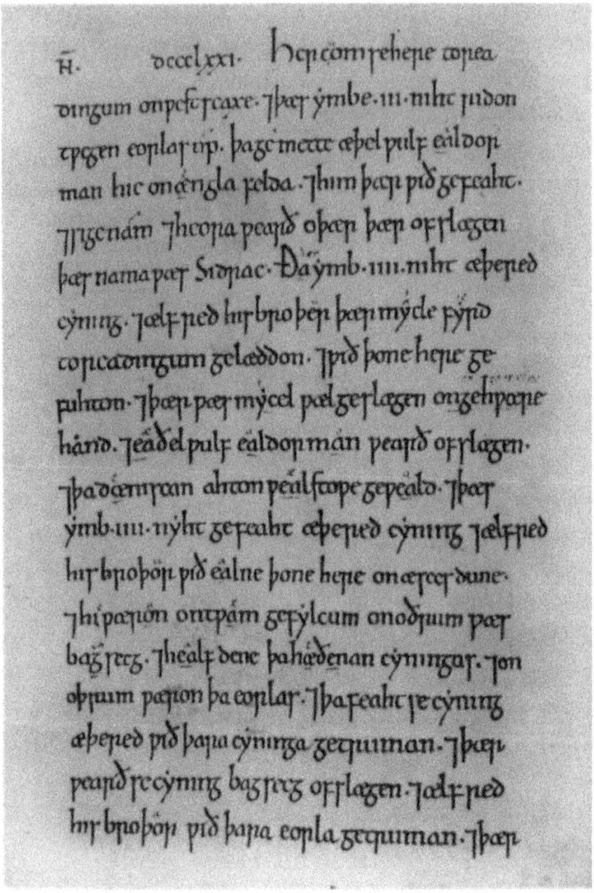

Figure 14 From Chronicle C, annal for 871. © The British Library.

article *se*, which implies the very specific title of 'the earl' (6, 28, 89, 146, 159, 165). The explanation offered by Cecily Clarke is the most convincing: Essex partly overlapped with the old Danelaw, which was essentially East Anglia. In a poem from this region, in which a number of the Englishmen even have Norse names, the Norse-influenced word dominated, anticipating the official change that was to take place later in the West Saxon regions.[8]

As the leader of the East Saxons, Byrhtnoth is described in a number of appropriate ways in the poem *Maldon*. In his working relation with his men, the poet describes him as *ealdor* 'prince' (11), *frea* 'lord' (16), *hæleða hleo* 'protector of men' (74), *ðeoden* 'prince' (120), *hlaford* 'lord' (189) and *leof* 'dear, well-loved' (208). As a fighting warrior he is *guð-rinc* 'battle-warrior' (138), *fyrd-rinc* 'army warrior' (140), *har hilderinc* 'grey-haired battle-warrior' (169), *modi man* 'brave man' (147) and *se beorn* 'the warrior' (154, 160). Finally, in relation to the king he is *Æþelredes þegen* 'Æthelred's thegn' (151); and the narrator's last word on Byrhtnoth is *þæs folces ealdor, Æþelredes eorl* 'the people's prince, Æthelred's earl' (202b–203a). The latter is an example of variation, in which Old English poets excelled, loving the challenge of varying their words in order to present different aspects of a person or event. Above all, the poem emphasizes the exalted position of Byrhtnoth, as a kind of prince, second only to the king in rank and status.

By contrast, the Vikings all seem to be regarded and presented as socially lower-status individuals. Even the messenger, spokesman of the Danish army, is not given any rank or status. And at line 132, to take another example, from the beginning of the violent passage that narrates Byrhtnoth's last fight, the poet embellishes his alliterative line with rhyme; where the hero is an *earl*, he pulls rank, for his enemy by contrast is merely a *churl*:

eode swa anræd,   eorl to þam ceorle,

[just as resolute, the earl advanced towards the churl]

The two nouns *earl* and *churl* have both undergone intensive semantic change in the history of the language. In legal texts on status, the meanings of *eorl* and *ceorl* are relatively neutral: 'nobleman' and 'freeman', respectively. But because *ceorl* denoted a land-owning member of the peasant class (a use still found in *Maldon*, 256), the word could easily acquire lowly, less prestigious connotations or even assume negative associations. The first record of it in a possibly pejorative use is a passage in the Anglo-Saxon Chronicle. Queen Emma, Æthelred's Norman queen, known by her title 'the Lady', has appointed one of her French supporters as reeve at Exeter, but when the city falls to the Vikings, the chronicler (Version C) is quick to lay the blame:

C 1003 Her wæs Exacester tobrocen þuruh þone frenciscan ceorl Hugan, ðe seo hlæfdige hire hæfde geset to gerefan, 7 se here ða þa buruh mid ealle fordyde 7 micle herehyðe þær genamon.

[The year 1003. Here Exeter was broken into because of the French churl Hugo, whom the Lady had appointed as reeve, and the Viking army completely destroyed the town and seized great booty.]

Here the word *ceorl* may be a negative epithet for an incompetent or treacherous reeve, not necessarily a literal mark of status or rank. Similarly in *Maldon*, the Viking who takes on Byrhtnoth in an exchange of spears is also a *ceorl* (132b). How are we to understand the connotations? Other epithets chosen by the poet for this nemesis figure vary in their evaluative force: he is *wiges heard* 'a man fierce in battle' (130a), and *særinc* 'sea-warrior' (134a), a variation on the usual description of the Danes as 'seamen'; later in the same passage he is *wlanc wicing* 'proud Viking' (139a) and neutrally also *hyse* 'warrior, youth' (141a). Finally he is *se færsceaða* (142a), a word occurring nowhere else except in this poem, meaning 'the sudden attacker', presumably because Byrhtnoth in this sequence has suddenly and unexpectedly been wounded by him. This compound *færsceaða* is formed in a similar way to the later more obviously derogatory *helsceaða*, 'hellish assailant', used to describe the devils in Byrhtnoth's final prayer when he prays for protection at line 180. It is also reminiscent of *Beowulf* (712), where the monster Grendel is termed *manscaða*, meaning 'evil assailant' and punningly perhaps also 'attacker of man'. On this evidence, the Viking *ceorl* in *Maldon* is decidedly a *ceorl* with at least some negative connotations attached to his status.

But Byrhtnoth the earl, though wounded by the churl's spear, nevertheless despatches him with his own spear and goes on to kill another as the fight moves on (lines 143–6). In narrating this violent action at length, the poet again resorts to rhetorical effect, linking the two opponents together through rhyme and repetition, for where the Viking is *se sæ-rinc* 'the sea-warrior' (134a), Byrhtnoth is *se guð-rinc* 'the battle-warrior' (138a). In addition, parallelism of syntax (especially the inverted verb-subject word order) and an envelope pattern serve to underline further the connections and the reciprocal actions of the two warring spearmen:

> Sende ða se særinc (134a)   [Then the sea-warrior sent]
> Gegremod wearð se guðrinc (138)   [The battle-warrior became enraged]
> Frod wæs se fyrdrinc (140a)   [The *fyrd*-warrior was experienced]

Byrhtnoth's mental state seems to change as this fight progresses, from anger, to experience and confidence, to happiness (146b) and finally to exultant laughter (147a) and gratitude to God (147b). For many modern readers the laughter must rank as the strangest moment in the whole of the poem. Byrhtnoth laughs. But laughter is not necessarily a virtue in Old English writing (the monster Grendel, for instance, laughs just before his last fight in *Beowulf* at line 730b). The reader may therefore suspect that this exultation is untimely, and with good reason, for now another Viking lets fly his spear and Byrhtnoth is wounded yet again, this time more seriously (149–51):

> Forlet þa drenga sum   daroð of handa,
> fleogan of folman,   þæt se to forð gewat
> þurh ðone æþelan   Æþelredes þegen.

> [Then one of the Vikings launched a javelin,
> flying from his hands, which advanced too far
> through Æþelred's noble thegn.]

This is another of those 'let fly' structures, discussed in Chapter 3, where the missile, once released from the hands into flight, takes on a life and agency of its own. The passage also neatly illustrates the theme of social hierarchies which this fight sequence from lines 130 to 172 seems to embody. The sentence begins with the Viking, the noun chosen being *dreng*, a Norse-derived term of a similar rank to *ceorl*; this may be defined as follows:

Sense 1: lad, warrior (perhaps reflecting the sense of ON *drengr* literally 'youth, lad; member of a ship's crew, military unit, or merchant fraternity; bold or worthy man')

Sense 1a: in (?post-Conquest) Northumbria: member of a class of free tenants holding land by a form of tenure the nature of which was partly military and partly servile.[9]

As well as narrating the fight action, the whole sequence (*Maldon*, 130–51) concerns rank and status and appropriately ends with 'Æþelred's noble thegn', the king's representative on the battlefield.

On the whole, then, the poet mostly uses neutral terms to designate the Vikings;[10] on the other hand, however, he avoids unduly positive epithets: no aristocratic terms are used to describe the Vikings, and twice they are termed free peasants. And this relatively low rank is appropriate, for according to the rules of the social hierarchy as outlined in the legal texts on promotion that were discussed in Chapter 3, the Vikings lack some of the prerequisites of 'thegnly' status. For example in the short treatise, akin to the Promotion Law, known as *Norðleoda lagu* ('The Law of the North People'), it is not enough for an upwardly mobile peasant to look the part of a thegn, he needs also to hold substantial land to prove his credentials. As paragraphs 9–10 of this treatise affirm, his legal value in cases of compensation (Old English *wergild*) is the same as that of an established thegn, but only if he fulfils the conditions correctly:

(9) And gif ceorlisc man geþeo, þæt he hæbbe V hida landes to cynges utware, & hine man ofslea, forgilde man hine mid twam þusend þrimsa. (10) And þeah he geþeo, þæt he hæbbe helm & byrnan & golde fæted sweord, gif he þæt land nafað, he bið ceorl swa þeah.

[(9) And if a *ceorl* prospers, that he has five hides of land on which he discharges the king's dues, and anyone kills him, he is to be paid for with 2,000 *thrymsas* (10) And even if he prospers so that he possesses a helmet and a coat of mail and a gold-plated sword, if he has not the land, he is a *ceorl* all the same.][11]

An analogy could be drawn with the knights of the later Middle Ages who needed to prove their membership of their social class not only by owning and wearing the required clothing and equipment – the mail hauberk on top of the padded tunic, the iron helmet, the wooden lances, the shield painted in the appropriate heraldic colours, the saddles and the horses – but also by their landholding and their running of a household (from which came the due provision of armed men as foot-soldiers for military service).

What the Danish seamen in *Maldon* do have is the weaponry, that is to say, the spears and swords, and – unlike the East Saxons of the *fyrd* who may be unarmoured behind their wooden shields – the Vikings are described three times explicitly as wearing byrnies, or coats of chainmail, as Brooks points out.[12] Indeed, this gives the opportunity for the poet to elaborate some impressive acoustic effects in his poetic descriptions of the prowess of the English fighters. Accordingly, Byrhtnoth is so strong – it is implied – that he is able, even after his first wound, to cause a Viking byrnie to 'burst apart' (line 144a); and later, in the section on Ætheric the 'noble companion' (280–5), there is the startling animism of the singing byrnie (284–5):

bærst bordes lærig,   and seo byrne sang
gryreleoða sum.

[the rim of the shield burst, and the mailcoat sang
a terrifying song.]

This use of the rare poetic compound *gryre-leoð* (terror-song) echoes lines 786–7 of *Beowulf*, where the defeated Grendel, here termed 'God's adversary', chants in his pain and weeping a 'terrifying song of defeat' (*gryreleoð galan godes ondsacan, / sigeleasne sang*). In *Beowulf* also there is the theme of the singing, ringing chainmail in the scene of arrival in Denmark, in a peaceful episode in which the potential *gryre* or 'terror' of the equipment is nevertheless highlighted in the description:

                    Guðbyrne scan
heard hondlocen,   hringiren scir
song in searwum,   þa hie to sele furðum
in hyra *gryre*geatwum   gangan cwomon.
Setton sæmeþe   side scyldas,
rondas regnhearde,   wið þæs recedes weal,
bugon þa to bence. Byrnan *hringdon* . . .

[The battle hauberk shone,
tough, linked together by hand, each bright ring-iron
sang in its chainmail as they advanced to the hall
in their *terror*-inducing armour.
The sea-weary men set down their wide shields,

the hardened metal bosses, against the wall of the building
and moved to the benches. Their mailcoats *rang* . . .]

Whether the *Maldon* poet is here consciously echoing the passages from *Beowulf* is open for discussion (and I will return to this question in Chapter 9).

What the Danish seamen in *Maldon* lack is *land*, and this arguably is why the poet mostly does not assign them any rank other than 'seamen'. Byrhtnoth of course makes a point of this in his major speech, the reply to the messenger, employing elegant variation to reinforce his point about defending 'this homeland, my lord King Æthelred's country, land and people' (52–4). Honour is at stake, for this is the king's land, and at the same time it is also 'our land' (55–8):

> It seems to me too shameful
> that you will take our money and return to your ships,
> without a fight, now that you have come in so far
> onto this our land.

It is land that the Vikings need to gain if they would enhance their status. And this is the crucial moment in the poem, the points where many critics disagree. Did the Vikings 'devise a plan' or 'use guile' (86a: *ongunnon lytegian*)? Did Byrhtnoth agree 'because of his exuberance' (89b), to take an interpretation of *ofermod* that is no longer in vogue, or, as is more likely, 'because of his pride'? Did Byrhtnoth 'allow them too much land' or 'grant them land, as he should not have done' (89–90)? Here are the crucial lines:

> Ða se eorl ongan   for his ofermode
> alyfan landes to fela   laþere ðeode.

> [Then because of his pride, the earl granted
> too much land to that hostile nation.]

The verb *alyfan*, 'to allow' or 'to grant', is often used in contexts where a king or other authoritative figure grants permission or allows someone to have land, food, support.[13] Byrhtnoth's full authority lies behind this decision in which he grants *upgang* 'passage' to the Danes; their response is brisk: 'the seamen advanced to the land' *wodon . . . lidmen to lande* (97a and 99a).[14]

Disputes over land

As an ealdorman active in the East Anglian region, Byrhtnoth often had to deal with litigation over land: this is not the first time in the literature of the period that we see Byrhtnoth in a verbal dispute over the right to hold land. The key text here is the *Libellus Æthelwoldi Episcopi*, 'the Little Book of Bishop Æthelwold', ascribed to Gregory, a twelfth-century Ely monk who was commissioned by Hervey, the first bishop of Ely (1108–31) to translate tenth-century Old English records and documents concerning the work of Æthelwold, the monastic bishop of Winchester in the reigns of Edgar and Æthelred, and the founder of the abbey at Ely.[15] This work was then incorporated into Book II of *The Book of Ely*. Recorded for posterity here are the many lawsuits that took place in the late 970s in the wake of King Edgar's death, when suddenly the royal government was no longer aligned with the monastic party, and when landowners and tenants tried to recover land that rightfully or wrongfully had been taken from them by the new monasteries.

In this context we find Byrhtnoth, in a complex case of litigation, defending the rights of Ely to a joint estate (the properties at Hauxton and Newton) that King Edgar had promised to the abbey shortly before his death. Hauxton had originally belonged to a certain Eadric the Tall, who had left it to the king in his will. But Eadric's brother, Ælfwold, and other kinsmen, had claimed part of this estate. Now came the difficulty: Ealdorman Æthelwine, the pious friend of Archbishop Oswald (see Chapter 11), had promised his support to Bishop Æthelwold, who wanted the land for Ely. But Æthelwine neglected to keep the agreement. In view of this, the community brought in Ealdorman Byrhtnoth, the other big authority in the region, who brokered a deal with Eadric's brother Ælfwold and arranged, at his own expense, an exchange agreement by which Ely ended up in possession of the disputed estates.[16]

The most spectacular of the seizures of monastic land in this period is recorded in Byrhtferth's *Life of St Oswald*. This is ascribed to the Mercian ealdorman Ælfhere (uncle of the nobleman Ælfwine who features in *Maldon*). Ælfhere seized the monastery at Winchcombe and ejected Abbot Germanus and his monks, who were forced out with few possessions onto the road and eventually given refuge at Ramsey Abbey. In his account of this episode, Byrhtferth makes much of the pathos and indignation this action caused:

> Qui prius solebant equis insedere faleratis et cum sociis concinere melli fluum carmen Dauitici regis, tunc cernere posses sarcinam pati, non uectos ut priscus patriarcha uehiculo in Egyptum, uel com sociis aut cum amicis ambulantes, 'sine sacculo, sine calciamentis'.

> Monks who were formerly accustomed to sit on caparisoned horses and with their companions to sing the melodious song of King David, could then be seen carting a burden, not being carried like the ancient patriarch on a carriage into Egypt, or walking about with companions and friends, 'without a purse, without shoes'. [Lk. 22.35][17]

Naturally Byrhtferth of Ramsey supported the East Anglian political faction in his writing, and so accordingly, at least at this point in the narrative, he makes Ealdorman Ælfhere the villain of the piece, the opponent of Æthelwine and Byrhtnoth, the two East Anglian ealdormen who he presents as the champions of the monastic cause, defending the monks from the rapacious thieves who try to steal their land after the death of their royal lord and protector King Edgar. In disputes over land such as these, however, much depended on which monastic house was keeping the records. A document from the Abingdon archives shows that in another context, Ealdorman Ælfhere could appear in a rather different light:

Ælfheah ealdorman becwæð Ælfhere ealdormenn .xx. hida æt Kingestune. Ða abæd Osgar abbud æt Ælfhere ealdormenn þæt he moste ofgan þæt land æt him mid sceatte. Ða tiþode se ealdorman him. And se abbod sealde him ða an hund mancosa goldes. Ða wes ofer Eastron micel gemot æt Aþelwarabirig 7 hit wes gesitolad ðar þam hlafardingan þa ðæron weron, þæt wes Adelwold bisceof, 7 Ælfstan bisceop 7 Æthelgar abb' 7 Eadwine, 7 Ælfric cild 7 Ælfric Sirafes sunu 7 Brihtric his broðor 7 swiðæ manega oðra ðegenas. And þis wes gedon on micelre gewitnesse 7 þysses gewrites geclofan nam se ealdorman Ælfhere to swytelunga.[18]

[Ealdorman Ælfheah bequeathed Ealdorman Ælfhere twenty hides at Kingston. So then Abbot Osgar petitioned Ealdorman Ælfhere that he might acquire the land from him by payment. The ealdorman granted him this. And the abbot gave him then a hundred mancusses of gold. Then during Easter there was a great assembly at Alderbury and the sale was declared to the lords present there, namely: Bishop Æthelwold, Bishop Ælfstan, Abbot Æthelgar, and Eadwine, and Ælfric Cild, and Ælfric Siraf's son, and Brihtric his brother, and very many other thegns. And this was done in front of many witnesses, and Ealdorman Ælfhere took the counterpart of this document as declaration of proof.]

This document shows Ælfhere cooperating very amicably with Osgar, the abbot of Abingdon (successor to Bishop Æthelwold, who is himself recorded in the witness list as present on the occasion of the agreement). The text incidentally is of interest in its mention of Ælfric Cild in the witness list – this man was the father of Ælfwine who features in the poem *Maldon*; he eventually became – for a short time only – Ælfhere's successor as Ealdorman of Mercia (we will return to this point in Chapter 6).

The discrepancy between the two pieces of writing is illuminating, for clearly one monastery could paint a character as black while another might praise the same man as a generous patron. As we have just seen, even the pious

Ealdorman Æthelwine, co-founder of the abbey of Ramsey, appears rather less than altruistic towards the monks of another abbey, Ely, in the pages of *The Book of Ely*. Whether by chance or design only Ealdorman Byrhtnoth appears in a favourable light in all these monastic land disputes.

Another classic example is the case of Bluntisham reported in the *Libellus* and *The Book of Ely*.[19] Here a certain Wulfnoth had promised land at Bluntisham (Huntingdonshire) to Bishop Æthelwold, but after Edgar's death the land was claimed by the sons of Broga of Hemingford on behalf of their uncle Tope and the latter's grandmother (their great-grandmother). The said lady was reputed to have claimed the land back in the time of the Viking wars of King Edward the Elder. But the 'wise and old men of that district', so the text asserts, 'who well remembered the time when earl Toli had been killed at the river Thames, pronounced all of this spurious'. To resolve the dispute Byrhtnoth became involved, and a great assembly was called:

> After this, the whole of Huntingdonshire was called together by Ealdorman Byrhtnoth and Ælfwold and Eadric. Without delay, a very great assembly was held. Wulfnoth was summoned to the meeting, as were the sons of Broga. When they had come, Wulfnoth brought there with him many loyal men, namely, all the better people of the six hundreds, and the monk Leofsige of Ely produced there the charter of Bluntisham. They explained the claim to the assembled people and aired and discussed the case. And when the truth of the matter had been determined, they took Bluntisham away from the sons of Broga by their judgement.[20]

The resolution of this case depended on oral testimony – the fact that people remembered the case and testified to the history of the land in question. There is also a sense of justice involving written evidence: 'that the person who had the charter was nearer to having the land than the one who did not have it'. But finally the decision was reached by the sworn testimony of 'a thousand men' who swore oaths in support of Wulfnoth, after which the sons of Broga withdrew from the litigation. Holding of land depended in this case on a hearing before the ealdorman, in which written evidence and the oaths of witnesses carry the day.

'Here stands . . .'

'Here stands an earl' is a classic trope of defiance, and its associations are not confined to the Middle ages; it recalls Martin Luther's *hier stehe ich*, 'here I stand', attributed to the German religious reformer at the Diet of Worms in 1517, when he refused to retract any of his statements.[21] The author of *Maldon* is a poet sensitive to dynamic movement and the meanings of verbs of action, and this is undoubtedly true for the everyday verb *standan*, which recurs no less than fifteen times in the text. Though its distribution in the poem is not entirely even or systematic, it nevertheless informs the themes and plot, in interesting ways, for it is mostly confined to the first half of the poem, up to the fall of Byrhtnoth at line 184.

Some select examples will serve to illustrate how the poet weaves a pattern around this simple verb 'to stand'. The exchange between the Viking messenger and Byrhtnoth, for example, is a classic case of scene-setting, and the poet creates a variant of the envelope pattern by introducing the two speakers as figures who 'stood' (OE *stod*) on opposite shores of the river channel (25–8):

Þa *stod* on stæðe,   stiðlice clypode
wicinga ar,   wordum mælde,
se on beot abead   brimliþendra
ærænde to þam eorle,   þær he on ofre *stod*.

[There *stood* on the river bank and called out sternly –
the messenger from the Vikings – spoke these words –
declaring, in a boast, the seafarers'
message to the earl where he *stood* on the shore.]

For further dramatic effect, the poet creates a chiasmus, a mirroring effect, not easily rendered in the modern English but very evident in the more flexible Old English word order that allows the chiastic pattern to emerge:

Þa *stod* **on stæðe** . . . þær he **on ofre** *stod*.

The scene is now set for the two long monologues that form the challenge and response, the exchange of views before the battle.

As the two armies subsequently line up on opposite shores, the poet again employs the verb *standan*, in its past tense form *stodon* 'they stood'. The verb is necessary to mark the sudden halt of the advance, for as the two armies gather, the high tide (which moves quickly in the Blackwater estuary) soon covers the causeway (62–4):

Het þa bord beran,   beornas gangan,
þæt hi on þam easteðe   ealle stodon.
Ne mihte þær for wætere   werod to þam oðrum;

[He ordered shields to be carried, men to advance,
until they all stood on the riverbank.
Because of the water the one army could not reach the other.]

Adhering to the rules of alliterative poetry, the poet here alliterates on key words *bord* 'shields', *beran* 'carry' and *beornas* 'men' in line 62, on *ea-steðe* 'river bank' and *ealle* 'all' in line 63, on *wætere* 'water' and *werod* 'troop' in line 64. But by adding embellishments not required by the metrical rules, he then adds a further half-rhyme effect on the initial syllables of *beran* and *beornas*. Half-rhyme also affects the *-an* endings of the infinitives and the *-um* dative plural endings of the nouns, both of which sound similar in late Old English. The result is that *stodon* and *oðrum* may well have rhymed: they probably sounded like 'stodon' and 'oðron', linking the two opposing ideas of 'they stood' and 'the other'. A few lines later, exploiting the form and structure of the Old English verse line, which invariably has a brief pause or caesura in the middle, the poet presents the following (68–71):

Hi þær Pantan stream   mid prasse bestodon,
Eastseaxena ord   and se æschere.
Ne mihte hyra ænig   oþrum derian,
buton hwa þurh flanes flyht   fyl genname.

[There by Panta stream they stood in force,
the vanguard of the East Saxons and the Viking army:
neither of them could harm the other,
except if someone through the flight of an arrow could cause a fall.]

The caesura here is iconic: it expresses the idea of 'separateness'. Following the variant verb *bestodon* 'they stood' are three lines in which the caesura serves to represent the space – visual or acoustic space – that intervenes between the one shore of the channel and the other. On the left are the Anglo-Saxons and on the right the Vikings. This also works syntactically: on the left 'neither of them could' – on the right 'harm the other'; on the left 'the flight of an arrow' – on the right, 'the fall of a man'. Such effects are hard to describe, but are easily seen on the pages of modern editions which, by agreed convention, signal the caesura with a visual space in the middle of the line. In oral performance at the time of the poem's composition, we can only imagine that a good speaker would achieve an equivalent effect by gesture, by careful pause and effect in voice and delivery.

'Standing and holding', and 'going forth'

In Chapter 3 it was argued that Byrhtnoth was still training the *fyrd* as he arranged them on the battlefield at the beginning of the poem, showing them how 'to stand'

and how 'to hold their position' (*bone stede healdan*). The noun *stede* implies 'station', 'standing' and derives, like modern 'stead' in 'homestead', from the verb *standan* 'to stand'. The idea of standing and holding, therefore, is a kind of loose collocation in the language of the poem.[22] Elsewhere, in two other places, we find the same verbs 'stand' and 'hold' in close proximity, both crucial to the action of the poem. The first is the scene where Byrhtnoth orders Wulfstan 'to hold' the bridge against any Viking bold enough to step onto it, an order he carries out with alacrity, supported by his two comrades Ælfere and Maccus, who 'stood with' him (79–80), the notion of 'standing with' being repeated in Byrhtnoth's last fight, where the warriors Wulfmær and Ælfnoth 'stood at his side' or 'stood by him' (152, 182). The other iconic moment of 'standing with' at the bridge comes after Byrhtnoth has agreed to grant them safe passage. As the poet presents it, the actual crossing begins with the verb *wodon* and ends with the verb *stodon*. The Vikings *wodon* 'advanced' (96a) across the water to the mainland where there 'stood' (*stodon* 100b) Byrhtnoth with his men (101a). To complete the pattern of standing and holding, Byrhtnoth immediately orders his men to form the shield-wall and 'to hold' the body of men together firmly against the enemy (101–3). The delayed rhyme on *wodon* and *stodon* here serves as a kind of envelope pattern, with *stodon* possibly marking the end of a section or verse paragraph within the poem.

In many of these scenes the 'stand' is brief and temporary: Wulfstan and his companions on the bridge fight 'for the time that they were permitted to wield weapons' (83), the latter phrase being repeated with variation at 236 in Offa's speech 'for as long as we are able to have and hold our weapons', and again at 272 in the passage on the Northumbrian hostage 'for as long as he was permitted to wield his weapons'. The chain of associations thus extends from standing, to standing with a person, to holding a position to holding or wielding a weapon (the latter idea emphasized by the two alliterating verbs 'have and hold' or the two rhyming verbs *wealdan* and *healdan*). All this culminates in the violent give-and-take of Byrhtnoth's last fight. And the sequence ends with Byrhtnoth, now wounded twice, attempting to draw his sword to fight off the would-be robber who wants to steal his equipment (161). But he falls as yet another Viking wounds him in the arm (165). There follows the final moment of the action and Byrhtnoth's penultimate speech, one of encouragement to his men to go forward (166–71). Here the various verbs we have seen – 'hold', 'wield', 'stand' – reappear in the same short passage of narrative:

Feoll þa to foldan   fealohilte swurd;
ne mihte he *gehealdan* heardne mece,
wæpnes *wealdan*.   Þa gyt þæt word gecwæð
har hilderinc,   hyssas bylde,
bæd gangan forð   gode geferan;
ne mihte þa on fotum leng   fæste *gestandan*.

[The golden-hilted sword fell to the earth;
he could no longer *hold* the fierce blade,
or *wield* any weapon. But still he spoke this word,
the grey-haired warrior, encouraged the men,
commanded the good companions to advance;
but he could no longer *stand* firm on his feet.]

This is the realistic, but at once also symbolic, narrative moment that was briefly considered in the Introduction to the present book, the moment when the sword fell to the earth. In its significance it might be compared to that moment when Sir Bedivere throws the sword Excalibur into the lake in the final stages of Thomas Malory's *Le Morte Darthur*.

Given the discussion earlier on patterns of synonymy and verbal repetition in the poem, we are now in a more favourable position to interpret the import of the fall of the sword in *Maldon*. The word denoting 'earth' here is the poetic term *folde* rather than *eorðe*, the prosaic synonym. In fact *eorðe* occurs much more often in the context of warriors 'lying' dead 'on the earth' (as used in lines 126, 157, 233, 286; with related expressions also at lines 200 and 315). The noun *folde*, by contrast, has connotations of homeland: it is used in poetic variation with the nouns *epel* and *eard* (both meaning 'homeland') in Byrhtnoth's speech to the messenger that was quoted at the beginning of this chapter (*Maldon*, 51–4). With hindsight, and remembering his stance and speech at that point in the narrative, we note that he can no longer stand and can no longer hold or wield his weapon: Byrhtnoth has in fact failed tragically in his intention 'to defend this homeland, my lord King Æthelred's country, land and people'. It would be tempting to highlight the symbolism by translating the line about the fallen sword as follows:

The golden-hilted sword fell to the home ground.

But in the end, I think, any rendering will lose necessary connotations and perhaps gain unwanted associations in the process of translation. To begin with, we may safely assert that the pre-modifier 'golden-hilted' here is too literally descriptive; it would work much better if the poet had written *goldhilted* as in Riddle 56, or *gylden hilt* as it appears in *Beowulf* (1677). But the poet's choice was *fealohilte*, which, despite also signifying the precious metal out of which the hilt has been constructed, also shifts the tone and mood of the description.

Colour terminology can vary considerably from language to language, and *fealo* is a notoriously difficult colour-word to define satisfactorily. Seeking to cover all the bases, the *Dictionary of Old English* opts for a long definition:

a colour-term of varied meaning; the corpus yields the most evidence for a colour basically yellow but variously tinted with shades of red, brown or grey, often pale but always unsaturated, i.e. not vivid; hence, 'tawny', 'yellow(ed)', 'yellowish-red', 'yellowish-brown', 'yellowish-grey' all appear as translations; the ModE reflex, 'fallow', is now obsolete except of the coat of an animal.

It is obvious that this definition suits very well the pale reddish colour of gold, but other associations are in play. There are the 'pale, fallow' waves of the sea, upon which the friendless man gazes in the elegy *The Wanderer* (line 46). There are the connotations of autumnal decline and fall as found in *The Phoenix* (lines 74–5) which, notably, shares some of its diction with the line from *Maldon*:

ne feallað þær on foldan fealwe blostman,
wudubeama wlite.

[nor do the blossoms, the beauty of the trees, fall brown to the ground.][23]

The Alfredian Prose Psalm 1 ('Blessed is the man') also captures something of the same elegiac mood with its verb *fealwian*, a derivative of the adjective *fealo*:

Eadig byð se wer þe ne gæð on geþeaht unrihtwisra, ne on þam wege ne stent synfulra, ne on heora wolbærendum setle ne sitt. (2) Ac his willa byð on Godes æ, and ymb his æ he byð smeagende dæges and nihtes. (3) Him byð swa þam treowe, þe byð aplantod neah wætera rynum. (4) Þæt sylð his wæstmas to rihtre tide, and his leaf and his blæda ne *fealwiað*, ne ne seariað; swa byð þam men þe we ær ymbspræcon eall him cymð to gode þæt þæt he deð. (5) Ac þa unrihtwisan ne beoð na swylce, ne him eac swa ne limpð; ac hi beoð duste gelicran, þonne hit wind toblæwð.[24]

[(1) Blessed is the man who does not walk in the counsel of the unjust, nor stands on the path of the sinful, nor sits in their seat of pestilence. (2) But his will is in the law of God, and about his law he will meditate day and night. (3) He is like the tree that is planted near the watercourses. (4) Which bears its fruits at the right time, and its leaf and foliage neither *fade* nor wither; so it is for the man of whom we spoke: that all comes to the good that he does. (5) But the unjust are not like this, nor do they also prosper in this way; but they are more like dust when it blows in the wind.]

So far, then, we have traced the final hours of Byrhtnoth the ealdorman, as presented in the poem *The Battle of Maldon*, from the moment where he arranges how his troops should stand to his own stance against the Viking messenger and then through to the end of his fight when he can no longer stand, and his sword falls like a fallow leaf to the ground, to 'this our land'. The context and associations of the fallen sword range from heroic poetry to documentary prose to psalmody and sermons. We will return to Psalm 1 in the next chapter, as we explore the notion of the 'blessed man' and the implications for interpreting Byrhtnoth's final prayer.

Figure 15 The Abingdon sword, early tenth century. © Wikimedia Commons / Geni (public domain).

Chapter 5

'Blessed is the man'

Byrhtnoth's prayer

He to heofenum wlat.
'Geþance þe   ðeoda Waldend
ealra þæra wynna   þe ic on worulde gebad.
Nu ic ah milde Metod   mæste þearfe,
þæt þu minum gaste   godes geunne,
þæt min sawul to ðe   siðian mote
on þin geweald   Þeoden engla,
mid friþe ferian;   ic eom frymdi to þe
þæt hi helsceaðan   hynan ne moton.'

THE BATTLE OF MALDON (172–80)

[He looked to the heavens:
'I thank you Ruler of nations,
for all the joyful times I have experienced in the world.
Now, merciful Providence, I have great need
that you may grant wellbeing to my spirit;
may my soul travel to you,
into your dominion, O Prince of angels,
may it journey under protection I entreat you,
that hellish assailants may not harm it.']

The prayer in *The Battle of Maldon*

The major argument of this book, presented from various perspectives, is that
the poet of *The Battle of Maldon* was writing, like many intellectuals of his day, in
the wake of the Benedictine Reform that was implemented in the reign of King

Edgar. This brought many advantages to a writer: increased access to books, to theology and liturgy, to classical and early Christian Latin poetry, to prose treatises and homilies written in Old English. The monastic environment, the regular life, the ways of thought, all influenced his ideas, values and modes of expression. At the same time, it must be emphasized, the author of the poem was steeped in traditional culture, the written and oral literature of his own language, *englisc* (Old English). This included the vernacular poetry that went back to the eighth century (and earlier, in the oral tradition). Inevitably, therefore, the poet also uses the language of the traditional verse: the metre and alliteration, the diction and vocabulary of the old poets, and this too influenced his ideas and modes of expression. The two streams of influence converge in the prayer in *The Battle of Maldon* that the ealdorman prays on the battlefield just before he is killed by the Vikings; this a prayer for protection, since he is concerned about predatory demons and the safe journey to the afterlife. But it is not sufficient to interpret the significance of the prayer solely in terms of its internal function within the poem. The source of this prayer it will be argued is Benedictine; in other words, it is an example of how external factors from the tenth-century world, in which the poet and the ealdorman lived, will again affect our interpretation of the poem *Maldon* and the character and status of its protagonist Byrhtnoth.

Let us begin first with stylistic features internal to the poem. In a poetic prayer addressed to God, we would expect to find set phrases used to address the deity, and indeed there are three such expressions:

> *ðeoda Waldend* 'Ruler of nations' (173b)
> *milde Metod* 'gracious Lord' (175a)
> *Þeoden engla* 'Prince of angels' (178b)

This is the heroic diction of Old English verse, as found in a poem such as *Beowulf*, sometimes with religious and sometimes with secular meanings. It will be noticed that the phrase *his þeoden* (his prince) is used at lines 120 and 158 in *Maldon* to reflect the purely secular relationship of a thegn or retainer to 'his lord' (there is a similar use at 294b). Such language, then, was originally secular, but was adapted to poetic prayers and hymns, and was then extended for religious purposes to epic narrative poems on the Old Testament patriarchs and heroes and on Christ and his saints. The practice had a long tradition behind it, going back at least to the texts of the poem *Cædmon's Hymn* that were added to manuscripts of Bede's Latin *Ecclesiastical History of the English Nation* in the eighth century. In Old English poetry, words like *Metod* (*Maldon*, lines 147a, 175a; *Cædmon's Hymn*, line 2a) or *Drihten* (*Maldon*, 148b; *Cædmon's Hymn* lines 4a and 8a) have been adapted from their more worldly uses in order to serve as epithets for 'God the Ordainer' (OE *Metod*) or 'God the Lord of Hosts' (*Drihten*).[1] Many Old English poems in the Exeter Book anthology illustrate this usage: there is the phrase *folca Waldend*

(Ruler of peoples) in the poetic paraphrase of *The Lord's Prayer I* (line 10b) that adheres to the same formulaic pattern as *ðeoda Waldend* (Ruler of nations) in *Maldon*. In the so-called Junius manuscript, a collection of biblically inspired epics in Old English (*Genesis*, *Exodus* and *Daniel*), we find that *Waldend* (Ruler) is a basic synonym for 'the Lord', and appears in many permutations such as 'Ruler of the Skies', 'Ruler of Victories', 'Ruler of Powers', 'Ruler of Angels' as well as 'Ruler of Nations' (cf. *Daniel*, line 360a). A similar practice is found in the Latin poetry that was studied or indeed composed in the tenth-century minster schools; authors on the syllabus included the late classical poet Aurelius Clemens Prudentius (348–413) or the early Anglo-Latin poet Aldhelm (639–709), both of whom use *Tonans* 'Thunderer' (in classical Latin an epithet for Jupiter) to refer to God in the Christian sense, with no question here of religious syncretism.[2] Prudentius, as we have seen, was popular in the tenth century: there are twelve manuscripts extant in Anglo-Saxon England containing the texts of his poems.[3]

But as well as these echoes of other poems, Byrhtnoth's prayer also sets up internal resonances within the text of the poem. Byrhtnoth prays that his soul may travel to God and 'journey under protection', or in Old English, *mid friþe ferian*, a phrase that also may be rendered as 'go in peace'. In alloting this speech to his hero at this point, the poet echoes the speech of the Viking messenger earlier in the narrative, who declares (lines 36–41):

> gyf þu þat gerædest   þe her ricost eart,
> þæt þu þine leoda   lysan wille,
> syllan sæmannum   on hyra sylfra dom,
> feoh wið freode,   and niman frið æt us,
> we willaþ mid þam sceattum,   us to scype gangan,
> on flot feran,   and eow friþes healdan.

> [And if you, sir, counsel this, who are the richest here,
> that you will redeem your people,
> give the seamen, on their terms,
> money in exchange for friendship, and make peace with us,
> we will take ourselves off with the payments to our ships,
> put to sea, and keep the peace with you.]

The poetic device to observe here is alliteration: the fact that Old English poets need two or three alliterating 'lifts' in their four-beat line in order to obey the basic rules of the alliterative metre. But like rhyming in later English verse, the device can be exploited to make emphases and connections between related concepts and ideas in the poem.

Accordingly, in the messenger's speech at line 39, we find 'f' alliteration on *feoh* meaning 'money' and on *frið* meaning 'truce' – a word that also has connotations of both 'peace' and 'protection'. The 'f' alliteration then returns at line 41 in order to connect *frith* with the notion of *feran* 'to go, depart'. The message is clear: if the Vikings are paid, then they will fare forth in their ships and keep the 'frith'; similarly, Byrhtnoth will, if his prayer for protection is heard, 'fare forth in frith' or 'go in peace' on his final journey. Another clause to add to this equation of peace, protection and path is found at lines 177–8, where the words for 'soul' (*sawul*) and 'journey' (*siðian*) are explicitly linked and connected by 's' alliteration. And the poet no doubt makes this connection because it is already predetermined by the patterns of his mother tongue: Old English writers frequently connect the ideas of 'soul' and 'sith', not only in verse, which invites such connections because of its alliterative metre, but also in literary prose, where the writer is free to choose whether or not to employ rhythmical alliterative phrases. This feature of his style, then, underlines the *Maldon* poet's skill, his ability to exploit the medium and the genre to allow form to underline content and contribute to the overall meaning of the passage.

Moving away from strictly poetic devices, we may also note that the passage belongs to the discourse of prayer, which like any other mode of language has its patterns and set phrases: the ealdorman looks to the heavens and prays to the Lord that He *may grant* his spirit 'well-being' or (as Bill Griffiths translates it) 'favour', namely, a safe journey into the afterlife.[4] The commonly occurring expression in a petitionary prayer in modern English is 'may grant'. The same idea is expressed with one word in Old English, namely the subjunctive *geunne* (or the imperative, which happens to have the same linguistic form, *geunne*). As a quick search through the corpus of Old English texts reveals, this has many parallels with other prayers, in both prose and verse. As a basic rule, then, *geunne* is a religious term: it predominantly appears in prayers, and then also, but only to a lesser extent, in lawbooks and lawcodes.[5] So for instance an eleventh-century biography of St Margaret makes a similar connection between looking-to-the-heavens and granting-of-a-favour, which appears to be a hagiographic motif.[6] The saint is in a tight spot, about to be drowned, she fears, by her persecutors:

Se [*sic*] eadega Margareta locade on heofonum and cwæþ: Drihten, God ealmihtig, þu þe eardest on heofonum, *geunne me* þæt þis wæter sy me to hælo and to lihtnesse and to fulwihtes bæþe unaspringende þæt hit me aþwea to þam eacan life, and awyrp me from eallum mine synne and gehæl me on þinum wuldre, forþon þe þu eart gebletsod on weorulde.[7]

[The blessed Margaret looked to the heavens and said: 'Lord, God Almighty, you who live in the heavens, *grant me* that this water should be my salvation and illumination and a bath of baptism unfailing, that it may cleanse me for eternal life and take from me all my sin and heal me for your glory, because you are consecrated for ever.']

Unexpectedly, this is not to be Margaret's last word, for her petition is in fact granted, but it follows the same pattern as Byrhtnoth's prayer. In both texts, the speech is introduced by the saintly gesture and action: *Se eadega Margareta locade on heofonum* or, in the case of Byrhtnoth, *he to heofenum wlat*. In the poem that gesture is possibly emphasized by the form, for the poet has apparently omitted a half-line here, perhaps to make the statement stand out as unusual.

The parallel between the two texts is instructive: it suggests that the language of the epic poem *Maldon* borders on the discourse of the saint's life, despite some valiant efforts by critics to purge Byrhtnoth of such saintly influences and make him more purely heroic.[8] But at this point, texts external to the poem tip the balance. Byrhtnoth, as we know from other sources, is fighting at an auspicious

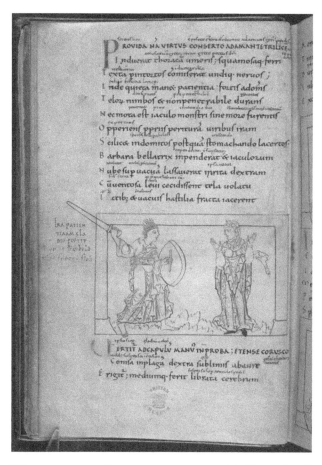

Figure 16 Patience at prayer as Anger attacks; in a manuscript of Prudentius, *Psychomachia* in London, British Library, Cotton Cleopatra C. VIII, folio 11v. © The British Library.

spiritual location (see Chapter 1 for the significance of the name of the battle site). And as Chapter 11 will show, particularly in Book V of *The Life of St Oswald*, Byrhtnoth belongs typologically alongside Dunstan in the account of their last days, just as the saintly Archbishop Oswald is compared even more explicitly to his pious friend Ealdorman Æthelwine, who dies chanting the psalter and is conveyed, so the author Byrhtferth believes, on 'the path of the saints' to 'the citizenry of Paradise'.[9]

A contemporary vernacular prayer

There is one more major statement to be made about the language of Byrhtnoth's final prayer in *The Battle of Maldon*. As Donald Scragg notes briefly in his critical edition, the actual wording echoes 'a contemporary vernacular prayer', published as a minor piece in a late-nineteenth-century issue of a scholarly journal.[10] In his note, Scragg cites two short extracts from the prayer. But as far as I am aware, no critic has taken Scragg's insight any further, neither has anyone analysed the parallels, nor examined the immediate context in which this prayer appears.[11]

The prayer is recorded in the Regius Psalter, so-called after its shelf mark in the British Library; this manuscript is an important one, for as recent research has demonstrated, it is associated very closely with the early years of the Benedictine Reform.[12] Dunstan, it will be remembered, was very nearly exiled by King Edmund at Cheddar, but the monarch's change of heart led to his appointment to the abbacy of Glastonbury. Once established as abbot, Dunstan set up a school with the help of the young, bright scholar, Æthelwold. Together the two men instigated a long and intense programme of literary, textual and theological study of some of the major texts of the monastic reform movement on the Continent, the results of which are recorded in various glossed textbooks and manuscript anthologies that have survived the years.[13] Once Æthelwold had become abbot in Abingdon, he continued such studies, focussing particularly on the study of the psalter.[14] The Regius Psalter, with its annotations and interlinear glosses, represents the fruit of Æthelwold's academic labours; and this manuscript contains the copy of the contemporary vernacular prayer.

Before taking a glance at the text itself, we will examine the context in a little more detail, for it is crucial to such questions as the literacy and spirituality of the period, the process of learning to read and the language of religion. The psalter was in fact one of the best-known texts in the period and one of the most widely occurring books. From Anglo-Saxon libraries there survives, for example, only one manuscript of *Beowulf*, but there exist no less than forty manuscripts of the Latin Psalms. Like the Gospels, the Psalms were of course very familiar, used every day as the basis of church services and music. For this reason, the psalter also became the elementary textbook of the middle ages. People learned to read and write with the Latin Psalms; a typical pupil in a monastery or cathedral school memorized a passage by heart and wrote it out with a stylus on a wax tablet (a wooden board the size of a notebook, covered with a layer of wax as a writing surface that could later be smoothed over once the text was learned). Furthermore, the psalter was a means of private prayer and meditation, as well as being the key to the monastic liturgy and the various 'hours' of the day in a monastic or cathedral community.[15]

Here is an example from the Psalm 1 of the Regius Psalter. For ease of reading, the Latin and Old English texts have been separated, but in many Anglo-Saxon psalters, the two languages worked in tandem, with the Old English words entered as individual glosses written over the top of the Latin words to which they referred.[16] In the extract here, the numbered verses are to assist comparison with modern texts of the Bible; the square brackets represent places where the editor, Roeder, found the text to be illegible in the manuscript:

1. Beatus uir qui non abiit in consilio impiorum et in uia peccatorum non stetit. et in cathedra pestilentiae non sedit.

    eadig wer se þe na eode on geþeahte arleasra on wege synfulra na stod 7 on heahsetle cwyldes uel wawan [---] sæt

2. Sed in lege domini uoluntas eius et in lege eius meditabitur die ac nocte.

    ac on e [---] willa his 7 on ǽ his smeað uel foreþæncð dæges 7 nihtes

3. Et erit tamquam lignum quod plantatum est secus decursus aquarum quod fructum suum dabit in tempore suo. et folium eius non defluet et omnia quecumque fatiet prosperabuntur.

    bið swa swa treow þæt planted is wið ryne wætra wæstm his selð on tide his leaf his na [---] ealle swa hwelce swa [---] beoð gesundfullude.[17]

Here, for convenience, is the translation of the Vulgate into Early Modern English from the Roman Catholic Douay Bible:

1. Blessed is the man who hath not walked in the counsel of the ungodly, nor stood in the way of sinners, nor sat in the chair of pestilence.

2. But his will is in the law of the Lord, and on his law he shall meditate day and night.

3. And he shall be like a tree which is planted near the running waters, which shall bring forth its fruit, in due season. And his leaf shall not fall off: and all whatsoever he shall do shall prosper.

Though the Hebrew Bible originally had a very different purpose, the three verses quoted here could not serve better as a primer of the early medieval monastic life. This is the epitome of 'the blessed man', living a spiritual life and flourishing, secluded from the world and its ways, engaged in meditation. In a medieval monastic context, he is the ideal monk. It is no surprise that two illustrated psalters in use at Canterbury in the late tenth century show the blessed man as dressed in a monk's habit or gown, with his hair shaven in the shape of a monastic tonsure.[18]

If, with this in mind, we now return to the text of the Regius Psalter, it will become clear that the glosses do more than simply function as a linguistic guide to the Latin text, they function also as its commentary and interpretation. The

Figure 17 Psalmist praying in Harley Psalter, illustration to Psalm 12: London, British Library, Harley 603, folio 7. © The British Library.

glossator takes the *beatus uir* of Psalm 1, verse 1, for instance, and interprets it in his Old English gloss as *eadig wer*: but the phrase is commonly found in saints' lives and chronicles meaning a 'holy man', that is, a saint, the aspirational goal of the medieval religious orders. In the C version of the Chronicle, in the annal for 44 AD, to give just one illustration from that genre, Saint Peter, in his promotion as Bishop of Rome is *se eadiga Petrus*, and in the passage just quoted from hagiography, Saint Margaret is *se eadega Margareta*.[19] The psalter, then, to put it bluntly, assists in the process of becoming more holy. Another key monastic practice can be extrapolated from verse 2: the glossator takes Latin *meditabitur*, 'he shall meditate', and provides it with two alternative interpretations separated by the little conjunction *uel*, which means 'or' (a common means of providing alternatives in these glossed texts). For our commentator, *meditabitur* is glossed *smeað*, from *smeagan*, literally 'to examine, penetrate, scrutinize, look closely into', but it also means *foreþæncð*, from *foreþencan*, 'to premeditate, consider, be mindful'. Taken together, these meanings encapsulate the practice of monastic meditation as it developed in the early medieval West generally, and with its own nuances in tenth-century English religious culture in particular. A meditating monk or nun learned a text by heart, mulled over it, looked closely into it, ruminated and digested it; all this was meditation.[20] Moreover, as Gretsch points out in her *The Intellectual Foundations of the English Benedictine Reform*, the psalter was also a higher-level text book; it could be used to teach the deeper problems of theology, literature and textual scholarship; a psalter glossed and annotated in a particular manner could and did represent a particular school of thought or a particular spirituality. The Regius Psalter is in this respect no exception: it represents some of the main theory and practices that lie behind the tenth-century Benedictine Reform movement. And like other psalters it can also serve as a kind of anthology, with additional, relevant texts added in blank spaces in the manuscript. Such is this vernacular penitential prayer, added to the manuscript of the Regius Psalter perhaps at some point in the second half of the tenth century.

To appreciate its cumulative style we need to hear some of the repetitions in the prayer over the course of an extended passage. Here is a section (my translation):

> My Lord, almighty God, glory be to you and thanks for what you have granted as favours to me or to others. My Lord, thank you that you created your angels as an adornment and as a joy to all the souls of the saints, the angels who praise your name for ever and ever. My Lord almighty, thank you that you were born in a human body and for all the humility which you suffered and made manifest for all mankind. By that humility grant me grace and favour for my sins. My Lord Christ, thank you that you ascended the font of baptism, innocent of all sins, for the great joy of humankind: grant me remission of all my sins that I

ever committed against any creature. My Lord, thank you that you fasted in the desert for the sins of mankind for forty days and nights, and that you overcame the vices and threw down the devil. Grant me through the grace of fasting remission of all my sins because I fasted too little for my sins, and overcome my vices that the devil may never reach my soul or my body. My Lord thank you that you allowed your innocent body to be taken and to be bound and whipped. Grant me for the sake of the blows with which the unfaithful whipped you and struck you that all I have been struck with, through the wounds of sin, that you heal all this, my Saviour, through your mercy. My Lord, thank you that you suffered for the love of human beings and that you stood before the throne of the earthly judge and suffered those judgements upon yourself.

The prayer is long and deliberately repetitive, a set of reflections on the life and passion of Christ followed by petitions for mercy that arise out of these reflections; overall, this is a prayer of penitence and forgiveness. Already, in comparison with Byrhtnoth's prayer, some minor similarities of theme might be teased out, but the real verbal and thematic parallels occur in the subsequent section:

> Min drihten sie þe þonc þæs þe þu þinne gast, þinum fæder bebude, þa þu woldest for monna cynne deaþ þrowian, forgif me for þære are þonne ic scyle of þisse weorulde feran, þæt þu þonne minum gaste onfo mid sibbe, and ic hine mote ðe bebeodan, þelæs þe hi se arwyrgda gast derian mote.

> [My Lord thanks be to you that you entrusted your spirit to your Father, when you desired to suffer death for humankind. Grant me, for that mercy, when I must pass from this world, that you will receive my spirit with peace, and that I may entrust it to you, so that the devil may not harm it.]

The similarities between the two texts are thematic rather than verbal: the thanks, the granting of mercy, the journeying (*ferian* in *Maldon*, *feran* in the Regius prayer), the safe arrival 'in peace' (*mid friþe* in *Maldon* but *mid sibbe* in the Regius prayer), the fear that the devil or demons might harm the soul or spirit. Nevertheless, despite the lack of exact verbal echo (usually a convincing sign of influence from one text to another) there are enough thematic parallels here to suggest that the two prayers inhabit the same thought-world. Byrhtnoth's prayer is Benedictine, and consonant with other prayers of the period.[21]

Byrhtnoth and the Benedictine Reform

Given the Benedictine influence on Byrhtnoth's prayer, this raises questions about the spirituality of both the anonymous poet and of Byrhtnoth himself. The channels by which Benedictine ideas reached eastern England were chiefly the monasteries themselves, Ely and Ramsey being the leading centres, founded, respectively, by the two reformers Bishop Æthelwold and Archbishop Oswald. *The Book of Ely* (II. 4–5) tells at length how Bishop Æthelwold refounded Ely, and the exchange of gifts that took place when he purchased the monastic land from King Edgar, who laid 'a golden cross, embellished with marvellous workmanship' together with 'a wonderful gospel-book' on the altar of St Æthelthryth, the patron saint of Ely and its abbey (II. 4).[22] The gospel book in question was later described as marvellously decorated and illustrated (*Book of Ely*, III. 50):

> This gospel-book has, along with a 'Christ in Majesty' and four angels and twelve apostles, its whole surface-area gilded with precious stones and enamels. The other side of the gospel-book is of silver with images of virgins.

In the foundation charter for the abbey at Ely, as reported in *The Book of Ely*, Edgar stresses the need for the monastic revival in order to preserve peace and stability in the country, 'so that by their prayer and lively religious observance of the service of God, we may be able to have the Ruler himself at peace with us' (II. 5).

We have already seen the role that Ely Abbey played in the life of Byrhtnoth, and then also in his death and burial; as *The Book of Ely* (II. 62) tells the story:

> But the abbot, on hearing the outcome of the fighting, went with some monks to the battle-ground and found Byrhtnoth's body. He brought it back to the church and buried it with great honour. And in place of the head he put a round lump of wax. Long afterwards, in [our own] times, he was recognized by this sign, and was honourably entombed among the others. But it was in the days of Edgar, Edward (king and martyr) and Æthelred, Kings of the English, that this pious and energetic man had his being, and he died in the fourteenth year of the reign of the same Æthelred, in the 991st year from the incarnation of the Lord.[23]

The epitaph 'pious and energetic' recalls the way Ealdorman Byrhtnoth is presented in Byrhtferth of Ramsey's *Life of St Oswald*, in one cameo appearance making a stirring speech on the value of the monasteries at a meeting in London in 977, at a time when some were under threat of closure during the so-called anti-monastic reaction following the death of King Edgar in 975. Here Byrhtnoth actively supports his like-minded colleagues, the two brothers Ælfwold the thegn and Æthelwine the ealdorman of East Anglia. Æthelwine, as will be seen in Chapter 11, features prominently in the biography as Oswald's close friend, and is even called *amicus Dei*, 'friend of God', because of his support for the monastic reform (IV. 14). According to Ealdorman Æthelwine, it is the monks 'qui omnem Christianitatem eu iuuante tenuerunt in regno' (who with his support maintain all Christendom in the kingdom; my translation), while for his brother Ælfwold 'it is only through their prayers that we can be snatched away from our enemies' (IV. 13). These are the pro-monastic attitudes of two prominent laymen, to which Byrhtnoth adds his contribution:

> Deinde surrexit Byrihtnoðus comes, 'uir religiosus et timens Deum', qui fieri precepit silentium et ait ad exercitum: 'Audite me, seniores et iuniores! Hoc quod eximius miles nunc dixit, cuncti uolumus et cupimus ut uos id desideretis.'

> Then Ealdorman Byrhtnoth, 'a religious man and fearing God' [Acts 10. 2], who asked for silence and said to the assembly: 'Listen to me, old men and young men! We all wish and desire that you also desire that which this excellent thegn has spoken just now.'[24]

The biblical citation comes from Acts 10. 1-5, in which Cornelius the centurion, a pious but secular soldier, is called to the service of God:

> And there was a certain man in Caesarea, named Cornelius, a centurion of that which is called the Italian band; [2] A religious man, and fearing God with all his house, giving much alms to the people, and always praying to God. [3] This man saw in a vision manifestly, about the ninth hour of the day, an angel of God coming in unto him, and saying to him: Cornelius. [4] And he, beholding him, being seized with fear, said: What is it, Lord? And he said to him: Thy prayers and thy alms are ascended for a memorial in the sight of God.

Such is the level to which Byrhtnoth had risen in the estimate of the ecclesiastical writers of the period; he is 'a religious man and fearing God', a new Cornelius, who assists the monastic bishops in the work of the church.

Chapter 6

'From a great kindred in Mercia'

Ic wylle mine æþelo   eallum gecyþan,
þæt ic wæs on Myrcon   miccles cynnes.
Wæs min ealda fæder   Ealhelm haten
wis ealdorman   woruldgesælig.

THE BATTLE OF MALDON (LINES 216–19)

[I wish to declare my lineage to all:
that I was from a great kindred in Mercia.
My grandfather was called Ealhhelm,
a wise ealdorman and prosperous in the world.]

The young warrior Ælfwine's rousing speech from *The Battle of Maldon* contains a proud declaration of his origins in the Mercian nobility, along with the name of his grandfather, a historical figure, named Ealhhelm. Implied in Ælfwine's speech also are the names of his various famous (and historically attested) uncles; in addition, the poet explicitly names Ælfwine's father as Ælfric, but paradoxically it turns out from sources external to the poem that this is the notorious Ælfric 'Cild', exiled in 985 for treason against his king and people. Intriguingly, Ælfwine ends his speech by mourning for Byrhtnoth not only as his lord, in social terms, but also as his *mæg* or kinsman, in terms of family connections (lines 220–4):

. . . Ne sceolon me on þære þeode   þegenas ætwitan
þæt ic of ðisse fyrde   feran wille,
eard gesecan,   nu min ealdor ligeð
forheawen æt hilde.   Me is þæt hearma mæst;
he wæs ægðer min mæg   and min hlaford.

[. . . and none of the thegns in that nation may reproach me
with wanting to desert this army
or seek out my own country, now that my prince lies
slain in battle. For me it is the greatest of sorrows,
for he was both my kinsman and my lord.]

The context for this speech is clearly important for the poem, and in this chapter we will explore the role of kindred, first in *Maldon* and then in heroic poetry more generally. Various texts from outside of the poem will also be brought to bear on identifying and explaining the role of Ælfwine in *The Battle of Maldon*.

The naming of kindred

The naming of both kinsmen and also the kindred group from which they come is certainly common in *Maldon*. According to figures suggested by Pauline Stafford, there are twenty-four men named in *The Battle of Maldon*, of whom arguably sixteen are introduced and identified by a kin relationship.[1] Usually the poet gives the name of the father, often in the form of a patronymic on the pattern 'X's son'; so Byrhtnoth is *Byrhtelmes bearn* 'Byrhthelm's son' (92a), Wulfmær is *Wulfstanes bearn* (155a) and the fugitives Godric, Godwine and Godwig are *Oddan bearn*, 'Odda's sons' (186a).[2] Alternatively the poet uses the term *mæg* 'kinsman': *Offan mæg* (5a), *Byrhtnoðes mæg* (114a), *Gaddes mæg* (281a) or the straightforward word for 'brother': *his broðru* 'his brothers' (191a), *Sibyrhtes broðor* 'Sibyrht's brother' (282a), *begen þa gebroþru* 'both the brothers' (305a).

Most of these references are to the immediate family of father and brother, some to the more distant relation of cousin and kinsman, but just occasionally the poet speaks of the *cynn*, which I have translated as 'kindred', as a term of wider coverage and meaning. The Toronto Dictionary of Old English, which offers the latest research on the Old English lexicon, gives for sense 1 of *cynn*, 'race, people, nation', while sense 2, 'referring to a family line', covers a whole range of relevant semantic distinctions, including a group of persons descended from a common ancestor; a clan or tribe; the tribes of Israel; the kinsmen and actual members of a family; the ancestors, forebears, and 'ancestral stock'.[3] A clear example of such a reference to the wider 'kindred' is the Northumbrian hostage, who we see engaging in the battle towards the end of the poem (265–7):

Him se gysel ongan   geornlice fylstan;
he wæs on Norðhymbron   heardes cynnes,
Ecglafes bearn,   him wæs Æscferð nama.

[They were eagerly helped by the hostage, who was of a fierce kindred in Northumbria, the son of Ecglaf: his name was Æscferth.]

Just as Ælfwine is 'of a great kindred in Mercia', so Æscferth is of 'a fierce kindred in Northumbria'.

Kindred in *Beowulf*

In brief, then, the hero is identified by his kindred. This is the norm in the heroic poetry of the period, which was still a popular part of 'tradition' in the tenth century, and clearly influential on the poet of *Maldon*. As ever, the touchstone is the classic poem *Beowulf*, which was still in circulation. How well known it was is a question that cannot be answered, but the manuscript of *Beowulf* was copied around the time of 'Maldon' by two scribes: there were at the very least two readers of this old poem in the late tenth century or the early eleventh century.[4] And in terms of identity, the plot of *Beowulf* begins with the Danish kings, the Scyldings ('sons of Scyld') and an account of their ancestral kindred: Scyld, who founded the dynasty, his son Beow, Beow's son Healfdene, then the latter's three sons, with alliterating names: Heorogar, Hrothgar and Halga the Good (the latter being an example of a by-name, like Edward 'the Tall' in *Maldon*). At the beginning of the main story, Hrothgar, the reigning king, is referred to as *wine Scyldinga* (line 170b), 'friend, i.e. lord, of the Scyldings', and *maga Healfdenes* (189b), 'son of Healfdene'.[5]

The interest in kindred continues into the main plot. There now begins *Beowulfes sið* (501b), 'Beowulf's journey', the main theme of the first half of the poem, which offers many opportunities for the travellers to meet new characters, who join the action and introduce themselves to Beowulf and his men as they make their way to their destination at Hrothgar's hall. The travellers first encounter the coastguard or watchman, 'guard of the Scyldings' (229b); later they are stopped by the doorman, who is introduced by his rank as 'Hrothgar's herald and officer' (335–6) and subsequently by his kindred as 'Wulfgar . . . who was a man of the Vendels'. This Wulfgar speaks of his king not by name but as 'friend of the Danes' (350b) and 'lord of the Scyldings' (351a).

At this stage in the story – the long, protracted testing of the stranger Beowulf at the Scylding hall – one new section (Fitt VI) starts as follows: the context is the doorman's announcement of Beowulf's arrival, and King Hrothgar's response

Hroðgar maþelode,   helm Scyldinga:
'Ic hine cuðe   cnihtwesende.
Wæs his ealdfæder   Ecgþeo haten'

(START OF FITT VI, LINES 371–3)

[Hrothgar made a speech, the protector of the Scyldings:
'I knew him when he was a boy.
His forefather was called Ecgtheow']

Once he has recognized Beowulf, Hrothgar identifies him more exactly by naming his 'forefather', that is, Beowulf's *father*. Interestingly, in terms of its syntax, the line is very reminiscent of Ælfwine's speech just quoted from *Maldon*:

Wæs min ealda fæder   Ealhelm haten . . .

[My grandfather was called Ealhelm . . .]

There is the same archaic word order, beginning the sentence with the verb 'was' and ending with the past participle 'called', and there is only a minor difference in form between the compound *his eald-fæder* 'his forefather' in *Beowulf*, and the adjective–noun combination of *min ealda fæder* 'my grandfather' in *Maldon*. Though these are fixed, formulaic phrases, this is one of the passages where it may be suspected that the *Maldon* poet is echoing *Beowulf*.

   Another example of naming close kindred is Beowulf's earlier response to the coastguard, where a similar case of parallelism occurs:

Wæs min fæder   folcum gecyþed

[My father was known to many peoples]

The full context is as follows. The coastguard asks *hwæt syndon ge?* Literally, 'what are you (plural)', that is, 'what kind of men are you?' (237–40a):

Hwæt syndon ge   searohæbbendra,
byrnum werede,   þe þus brontne ceol
ofer lagustræte   lædan cwomon,
hider ofer holmas?

[What kind of men are you, bearing weapons,
protected by your mail-coats, guiding your broad ship
over the sea-road, coming here
across the high seas?]

In his reply, Beowulf talks first of his close kindred (260–4):

We synt gumcynnes   Geata leode
ond Higelaces   heorðgeneatas.
Wæs min fæder   folcum gecyþed,
æþele ordfruma,   Ecgþeow haten.

Gebad wintra worn,   ær he on weg hwurfe,
gamol of geardum;   hine gearwe geman
witena welhwylc   wide geond eorþan.

[We are of the great kindred of the people of the Geats and Higelac's hearth-companions. My father was known to many peoples, a noble leader called Ecgtheow. He had experienced a multitude of winters before he went on his way, an old man, from the courts, every wise counsellor remembers him well, far and wide across the earth.]

Beowulf first identifies himself and his men by kindred as *gumcynnes Geata leode* ('by kindred we are people of the Geats') and then by lordship: he and his men are *Higelaces heorðgeneatas*, 'Hygelac's hearth-companions', just as in the later poem *Maldon* the members of Byrhtnoth's retinue are described as his *heorðgeneatas* (see Chapter 3); Beowulf concludes with kinship, naming his father and reciting his achievements. Citing the passage on kindred from *Maldon* again, we can see that it follows a similar model, almost as though it were an echo and summary of the extract from *Beowulf* (see Chapter 9 for other parallels between this passage and *Beowulf*):

I wish to make known my origins: I was from a great kindred in Mercia. My grandfather was called Ealhhelm, a wise ealdorman who prospered in the world.

This is the correct protocol, this is how people in heroic poems should introduce themselves, naming their kindred, then their forefather, then his fame in the world.

Ælfwine's father

But there is a discrepancy in Ælfwine's declaration of origins. The young nobleman Ælfwine is a historical person, whose name occurs in a document of the period alongside the names of his uncles and other family; here is the relevant passage, from the will, written in the year 971, of one of his uncles, Ælfheah, ealdorman of Hampshire, who names him as *his swustur suna*, 'his sister's son Ælfwine':

And he grants to his brother Ælfhere the estates at Faringdon and Aldbourne. And to his son Godwine the estate at Tudingatune and Purton to Ælfweard and Wycombe to his kinsman Æthelweard; and Froxfield to his *sister's son Ælfwine*.[6]

Various other names in this bequest can be identified with confidence: in particular we should note the will-writer's brother Ælfhere, who became a famous, and in some circles infamous, ealdorman of Mercia. But these two uncles are not mentioned in the poem. The fact is that the character Ælfwine in the poem chooses to celebrate the name of his grandfather Ealhhelm as the representative of the Mercian kindred to which he belongs.[7] It is only the poet-narrator who actually names Ælfwine's father, in his usual manner (209–11):

> So he encouraged them, the son of Ælfric,
> [he was] a warrior young in winters, these words he declared,
> Ælfwine then said – speaking boldly.

From an internal point of view, looking only within the poem itself, there is no discrepancy: it is quite normal for the poet, as we have seen, to insert a transition before the speech of a character in the poem mentioning his kindred and his status.

But if we now apply texts and information from outside the poem, the picture looks rather more complex. Ælfwine's father was called Ælfric Cild (the by-name, meaning literally 'child', implies noble rank) and is mentioned as witness to an exchange of lands in an Abingdon charter.[8] He was of course one of several men at this time named Ælfric. For a brief period, however, this Ælfric also became an ealdorman, but apparently he was not regarded as a wise ealdorman, and he was not one who prospered in the worldly affairs of the kingdom. Here, by way of illustration, is Version C of the Anglo-Saxon Chronicle and its annals for the years 983–5:

> 983 Her forðferde Ælfhere ealdorman, 7 feng Ælfric to þam ilcan ealdordomscipe, 7 Benedictus papa forþferde.

> 984 Her forðferde Aþelwold bisceop on Kalendas Agustus.

> 985 Her wæs Ælfric ealdorman ut adræfed of earde, 7 on þam ilcan geare wæs Eadwine to abbode gehalgod to þam mynstre æt Abbandune.

> [983 Here Ealdorman Ælfhere departed this life and Ælfric succeeded to the ealdordom. And Pope Benedict passed away.

> 984 Here Bishop Æthelwold passed away on the Kalends of August.

> 985 Here Ealdorman Ælfric was exiled from the land. And in the same year Edwin was consecrated as abbot of the monastery at Abingdon.]

These annals cover a range of events from the international to the more local: there is the record of the Pope's death in 983 and the appointment of a certain Edwin as abbot of the local monastery at Abingdon. But the annal for 984 is of national interest: it marks the passing of Bishop Æthelwold, famously one of the most prominent of the Benedictine reformers and, along with Dunstan, the principal adviser to the king and his council. In addition, in the secular political sphere, the death is recorded in 983 of Ælfhere, ealdorman of Mercia. This man, as we have just seen, is the uncle of the Ælfwine 'young in years' who fights at *Maldon*. Ælfhere is now succeeded by his brother-in-law Ælfric Cild. But we can see from the annal for 985 that only two years later this Ealdorman Ælfric (who is Ælfwine's father) was sent into exile. A slightly later royal charter gives the reason, at least from the king's perspective; the king is speaking here of three estates which he has given to Abingdon Abbey:

> These portions of land Ælfric, surnamed 'Child', forcibly withdrew from a certain widow called Eadflæd, but later, when in his office of ealdorman he was convicted of crime against me and against all my people, these portions which I have mentioned and also all the landed possessions which he owned were assigned to my control, when all my leading men assembled together to a synodal council at Cirencester, and expelled the same Ælfric, guilty of high treason, as a fugitive from this country.[9]

It has been suggested that Ælfric Cild opposed the new policies of the king, who was seeking to throw off the influence of the advisers of his youthful years.[10] But historically, the official picture is that the Ælfwine of *Maldon* is the son of a convicted traitor.

Interestingly, it will be recalled that the leading thegn in the poem, Offa, responds to Ælfwine's rousing speech of encouragement by lamenting the betrayal they have just experienced and the consequent flight of the *folc*: 'Godric, cowardly son of Odda, has betrayed us all' (lines 237–8). But paradoxically, here we have the son of the traitor Ælfric Cild now placed prominently at the head of the brave retinue of men who have refused to flee the field and are now seeking to avenge the death of their lord and friend. If Ælfwine really fought and fell at the battle in Maldon, and I see no real reason to doubt this, then we have to see it as an example of the role of kindred as a necessary supportive mechanism in the practice of running society in the period. Ælfwine in the year 985 was perhaps only fifteen years old, and bereft of both maternal uncle and father, one by death and one by exile. Nevertheless the poem implies that he had been taken in by his more distant kinsman Byrhtnoth and given a prominent place in his retinue, as one of his commended men. A passage in the poem *Solomon and Saturn* (lines 391–2) outlines the process by which a young man like Ælfwine, whose family were wealthy, may have expressly sought out Byrhtnoth as his lord:

> Him mæg eadig eorl   eaðe geceosan
> on his modsefan   mildne hlaford,
> anne æðeling.   Ne mæg don unlæde swa.

[A wealthy nobleman may easily choose
according to his own inclination a gracious lord,
even a prince. But a poor man may not do so.]

In this way, the poet of *Maldon* presents Byrhtnoth as a hospitable and gracious lord, and a patron and friend to his kinsmen.

Chapter 7
Feud and friendship

> 'Me is þæt hearma mæst;
> he wæs ægðer min mæg and min hlaford.'
> Þa he forð eode, fæhðe gemunde
> þæt he mid orde anne geræhte
> flotan on þam folce, þæt se on foldan læg
> forwegen mid his wæpne. Ongan þa winas manian,
> frynd and geferan, þæt hi forð eodon.

THE BATTLE OF MALDON (223–9)

> ['For me it is the greatest of sorrows,
> for he was both my kinsman and my lord.'
> Then he went forward – directing his mind to the feud,
> so that with his spear he wounded
> a seaman in the crowd, who lay there on the earth,
> killed by his weapon. He urged his fellows,
> friends and companions that they move forward.]

In *Maldon*, as we have just seen, the young nobleman Ælfwine declares the high origins of his family. But that is only one side of his declaration. The other theme is friendship, and he makes it very clear that his kinsman and lord was also his friend, and his loss is the 'greatest of sorrows'. It prompts him immediately to take revenge, but it also prompts him to urge on the other men, and the poet emphasizes that friendship here too plays an important role: these people are his 'friends and companions' (the poet uses both the poetic term *winas* 'friends' and the more everyday word *frynd*, the irregular plural of the noun *freond* 'friend'). The question then arises: Who are these friends and companions? Dealing with this issue in terms of social class, the historian Pauline Stafford writes:

> The audience along with the date of the poem is much debated, but the
> lesser nobles who feature so prominently in it seem its likely hearers; it is their

actions which are presented, no doubt to their satisfaction, within older epic forms.[1]

The lesser nobles so named are the new thegnly class, already referred to earlier, in the discussion of hearth and home in Chapter 3. A well-known study by the literary critics Busse and Holtei follows a similar line to that of Stafford and takes the argument further, making a case for the poem as an expression of the social mobility of the new thegnly class, with a good deal of levelling.[2]

In *Maldon*, Ælfwine's speech is followed by a response from Offa, Ealdorman Byrhtnoth's leading thegn, who responds explicitly to Ælfwine, likewise in thirteen lines of poetry, suggesting there is parity of rank between them. Conversely, Dunnere the simple *ceorl* is given only two lines to make his speech of encouragement. Nevertheless, leaving out the high and the low characters, we see that the case for social levelling is strong, and this chapter will be concerned with how our poem presents these equal-standing members of the lesser nobility: the thegns who feature in the speeches and brief scenes of action that make up the latter part of the poem *Maldon*. These are also the 'thegns' in the home region to whom Ælfwine refers in his speech (lines 220–3):

> . . . and none of the thegns in that nation may reproach me
> with wanting to desert this army
> or seek out my own country, now that my prince lies
> slain in battle.

Among the administrative documents of the period which mention this class of people there are the wills, writs and charters, some of which we have already examined, while the chronicles tend to focus on the big players: the princes and ealdormen, the archbishops and bishops. In Chapters 3 and 4 we considered the 'vertical' lines of lordship and authority in *Maldon*; it is time now to look at the 'horizontal' links that bind society together, as implicitly presented in the poem. One type of document that has not featured in the discussion so far is the rule-book of the *guilds*, that is, the set of regulations or statutes concerned with the everyday practices and provisions of associations of lay people and thegns. The statutes describing the activities of these guilds, which started to proliferate in the tenth century, are a little-known window on the cultural conditions of the time.

The Thegns' Guilds

In a later medieval context, guilds are either groups of merchants who need to protect their trade or specialized craftsmen such as bakers, shoemakers and weavers, who bond together for security, mutual protection and economic benefit. Etymologically, the word 'guild' derives from the Old English noun *gyld* or *gild*, meaning literally 'payment' – this continues to be its basic meaning in many Old English texts and contexts, where it can refer variously to a large tax, a tribute or the ubiquitous *wergyld* or *wergild*, that is, 'man-payment', a compensation payment paid in legal cases involving injury or death, as a way of appeasing the victim's kindred and preventing a feud. In the tenth century, there appear the first references to *gyld* or *gegyld* meaning 'an association of dues-paying members', with the derivative *gegylda* meaning a member of such an association.[3]

The purpose of these guilds or fraternities was to call regular meetings in order to organize the following activities: communal feasts, church festivals, charitable almsgiving to the poor, and burials and regular commemorations of the dead – for which purpose monks were employed to chant psalms and priests to say masses, all for the benefit of the souls of the dear departed members of the guild.[4] As the various surviving statutes show, the guildsmen paid regular membership fees and shared other costs, hence the name *gegylda*, literally, 'the one who pays'. The texts go into precise and even vivid detail on the preparations for the feast, including requirements for individual items of food and drink. The Guild Statutes from Abbotsbury in Dorset, for instance (the fullest and most detailed example of this genre), demonstrate the meticulous preparations required for the annual feast of 'St Peter's Mass', which must have taken place either as the Feast of St Peter and St Paul on 29 June or the Feast of St Peter in Chains on 1 August.[5] The costs incurred by the guild-members were many and varied: five weeks before the feast each guild-brother paid one sester of wheat, then three days before the feast one penny, or one pennyworth of wax, to St Peter's Minster.[6] And on the evening before the actual feast the guildsmen were required to cooperate in pairs in order to deliver a loaf of bread, but the quality had to be assured, in very particular terms:

> ænne bradne hlaf well besewen and well gesyfled to urum gemænum ælmyssan.

> [one broad loaf, of good quality and well supplied with something to eat with it, for our common almsgiving.][7]

As with the food, so with the drink, no sympathy was to be had for any member whose brewing was below the expected quality; the festival ale had to meet the high standards of the guild:

> And se ðe bryðene underfehð, & þæt gecweme ne deð, beo he his inganges scyldig, and þær ne beo nan gyfu.

> [And he who undertakes a brewing and does not do it satisfactorily is to be liable to his entrance fee, and there is to be no remission.]

The *ingang*, or entrance fee, was three sesters of wheat, a large measure, hence a considerable fine for the hapless brewer. Other regulations match this severity. There seems to be some fear that trouble could ensue at the feast, which probably took place in the purpose-built *gegyldhealle* or guild-hall that the leading thegn Urki (also spelled Orcy) had donated to the fellowship. For this reason, the statutes are designed to preserve law and order. A guild-member who insults another is liable to a fine of one *ingang*, payable to the fraternity in addition to paying compensation to the man he had insulted. And if he refuses then he will be excluded from the guild-fraternity. Not unlike festivals today, there is a similar fine of one *ingang* for anyone who brings in more guests than he should, 'buton ðæs stiwerdes leafe and ðæra feormera' (without the permission of the steward and of the purveyors).

So much for the Feast of St Peter, but this was not the only or even the major function of the guild. It had in addition the far more serious purpose of arranging the burial of the dead. In an age of increased lay piety and a concern for penance and the state of the soul, at a time when thegns owned their own small chapels or churches within their own walled manor or *burh* (see Chapter 3), the guild made elaborate arrangements for prayers for the souls of the departed. In this respect, the Abbotsbury Statutes are characteristically very insistent about the details. In the actual presence of the deceased, the guild-members would assemble, and each was to offer a penny to help pay for the prayers, the masses and the psalters that were to be said for him or her. If the person had died even as far as sixty miles away, the guild steward would delegate up to thirty members of the guild to bring the deceased person to his or her chosen resting place. The statutes offer the following raison d'être for this, essentially the main function of the guild:

> Let us pray God Almighty eagerly from our inmost heart, that he have mercy on us, and also his holy Apostle St Peter, that he intercede for us and clear our way to the eternal rest, because we have assembled this guild for his sake.[8]

The last clause is slightly toned down in Whitelock's translation, for the text reads:

> Forðan ðe we for his lufon þis gegyld gegaderodon.[9]

This should rather be translated: 'therefore for his love we have assembled this guild'. The love of God and St Peter is the impetus, and this guild, despite its strong material concerns, is a very spiritually motivated fraternity.

As I have already noted, the Abbotsbury Guild depended on the patronage of the layman Urki, aided also, it seems, by his wife Tole; both were guiding lights in this part of Dorset, and Tole even gave her name to the nearby village of Tolpuddle. Although this is a later source, since this married couple were active in the 1040s, the regulations of earlier guilds certainly anticipate these statutes in their basic content, and even if they lack the vividness they occasionally add further details. The mid-tenth-century statutes of Bedwyn in Wiltshire, for instance, are fragmentary, but we have the opening regulations.[10] And these come straight to the point, that is, that any deceased guild-member will have five masses and five psalters said for them, and the other guild-members, organized into pairs, will provide the means to finance this, including two pence or a young sheep from each pair to go to the mass-priest employed for the occasion. Other details not found at Abbotsbury include insurance that the guild-brothers will provide in case of a house-fire (most houses were of course made of wood in this period).

The Exeter guild material also includes a set of guild statutes, similar in content but briefer than those of Abbotsbury, written on the blank page of a gospel book from Exeter; the additions are dated to the first half of the tenth century.[11] These have been thoroughly studied by Patrick Conner, who highlights the requirement that 'the members of the guild contracted with the monastic community for liturgies (forms of worship) during three regular meetings per year' (at Michaelmas, on the Feast of St Mary at Christmas and on the Feast of All Saints after Easter).[12] On this basis, according to Conner, the guild-members provided for the welfare of each other's soul, in this life and the next, and such practices pre-empted any criticism that guild-brothers were hoarding their wealth.[13] Taking this contractual obligation that they had with the monastic community as the context, Conner posits fascinating literary connections with the tenth-century Exeter Book anthology of Old English poetry. For Conner, the Exeter Guild Statutes resonate explicitly with the following verses from *The Seafarer* (lines 68–80a). This is the part of the poem following the section on 'the solitary flier', whose cry urges the poet-speaker's spirit to fly out over the sea, 'for the joys of the Lord are warmer to me than this transitory life on earth':

Simle þreora sum þinga gehwylce,
ær his tid aga, to tweon weorþeð;
adl oþþe yldo oþþe ecghete
fægum fromweardum feorh oðþringeð.
Forþon þæt bið eorla gehwam æftercweþendra
lof lifgendra lastworda betst,
þæt he gewyrce, ær he on weg scyle,
fremum on foldan wið feonda niþ,
deorum dædum deofle togeanes,
þæt hine ælda bearn æfter hergen,
ond his lof siþþan lifge mid englum
awa to ealdre, ecan lifes blæd,
dream mid dugeþum.

Conner translates as follows:

> Each of three things is always uncertain before its time arrives; illness or age or violence will take life from a doomed and dying man. And so for every man, the praise of the living – those who speak after he is gone – is the best testimonial, which he may bring about before he must be away, with accomplishments on earth against the fiends' devising, with worthy deeds against the devil, so that the sons of men may afterwards praise him, and his praise – the joy of eternal life and delight among the hosts – may then live with the angels always and forever.[14]

This passage and various other extracts from *The Wanderer* and *Resignation* prompt Conner to reconstruct a reading context and audience in the guild-hall

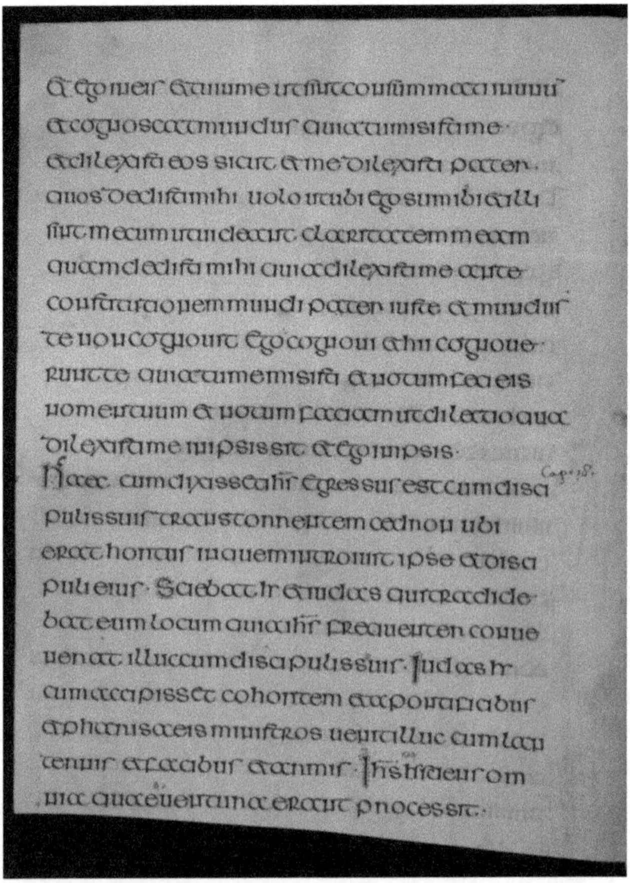

Figure 18 Page from Ely gospel book, now at Cambridge, University Library Kk. 1. 24. © Reproduced by kind permission of the Syndics of Cambridge University Library, UK.

for the elegies of the Exeter Book. On this approach these classic poems are conditioned by their concern with 'the way in which eternal life is supported by those living on earth', as Conner describes it, and he pushes for an interpretation in which the guild-brothers, as they listen to a reading of these poems, are exhorted 'to participate in purchasing the production of the monastery'.[15] Conner's reading depends partly on whether one can accept his conclusion that the Exeter Book was actually copied at Exeter in the tenth century rather than, as Gameson tentatively argues, a large and established monastery such as Glastonbury.[16] Some readers may also feel that Conner pushes the 'commodification' theory of saving the soul too far, so that other features of the elegies – such as the powerful imagery of the seascape and the journey – may be neglected. But I think that Conner's insight into the relevance of guild statutes and the new tenth-century thegnly class as a readership for poetry is a very illuminating one, which can certainly be taken further and applied to other contexts. For my purpose in this chapter, therefore, I propose to explore another set of guild statutes, little studied, and not mentioned by Conner because they are outside his area of interest, given that his focus is on Exeter.

The manuscript in question is another gospel book in Latin, written in an elegant script of the eighth century; it is the later additions which make it relevant to *Maldon*. Its origin and provenance are at Ely: in other words, the book was copied at Ely and kept in the monastic library over the centuries. In the late tenth century, on a blank page that was once part of the gospel manuscript, a scribe in the late tenth century added two texts in Old English; evidently he wished to preserve the documents for posterity, and it was common practice to use a precious gospel book as a repository for important documents.[17] Of the two texts, the first is a grant of land by a man called Ælfhelm to his goldsmith; one of the witnesses to the transaction is 'Byrhtnoþ abbod' and this is most likely Byrhtnoth, the Abbot of Ely from 970 to 999, who features frequently in the pages of *The Book of Ely* and who of course shares the same name with the ealdorman who fought at Maldon in 991. According to the researches of Margaret Locherbie-Cameron into Ealdorman Byrhtnoth and his family, there are grounds for thinking that the abbot was Ealdorman Byrhtnoth's cousin.[18] The other text added on the same blank page of the gospel book is the Statutes of the Thegns' Guild in Cambridge. There is potential here for connections with Ealdorman Byrhtnoth: the dates and the locations are both relevant. Even if the identification of the two men as cousins is speculative, the ealdorman certainly knew the abbot, as *The Book of Ely* makes clear, and the Cambridge connection is relevant, for *The Book of Ely* also shows that many of Ealdorman Byrhtnoth's landholdings were in the Cambridge area.[19]

The Statutes of the Thegns' Guild in Cambridge contains many of the same sorts of regulation as those of Abbotsbury, Bedwyn and Exeter: there is a rule about bringing a deceased guild-member to his desired place of rest and paying for half of the funeral-feast, there are statutes on almsgiving and regulations on keeping the peace indoors, presumably in the guild-hall or meeting-house. What this text lacks is the sense of genuine piety that is expressed in the text from Abbotsbury; there is a more secular tone to most of the provisions. But very striking, above all, is an emphasis on compensation for acts of violence, which if necessary would be pursued as a feud if the culprit scorned to pay the requisite amount.[20] Before we consider further the relevance of these Cambridge guild-brothers and their meetings, however, let us turn back to the poem and its references to the *gemot*, the moot, the council or assembly of thegns.

The moot or gathering

It will be clear by now that the crucial moment in *The Battle of Maldon* comes when Byrhtnoth falls in the fight and the traitor Godric takes the ealdorman's horse and leaves the field with his brothers. At this turning point, the poet-narrator pauses his narration, and for the space of a few lines he reminds us of what had happened earlier (i.e. before the extant text of the poem begins). There had been a council. Probably a call had gone out through the region to summon the men of the *fyrd*. At this mustering of the men, the high-ranking thegn Offa had admonished them to keep to their word and put their vows and promises into action. Offa, it seems from the poet's account, is Byrhtnoth's astute and cautious right-hand man, and his prominence is underlined by the poet's regular and frequent mention of him. All told, the name appears five times in the text.[21] Here, then, is the poet's report of Offa's speech at that crucial moment when the traitors flee (*Maldon*, 198–201):

> Swa him Offa on dæg   ær asæde
> on þam meþelstede   þa he gemot hæfde
> þæt þær modiglice   manega spræcon
> þe eft æt þearfe   þolian noldon.

> [So Offa had declared that day
> at the Place of Parley, when they had had their council,
> that many there spoke boldly
> who afterwards in time of need would be unwilling to endure.]

Clearly the levies had been summoned to war from their usual peacetime occupations, for the month was August, and most of the men were likely to be at work on their farms bringing in the harvest. No doubt they were instructed to assemble, perhaps given a day or two to prepare and then make the journey.

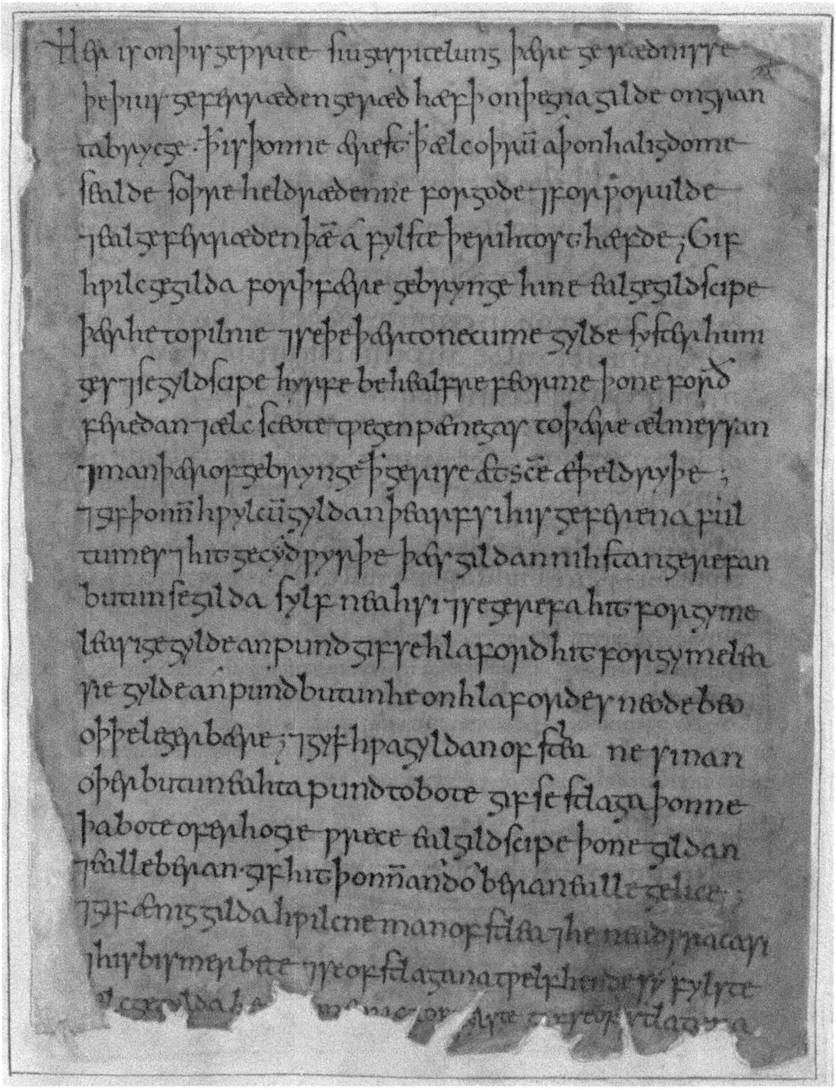

Figure 19 The Cambridge Guild Statutes added to the Ely gospel book, now bound with other writings in London, British Library, Cotton Tiberius B. V, f. 74. © The British Library.

As presumably told in the now missing lines of the poem, the men gathered at the *methelstede*, where they began to make their promises and vows. They then set off riding to the battlefield, and this is the situation as the narrative in the extant text begins. The poet-narrator refers specifically here to the *gemot*, the 'moot' or assembly of the troops, like a council of war, located at the *meþelstede* ('methelstede'), literally, 'the place of speech' – the noun deriving from the verb for 'to speak formally', *maðelian* (cf. 42 and 309). The noun *moot* is defined by the *Oxford English Dictionary* as 'a meeting, an assembly of people, *esp.* one for judicial or legislative purposes. Also: a place where a meeting is held.' According to its etymology, a *moot* (Old English *gemot*) is connected with the verb *maðelian* 'to speak, declaim, say'.[22] The obvious translation then is 'a council', where people speak and advise. One might compare the term that came later in English history, the *parliament*, and its relation to the word *parley* (both derived from French *parler* 'to speak').

The location of the *methelstede* is not made clear, either in the poem or in any other accounts of the battle. Space within the town may have been limited for such an army, and another possibility is that a local landmark in the countryside was chosen as the gathering place instead. As documents of the period show, the regular assemblies of the hundred moot, town moot and shire moot were often located at ancient mounds, standing stones or other prominent landmarks. People arrived with their tents, pitched camp and attended the meeting. In addition to the moots, such sites were used for the mustering of armies. Examples include 'Cwichelm's Barrow' in Berkshire, where the shire assembly used to meet, and where in 1006 the Viking *here*, as it was known in the texts, which may be translated 'the Army' or 'the Host', purposefully gathered, rather brazenly aiming to challenge the English to a pitched battle, but no English army came to meet them.[23]

To sum up, according to the speech by Offa reported at lines 198–201, the battle at Maldon began with a council of war. If that reconstruction of the poem is accurate, then this was Byrhtnoth's last experience of a council before he fell in the battle. But for the poet, the 'moot' was not yet over, and drawing on a tradition of litotes (ironical understatement) that Old English poets had developed, in which for example a *grimme guðgemot*, literally 'grim battle assembly', was a synonym for a 'terrible battle', he returns to the word 'gemot' as a kind of figure for the battle itself, in which Byrhtnoth's men have their own 'stern council' to endure (301–2):[24]

Þær wæs stið gemot;   stodon fæste
wigan on gewinne,   wigend cruncon,
wundum werige.   Wæl feol on eorþan.

[That was a stern council there. They stood firm,
soldiers in battle. Warriors fell,
weary with wounds. The dead fell to the earth.]

Rather grimly, the poet goes on to tell us that the men at this moot stood firm, grew weary, then fell. The battle is coming to an end for these remaining English warriors, and weariness has set in – the passage paves the way for the famous statement eleven lines later by the old retainer Byrhtwold, who declares that their courage should be greater as their strength diminishes. The implications of that particular speech will be considered shortly.

Going forth

Before that, however, we need to attend to the ealdorman's penultimate speech, the injunction to his men to advance, move forward, go forth, an encouraging last word that he leaves with them before he prays and passes on. It will be seen to have considerable influence on the behaviour of the last few who remain on the field. As we know, the immediate response to the ealdorman's death is the desertion of Godric and the brothers and the breakdown of the shield-wall, along with the flight of many of the others of the *fyrd*. But those who stay, the hearth-companions, respond to the desertion by heeding Byrhtnoth's last command *gangan forð* 'to go forward'. Though many critics casually speak of the end of the poem as the 'last stand', this is far from being the appropriate phrase to describe the shift in the plot. This is certainly not a variant on 'Custer's Last Stand': the scene is filled with forward movement, with the adverb *forð* 'forth' being the leitmotif that invigorates the action, associated with many of the characters whose words and deeds we now follow through to the end: Ælfwine (209, 229), Leofsunu (247), Dunnere (260), Æscferth (269), Wistan (297).

At first the main motivation for moving forward (line 205) is *leofne gewrecan* 'to avenge the man who was dear to them' (line 208). We are told, accordingly, that Ælfwine after his speech *fæhðe gemunde* 'remembered the feud' (225). The intention is repeated in Leofsunu's speech when he vows to go not only 'forth' but 'further' as well, his purpose being 'wrecan on gewinne minne wine-drihten' (to avenge in the fight my friend-and-lord (*wine-drihten*)) (263). And the peasant (*ceorl*) Dunnere too is wholly after vengeance, without a care for his life (lines 258–9). The idea of vengeance is part of the practice and culture of the feud, an ever-present feature of tenth-century English society, for where compensation was not to be had, then the only alternative was to perpetuate the feud, as here. Though the Laws of King Edmund (who reigned from 939 to 946) had attempted to limit the feud and prevent its escalation, it had not been abolished. An indication of how deep-seated the feud lay is that it is not felt to be anti-Christian: at lines 262–3 of *Maldon*, for instance, the men even pray that God will help them to avenge their friend and lord (*wine-drihten*). The relevant text here is again the Statutes of the Thegns' Guild in Cambridge:

> And if anyone kill a guild-brother, nothing other than eight pounds is to be accepted as compensation. And if the slayer scorn to pay the compensation, all the guildship is to avenge the guild-brother and all bear the feud.[25]

Given Byrhtnoth's connections with Ely and Cambridge, one could imagine that the lesser thegns who feature at the end of *Maldon* are exactly the right class of people to have been members of such a guild, with its emphasis on mutual support:

> Here in this writing is the declaration of the enactment which this fellowship has determined in the thegns' guild in Cambridge. Firstly, that each was to give to the others an oath of true loyalty, in regard to religious and secular affairs, on the relics, and all the fellowship was ever to aid him who had most right.

Of course there is no proof; it could be that none of the lesser thegns of *Maldon* lived in or near Cambridge. (As we have seen in Chapter 3, the only named location in the text is Sturmer, where Leofsunu has his origins, which is located on the Suffolk-Essex border, perhaps halfway between Cambridge and Maldon.) The point of such comparisons is not to establish absolute facts, but to experience vicariously something of the scope and quality of life which these thegns, or men like them, enjoyed.

By way of conclusion to this chapter on Byrhtnoth's men, it should be stressed that there is one further theme that recurs throughout the final scenes of the poem, namely friendship. We have already noted the adjective *leof*, (dear, beloved), associated with the hawk in the opening sequence (line 7). But otherwise *leof* is an index of love and affection for Byrhtnoth in the narrator's comment at line 208 and then, right at the end, in the famous last call to arms of Byrhtwold (line 319). But the affection that Byrhtnoth has for his men, and they for him and each other, is expressed in a number of ways in the set-piece speeches and the narrator's comments. Byrhtnoth himself in his last word of encouragement to his men calls them *gode geferan*, 'good companions', the *ge-* prefix on *gefera* expressing togetherness, the notion that companions are literally ones who engage in travel (*feran*), ones who journey together the same route. In his monologue, Ælfwine, the top-ranking thegn and first of the men to respond in words to the fall of Byrhtnoth and the dispersal of the *fyrd*, is described as encouraging and urging on '*winas frynd and geferan*' (his fellows, friends and companions) (228–9). Similarly, Leofsunu of Sturmer speaks of Byrhtnoth as *min wine*, 'my friend' (250b), the word being a poetic synonym for the more usual everyday word *freond*. Finally, there is Byrhtwold, whose famous lines on fortitude were discussed in the introduction and will be reconsidered shortly in Chapter 8. Unlike that stirring call to continue the fight (312–13), however, the later lines of his speech are less often cited, but they are less rhetorical, less patterned, an almost colloquial expression of friendship felt by one seasoned veteran for another (317–19):

Ic eom frod feores;   fram ic ne wille,
ac ic me be healfe   minum hlaforde,
be swa leofan men,   licgan þence.

[I have some experience in life. And I will not go from here.
Instead I mean to lie next to my lord,
a man we held in such great affection.]

Chapter 8
The Battle of the Holme

Byrhtwold maþelode,   bord hafenode
(se wæs eald geneat),   æsc acwehte;
he ful baldlice   beornas lærde:
'Hige sceal þe heardra,   heorte þe cenre,
mod sceal þe mare,   þe ure mægen lytlað.
Her lið ure ealdor   eall forheawen,
god on greote.   A mæg gnornian
se ðe nu fram þis wigplegan   wendan þenceð.
Ic eom frod feores;   fram ic ne wille,
ac ic me be healfe   minum hlaforde,
be swa leofan men,   licgan þence.'

BATTLE OF MALDON (309–19)

[Byrhtwold made a speech, raised his shield,
(he was an old retainer), brandished his ash-wood;
very bravely he exhorted the men:
'Thought must be harder, heart the keener,
courage the greater, as our strength diminishes.
Here lies our prince, cut down by swords,
a good man on the ground. A man will regret it forever
if he means to turn from the battle-play now.
I have some experience in life. And I will not go from here,
instead I mean to lie next to my lord,
a man who we held in such great affection.']

The famous passage from *The Battle of Maldon*, with its insistence on courage and endurance despite increasing weakness, seems to express some long-held ethical stance. There is the heroic resolve not to flee, and with it an insistence on being guided by the bonds of affection and loyalty to the man who had been their leader. Mentions of treachery, going home, holding the land and taking revenge – all these now fade away, and there is no more talk of them as motivating factors. Instead the poem offers this stoic attitude of perseverance, perhaps best labelled fortitude, which prevails from line 295 onwards, right up to end of the poem as we now have it at line 325. It is the time of 'the breaking of shields' (295a), 'a stern council' (301a), a time 'to endure' (307a).

This was not a new attitude in the 990s.[1] Similar behaviour is observable in the narrative 'Cynewulf and Cyneheard', a story of a feud in an extended version of the annal for 755 that was added to the Anglo-Saxon Chronicle in the ninth century. This particular feud involves a parallel plot in which men choose to remain loyal to their secular lord and die in battle rather than surrender to their kinsmen in the opposing forces.[2] That story was apparently well known in the tenth century, available in copies of the Chronicle, and retold in the 980s in Latin by Æthelweard the Chronicler in his own, Latin version of the Chronicle.[3] As ealdorman of the western provinces, Æthelweard knew Byrhtnoth, and duly assisted in the peace settlement with the Vikings in the aftermath of Maldon; thereafter, he was to become the leading ealdorman in England of the 990s. As a writer himself (and patron of the monastic writer and homilist Ælfric of Cerne Abbas) Æthelweard was 'the kind of man to relish literary celebration of aristocratic values in the era of The Battle of Maldon'.[4]

But apart from 'Cynewulf and Cyneheard', there exists another, equally valid account of die-hard heroism, which is relatively little studied. This is 'The Battle of the Holme' from the early years of the tenth century, also extant in the Chronicle – to be explored here in this chapter. I will argue that the ideology of heroism that so influenced the behaviour of the Kentishmen, as told in the account of 'The Battle of the Holme', was still being celebrated ninety years later in the behaviour of Byrhtnoth's 'hearth-companions' in Maldon.

The rebellion of the Ætheling Æthelwold

It is an uncomfortable feature of tenth-century English history that the death of a king and the accession of a new king almost inevitably led to trouble: at the very least a dispute over the succession, at the very worst an invasion or war. As the century progressed, the pattern can be seen at several moments of transition from one king to the next. One of the severest of these transitions followed the reign of King Alfred the Great (871–99). Alfred, later known as Alfred the Great, is arguably the most famous of the early English kings, for compelling reasons. As ruler of the kingdom of the Angles and Saxons, an enlarged kingdom of Wessex centred on Winchester, he was remarkably successful in defending his realm against the Danish Vikings, or to put it in words that may well be his own formulation, he was successful both internally and externally: reforming education and literature at home and extending his kingdom outside Wessex. The chronicler of his reign even claimed that Alfred had ruled *all of England*, 'except', he added (almost grudgingly), 'for the part ruled by the Danes'.[5] That exception was the region known as the Danelaw, situated in the north, eastern Mercia, and East Anglia (and bordering in fact on Essex); this was the area of mixed Anglo-Danish population that came about after the Peace of Wedmore in 878. Alfred had halted the Danish Viking incursions into his realm by reaching an agreement whereby the Danes were permitted to settle and found their own kingdom in East Anglia (to match the already existing Viking kingdom of York).

In 899 Alfred died, leaving the throne in the capable hands of his son Edward, called 'the Elder' to distinguish him from the later Edward 'the Martyr'. In Chapter 1, we saw Edward building fortified boroughs in East Anglia, including a strong and ultimately well-defended *burh* at Maldon in 917. But when he first came to the throne, Edward faced a crisis as the new ruler, for he was in a disputed succession with his cousin Æthelwold, the son of Alfred's older brother Æthelred, who had ruled immediately before Alfred from 865 to 871. Æthelwold was not easily appeased. The Anglo-Saxon Chronicle reports a stand-off scene with Edward at Wimborne in Dorset, a family property and also the resting place of Æthelwold's late father. I have discussed this scene at Wimborne elsewhere, and that discussion paid only slight attention to the chronicler's use of poetic language.[6] But it is clear that the chronicler at this point is aiming for deliberate stylistic effects: if not waxing lyrical, he is striving for a heroic tone. In the opening scene, for example, these are the words that Æthelwold speaks as he defies Edward's army from behind the walls and stockade of the fortress at Wimborne (the full text of the story is printed in Appendix 2):

> sæde þæt he wolde oðer oððe þær libban oððe þær licgan.
>
> [he said that he would do one of two things: live there or lie there.]

The situation, a parley before battle, is common in various heroic narratives that have survived from the period.[7] In addition, however, the heroic alliterative style of the phrase 'live there or lie there' recalls a scene in *The Battle of Maldon* (312–19), the famous speech of heroic defiance and determination delivered by the veteran Byrhtwold. The actual parallel occurs quite late in Byrhtwold's speech (*Battle of Maldon*, 317–19):

> Ic eom frod feores;   fram ic ne wille,
> ac ic me be healfe   minum hlaforde,
> be swa leofan men,   licgan þence.

[I am experienced in life: I will not depart from here.
Instead I mean to lie next to my lord,
a man we held in such great affection.]

It is the verb *licgan* 'to lie' that the two texts share in common. This is a heroic use of the word: the 325-line poem *Maldon* uses the verb some thirteen times, always with the connotation 'to lie slain'.[8]

Yet another resonance between 'The Battle of the Holme' and *Maldon* is the heroic determination, the choice-that-is-not-a-choice which the hero makes, expressed in terms of doing 'one of two things':

He said that he would do one of two things: live there or lie there.

In *Maldon*, it is the narrator himself who employs this figure of speech, describing how the men react to the fall of their leader (lines 205–8):

Þa ðær wendon forð   wlance þegenas,
unearge men   efston georne,
hi woldon þa ealle   oðer twega
lif forlætan   oððe leofne gewrecan.

[Then and there the proud thegns went forward, undaunted men hastened eagerly, for they all wanted one of two things: to give up their lives or avenge the lord they had loved.]

We are surely dealing here with another example of what Tolkien termed the 'ancient and honoured expression of heroic will'.[9] A very similar turn of phrase occurs in *Waldere*, a two-page fragment of a poem that has only survived by sheer good luck and chance. It is a short extract from a likely much longer poetic retelling of the old legend of Walter of Aquitaine, which covers some of the same heroic material from ancient times that is found in *Beowulf*; the speaker, it is worth saying, is a woman, for this is not exclusively a masculine attitude:

Is se dæg cumen
þæt ðu scealt   aninga oðer twega,
lif forleosan   oððe langne dom
agan mid eldum,   Ælfheres sunu.

[The day is now come
when you must simply do one of two things:
let go your life or have lasting fame
among men. Son of Ælfhere!][10]

This is the world of the old heroes who valued fame and honour above life and limb. I have already suggested that the old poetry was still current in the tenth century, still being read or heard and performed. It is one of the sources, we must assume, of ethical attitudes that lie behind the actions and motivations of the men and women of the period.

In the Chronicle, to return to the account of Æthelwold's rebellion, there is a touch of irony in the scene where Æthelwold makes his vaunt, since he did not fulfil it. Under the cover of night, so the Chronicle reports, he fled to the north, where he was able to gain recognition as king. He now successfully recruited a large army consisting of Danish Vikings supported by Mercians and other northern English loyal to Æthelwold. In the manuscript of the Chronicle most sympathetic to the Mercian cause, Version B, the annal is reported as follows (it will be seen that the numbering of the year in the annals appears to have gone awry in the course of copying the manuscript):

> B 904 Her com Aþelwold hider ofer sæ mid eallum þæm flotan þe he begitan mihte 7 him to gebogen wæs on Eastsexum.

> [904 Here Æthelwold arrived by sea with all the ships he was able to obtain and they submitted to him in Essex.]

It has been suggested that Æthelwold had a particular purpose here, to persuade the people of Essex to join him in his rebellion.[11] But in addition, there is for readers of *The Battle of Maldon* a kind of dramatic irony in this arrival *on Eastsexum* 'among the East Saxons', that is, in Essex; perhaps Æthelwold and his Anglo-Danish allies in their *flotan* landed in the very same navigable Blackwater estuary as Swegn and/or Olaf and his *flotan* in 991, a harbinger of what was to happen ninety years later. At this stage Æthelwold was unopposed (the fortress or *burh* at Maldon was not yet built), and he proceeded inland with his army; in Chronicle B a long annal now follows, which summarizes the subsequent events leading up to 'The Battle of the Holme':

> B 905 Her gelædde Æþelwold þone here on Eastenglum to unfriþe þæt hie hergodan ofer eall Myrcna land þæt hie coman to Cracgelade 7 foran þær ofer Temese 7 naman ægþer ge on Bradene ge þær onbutan eal þæt hie gehentan mihtan ond wendon þa eft hamweard; ða for Eadweard cing æfter swa he raðost mihte his fyrde gegaderian 7 oferhergode eall heora land betuh dicon 7 Wusan eall oþ fennas norð.

> [B 905 Here Æthelwold led the Host to war in Essex, so that they plundered all the way through Mercia until they came to Cricklade, and there they crossed the Thames and seized all that they could in Braydon and the surrounding area, and then turned for home. Edward then pursued them, as quickly as he could gather his defence force, and he plundered all their land between the dykes and all the Ouse as far as the northern Fens.]

Figure 20 Marshland in East Anglia. © Mark Atherton.

The word the chronicler chooses for 'war' is the noun *frith* 'peace', its meaning reversed by the negative prefix *un-*; peace and protection are conspicuous by their absence. And there follows in the narrative a war of attrition: the Anglo-Danish *here* ('invasion host') first plunders Mercia, and Edward retaliates by plundering and laying waste the Danelaw. As in many of the reports on the Viking wars, the English first have to gather a *fyrd*, a defence-force consisting of local levies, before they can proceed. This *fyrd*, as we have seen, is the standing army; it was in fact instituted by Edward's father King Alfred for just such an eventuality, a *here* or invasion. The pattern, it seems, will be repeated on many occasions in the tenth century, including the Maldon campaign of 991 (for more discussion of the *fyrd*, see Chapter 4).

The same annal of Chronicle B continues the story, for it now comes to a battle, in fact to an unplanned battle, at a *holm* (an Old Norse word for 'island') situated somewhere in the waterlogged Danelaw Fens.[12] It seems that the Danes are pushed back along the Icknield Way and forced to retreat into the Fens until they are trapped on this island, where they turn and stand. But cautious and wary, Edward withdraws his army. The honour of the Kentish vanguard is at stake, however, and they refuse to comply. Repeatedly ordered to withdraw, they repeatedly refuse to retreat; as Chronicle B for the year 905 (actually 902) continues:

Ða he eft þonon faran wolde, þa het he beodan ofer ealle ða fyrd þæt hie foran ealle ut ætsamne; ða ætsætan ða Centiscan þær beæftan ofer his bebod; 7 .vii. ærendracan he him hæfde to onsend; þa befor se here hie þær, 7 hie þær gefuhtan;

[When he (Edward) wanted to move out from there, he sent out orders throughout all the defence force that they should all retire together. But the Kentishmen remained in their rearguard position in defiance of his order, though he had sent seven messengers to them. Then the Host came upon them there, and there they fought.]

This is the kind of glorious, even foolhardy, steadfastness that the poet of *The Battle of Maldon* will celebrate in the second half of his poem ninety years later. It is a warrior's stoicism, sometimes called the 'heroic way of life', very evident here in the behaviour of the Kentish contingent.

The annal is not yet complete, for it moves to a conclusion and presents a list of six of the chief Kentishmen who fell in the battle, and there is a touch of the personal in the chronicler's assuming a first-person heroic style. Quite explicitly he declares 'though I have named only the most distinguished', the superlative here hitting the right heroic note, not unlike the eulogy for the hero in the last two lines of *Beowulf*. And so the chronicler proceeds to name their names and their ranks in society, one by one, each name preceded by a pause in the roll call marked by the abbreviation '7' for the conjunction 'and' in the syntax. It will be noted that even an abbot is numbered in the list of the fallen:

7 þær wearð Sigulf ealdormann ofslegen, 7 Sigelm ealdormann, 7 Eadwold cinges þegn, 7 Cenulf abbud, 7 Sigebriht Sigulfes sunu, 7 Eadwold Accan sunu, 7 manige eac to him, þeah ic þa geþungenestan nemde;

[And there Ealdorman Sigulf was slain, and Ealdorman Sigelm and Eadwold the king's thegn, and Abbot Cenulf (Cenwulf) and Sigebriht Sigewulf's son, and Eadwold Acca's son, and many others with them, though I have named only the most distinguished.]

There are three men here with alliterating names. Like the list of Mercians in *Maldon*, they are all members of the same family or kindred group: Sigulf, a short form of the name Sigewulf, and his son Sigebriht, and Sigelm (Sigehelm). These are the leading men of Kent. 'And on the Danish side', so the author continues, there are also six names to name, with their rank and status, even in some cases their specifically Danish rank (the chronicler knows his enemy well):

7 on ðara Deniscra healfe wæs ofslegen Eohric cing, 7 Aþelwold æþeling, þe hie him to cinge gecuron, 7 Byrhsige Byrhtnoðes sunu æþelinges, 7 Ysopo

hold, 7 Oscytel hold, 7 swiþe manig eac mid him þe we nu genemnan ne magon; 7 þær wæs on gehweþere hand mycel wæl geslegen, 7 þara Deniscra wearð ma ofslegen, þeah hi wælstowe geweald ahton.

[And on the Danish side King Eohric, the ætheling Æthelwold that they had elected as their king, and Byrhtsige, the son of the ætheling Byrhtnoth, and Ysopo the *holdr*, and Oscytel the *holdr*, and many others with them, though we cannot name them all now. And there was slain there a great number on each side, and more of the Danish army were slain, although they held possession of the battlefield.]

It is in this list that we find honourable mention of the two English æthelings who fought on the *other* side, the first is a West Saxon, the other a Mercian, namely Æthelwold son of Æthelred I, and Byrhtsige, son of Byrhtnoth. These names and their family connections will recur three generations later in the poem on the battle at Maldon, when Byrhtnoth son of Byrhthelm fights his last battle for Æthelred II, the third son of Edgar the Peaceable.

Indeed, the roll call of the names of the fallen in 'The Battle of the Holme' has resonances with the second half of *The Battle of Maldon* (lines 209–325), in its enumeration of the heroes after the death of Byrhtnoth. This is a common practice in heroic literature, which tends to follow common patterns even when there is no case of influence or borrowing. Unsurprisingly, it is also Homeric, and the modern British poet Alice Oswald has recently given voice to this commemorative naming of men in her poem *Memorial*. This is a kind of tribute to the men who fell in the Trojan War: Protesilaus, Echepolus, Elephenor, Simoisius and so on. So the list goes on, as recorded originally in Homer's *Iliad*, but transformed here into a modern English idiom, with extended similes to honour each of the slain in turn, beginning with Protesilaus:[13]

Like a land-ripple
When the west wind runs through a field
Wishing and searching
Nothing to be found
The corn-stalks shake their green heads.

As the author makes clear in her introductory remarks (pp. 1–2), the naming of names may be seen as a recollection of laments, perhaps women's laments, woven into the main narrative of the epic. Alice Oswald sees Homer's poem as vocative and invocative, 'as if speaking directly to the dead' (*Memorial*, p. 2). Interestingly, and coincidentally (although there is no question of tenth-century English writers reading Homeric Greek), the critic Ute Schwab has proposed a similar 'memorial' practice for the final scenes and speeches of *The Battle of*

Maldon, where the men appear to speak their own epitaphs as they make their final speeches.[14] If, as will be suggested in Chapter 12, the *Maldon* poet knew the commemorative tapestry made in memory of Byrhtnoth, his or her poem may have been a spoken response to the images of the men he or she saw there.

As a literary work of commemoration, the striking difference between *Maldon* and 'The Battle of the Holme' is that the latter gives equal weight in its eulogy to both sides in the struggle (as also does Homer's *Iliad*), whereas in *The Battle of*

Figure 21 Tenth-century tower at St Mary's Church, Burnham Deepdale, Norfolk. © Mark Atherton.

Maldon the eulogy is reserved only for the English. Naming the Danes in *Maldon* would have conferred rank and status upon them, but unlike the chroniclers, who are compelled by the constraints of their genre to record objectively for posterity, this is not the *Maldon* poet's concern, for one of his themes is, as we have seen, the allowing of 'too much land' to people who were not entitled to it (see Chapter 4). This, I would argue, explains the one-sidedness of the *Maldon* poet's poetry of praise.

There is, however, one other reason for our comparing the two accounts of battles at the Holme and at Maldon, other than the verbal and thematic parallels. It has been suggested that 'Byrhtsige, the son of the ætheling Byrhtnoth' is Byrhtnoth of Essex's great-grandfather.[15] This is by no means a proven fact, but what is sure is that Byrhtsige, son of a Byrhtnoth from an earlier generation, had, as a Mercian, become fatefully involved in the dynastic in-fighting of the West Saxon kindred, which was now the dominant force in the politics of southern Britain. In the past, before the time of Alfred, and occasionally afterwards, Mercians and West Saxons had been rivals and enemies, although cooperation and inter-marriage between the two royal houses had helped to heal the rift. All this has ramifications for our understanding of the figure of Byrhtnoth in *Maldon*, who must be seen as a unifier: a focal point around which there could gather the various groups and groupings that made up the English side in the fight against the Danes. In *The Battle of Maldon*, Byrhtnoth as a lord and leader is able to inspire selfless loyalty and unite East Saxons, Mercians and Northumbrians in the defence of the West Saxon monarch's English kingdom.

Chapter 9

Beowulf and *Maldon*

> He æfter recede wlat;
> hwearf þa be wealle,   wæpen hafenade
> heard be hiltum   Higelaces ðegn,
> yrre ond anræd.

BEOWULF (1572B–1575A)

> [He looked about the hall,
> walked along the wall, raised his weapon
> held hard by the hilt – Hygelac's thegn,
> angry and resolute.]

> Byrhtnoð maþelode,   bord hafenode,
> wand wacne æsc,   wordum mælde,
> yrre and anræd   ageaf him andsware

BATTLE OF MALDON (42–4)

> [Byrhtnoth made a speech, raised his shield,
> brandished his slender ash, declared in words,
> angry and resolute, he gave him an answer]

In the above two passages from the epic *Beowulf* and *The Battle of Maldon* there are a number of strikingly similar phrases and expressions. Each hero is *yrre and anræd* 'angry and resolute' and each *hafenode/hafenade* 'raised' his weapon. As electronic searches of the whole corpus of Old English texts demonstrate, the collocation *yrre and anræd* only appears here, in these two passages from *Beowulf and Maldon*. And again, while there are 174 instances of a past participle *ahafen* 'raised' (often combined with the verb *to be* or similar passive structure, as 'is raised', 'was raised' etc.), the past tense verb *hafenode/*

hafenade appears uniquely in these two passages from *Beowulf* and *Maldon*. Is this a case of *Beowulf* serving as a model for the poet of *Maldon*?

For a long time critics have been aware that Old English poetry employs a whole range of variable poetic compounds, lexical phrases and formulaic expressions. In his edition of *The Battle of Maldon*, E. V. Gordon pointed out that *Maldon* shares many such phrases with *Beowulf*: there is the epic formula *gehyrde ic* in *Maldon* (117a) and the similar *hyrde ic* 'I heard' in *Beowulf* (62a);[1] in both poems a sword or knife is *brad and brunecg* (*Maldon* 163a; *Beowulf* 1546a); Byrhtnoth is *Æþelredes þegen* (151b) just as Beowulf is *Higelaces ðegn* (1574b). As Gordon recognized some time before oral-formulaic theory became fashionable in the 1950s and 1960s, these are 'minor epic formulæ'.[2] Such a formula is usable in any poem, normally in the same position in the poetic line, as in the earlier examples, and its use does not imply that one poet is borrowing from the other. Rather, both poets are working in the same tradition and using a similar method of composition.[3] In *Maldon*, for example, the peasant farmer Dunnere declares that he who intends to avenge their lord should not flinch, 'nor must he worry about his life' (*ne for feore murnan*; line 259b), which seems to echo the clause 'nalles for ealdre mearn' (he did not worry for his life) in the scene where Beowulf prepares himself for battle in the mere (*Beowulf*, 1441–2):

> Gyrede hine Beowulf
> eorlgewædum,   nalles for ealdre mearn.

[Beowulf put on / a nobleman's armour, he did not worry about his life.]

As 'oral-formulaic' theory would explain it, the similarity here may well lie in the situation of preparation for battle, which generates similar motifs and language in two separate poems.

On the other hand, recent theory also emphasizes the learned intellectual quality of Old English poetry, and thus it cannot be ruled out that one poet has read the work of the earlier poet and is consciously borrowing from his or her work.[4] If, as has been argued recently, the poet of the epic saint's life *Andreas* borrowed from *Beowulf*, then the same question may also be asked of the *Maldon* poet. One way of doing this is cumulative – to count the sheer number of parallels. Accordingly, in the descriptions of fighting we see the same idea of 'reaching' the life of the enemy 'with the point' (OE *ord-e*) of the weapon (*Beowulf* 555, *Maldon* 226) or that the weapon 'went through' (OE *þurhwod*) the 'fated' (OE *fæge*) body (*Beowulf* 1567–8, *Maldon* 296–7); and we find the same images of 'breaking the shield-wall' (*Beowulf* 2980, *Maldon* 277) and, with a parallel here in the poet Cynewulf, the 'breaking of shields' (*Elene* 114, *Maldon* 295).[5] It is tempting to state that the *Maldon* poet wanted to 'sound like' *Beowulf*. The other method is to think contextually and look more broadly for thematic and structural devices accompanying the parallel phrases in the narration. In this respect, a profitable area of influence is the section on the fight with the dragon (Beowulf's last battle): the theme, it will be argued in this chapter, seems to generate a good deal of parallels with Byrhtnoth's last fight in *Maldon*. Some of the parallels adduced are conventional and easily explained by the style and mode of Old English poetry, while others are thematic and content-based, and cannot be accounted for quite so easily.

The dragon fight and the fall of Byrhtnoth

Before Beowulf goes to face the dragon in mortal combat, the poet introduces the speech with a familiar preamble (*Beowulf*, 2510):

> Beowulf maðelode,   beotwordum spræc
>
> [Beowulf made a speech, spoke words of boasting]

The compound *beot-wordum* (in words of boasting) used here to mark the onset and manner of the speech remind us of the Viking messenger in *Maldon* (25–8), who speaks *on beot* (in the form of a boast) while the verb phrases recall Byrhtnoth himself as he prepares to reply (*Maldon*, 42–3):

> Byrhtnoð maþelode . . . wordum mælde
>
> [Byrhtnoth made a speech . . . declared in words]

The parallels are there but not normally worthy of notice, for these verbs are epic formulas, conventional ways of introducing a new speech in Old English narrative poetry. But as Beowulf continues his speech, the content of what he promises, rather than the manner, becomes the focus of attention (2524–5):

> Nelle ic beorges weard / forfleon fotes trem,
>
> [I will not flee from the guardian of the barrow, / not even a footstep]

This is the refusal to flee even a footstep which features twice in *Maldon*, for both Leofsunu of Sturmer and Edward the Tall refuse to flee 'even by the space of one foot' (lines 247 and 275), and the idea is echoed once in *The Book of Ely*, where Byrhtnoth hurries to the battle 'lest the enemy army should occupy so much as one foot of land in his absence' (see Chapter 12 for further discussion). And now the parallels start to proliferate as Beowulf shouts out and incites the dragon to come out of its lair and face him in battle: he draws his sword, *gomele lafe*, an 'ancient heirloom': but though the theme is the same, the diction is more poetic than Byrhtnoth's prosaically expressed *ealde swurd*, literally 'old swords' (*Maldon*, 47b).

Unsurprisingly, perhaps, the *Beowulf* poet assures his readers that 'to each of them intent on destruction there was danger from the other', a rather more mannered way of saying, in the plainer words of the *Maldon* poet, that 'each intended evil to the other' (133). Immediately thereafter, in a sequence that has been much admired for its poetic skill, the *Beowulf* poet presents the dragon coiling itself up, ready for a speedy surge forward against the lone warrior who 'stood resolute . . . waiting in his armour'. The variation on the notion of 'he stood', 'they stood' is a feature to note here, for it seems to have influenced the *Maldon* poet, who, as we saw in Chapter 4, also rings the changes skilfully on the idea of 'stand'. Here, at lines 2565–8, is the first of three passages from *Beowulf* that employ a similar device:

Stiðmod gestod   wið steapne rond
winia bealdor,   ða se wyrm gebeah
snude tosomne;   he on searwum bad.

[Sternly resolute he stood braced against the tall shield – the lord of men – as the dragon coiled quickly together; behind his armour he waited.]

It is hard not to think that both the rhyming in the first phrase *stiðmod gestod* 'he stood sternly resolute' and also the envelope effect at the end of the sequence with *he on searwum bad* (literally: 'he in his armour waited') are echoed by the *Maldon* poet in passages where Byrhtnoth explicitly 'stood' waiting. Interestingly, some of these resonances are acoustic rather than thematic. For example, the passage when Byrhtnoth and his men wait for the Vikings to cross the bridge is remarkable for the number of inflectional endings that create the effect of partial end-rhyme. This is in addition to the full rhyme of the first and last words of the sequence, in the past tense verbs *wodon* and *stodon* (*Maldon*, 96–100):

Wodon þa wælwulfas,   for wætere ne murn*on*,
wicinga werod,   west ofer Pant*an*,
ofer scir wæter   scyldas weg*on*,
lidmen to lande   linde bær*on*.
Þær ongean gramum   gearowe *stodon*

The sound effects, here italicized, are surely deliberate. It looks like the brief rhyming phrase in *Beowulf* has inspired an all-out onslaught of rhyme in the *Maldon* poet's treatment of the similar theme, namely, 'the hero stood waiting'.

If this is not yet enough to convince the reader that this is conscious borrowing, let us now take the second example, a passage already examined in the discussion of the verb 'stand' in Chapter 4. For convenience, and focussing on the alliteration in the first and last lines of the envelope sequence, we may take the following lines from *Maldon* (122–7):

> *Swa stem*netton   *stið*hicgende
> hysas æt hilde,   hogodon georne
> hwa þær mid orde   ærost mihte
> on fægean men   feorh gewinnan,
> wigan mid wæpnum;   wæl feol on eorðan.
> *Stod*on *stæde*fæste;   *stih*te hi Byrhtnoð,

> [So they prevailed, sternly determined,
> the men in battle, they directed their thoughts eagerly
> as to who first at weapon point
> would win a life from fated warriors,
> men at arms; the dead fell to the earth.
> Steadfast they stood, Byrhtnoth encouraged them]

Again, this passage of standing and sternly waiting appears to have been inspired by the *stiðmod gestod* of *Beowulf* line 2655a, but it is taken further by the *Maldon* poet and developed in his own idiosyncratic way.

One more pattern of variation on the verb 'stand' in *Maldon* was noted in Chapter 4; this is the phrase 'stood by' or 'stood near'. This, I would argue, was influenced by the passage in Beowulf's dragon fight where the dragon recovers its breath and engulfs his enemy, the warrior Beowulf, in a cloud of fire and flame (2591–5). In a kind of understatement in the negative form, the poet now informs us of what Beowulf's retainers did *not* do, before telling us that they then fled to the woods (2596–9):

> Nealles him on heape   handgesteallan,
> æðelinga bearn,   ymbe gestodon
> hildecystum,   ac hy on holt bugon,
> ealdre burgan

> [His close companions, sons of nobles, did not stand by him in a troop valorously, but they retreated to the wood to save their lives.][6]

Once again, it will be apparent that the *Beowulf* poet's choice of word is suggesting phrases and ideas to the *Maldon* poet. In particular, the two parallel clauses with the past tense verbs, 'ac hy on holt bugon' (but they turned to the woods) and 'ealdre burgan' (they protected their lives), both find a place in the scene in *Maldon* where first Godric, and then the two brothers, flee the field (185–97). Notably, the same two alliterating verbs in the past tense, *bugon* and *burgon*, separated here to form another kind of envelope structure, are used to narrate the flight of the brothers and to supply their motivation:

> Hi bugon þa fram beaduwe   þe þær beon noldon,
> þær wearð Oddan bearn   ærest on fleame,
> Godric fram guþe,   and þone godan forlet
> þe him mænigne oft   mear gesealde.
> he gehleop þone eoh   þe ahte his hlaford,
> on þam geræedum   þe hit riht ne wæs,
> and his broðru mid him   begen ærndon,
> Godwine and Godwig,   guþe ne gymdon,
> ac wendon fram þam wige   and þone wudu sohton,
> flugon on þæt fæsten   and hyra feore burgon.

> [Then they turned from the battle – those who did not want to be there –
> Odda's son was the first in flight –
> Godric fled the battle and abandoned the good prince
> who had often given him many a horse:
> he mounted the steed that his lord had owned,
> with all its harness and trappings, though it was not a just action,
> and his brothers both ran off with him,
> Godwine and Godwig, who did not care for battle
> but turned from the war and sought the woods,
> flew to safety and protected their lives.]

Moreover, in these analogous scenes of disaster and flight from the battle in the two poems, we also have the perspective of the loyal and brave men, who see the others fleeing but refuse to join them (*Beowulf*, 2602–9; *Maldon* 203–8). In *Beowulf*, the loyal man watching is Wiglaf, who cannot restrain himself any longer (line 2609):

> Ne mihte ða forhabban;   hond rond gefeng

> [He could not restrain himself: hand grasped shield]

The immediacy, the unusual agency of 'hand grasped shield' (the 'hand' is the agent of the action of grasping rather than the man), is well conveyed here by the rhyming monosyllables and the metrical rhythm (Sievers D verse on the pattern //x\). There is no similar use of language in the equivalent scene in *Maldon*, for at this point, at lines 203–8, the poet uses very different techniques of narration, but what may be an influence is the rhyme of *hond rond gefeng*, which recalls the similar effect of rhythm and rhyme of *stiðmod gestod* (type E) that I discussed earlier. This pattern appears in *Maldon* in the phrase *ord in gewod* (157a), with its assonance, rather than rhyme, of *ord* and *wod* and the same D-type rhythm. The scene in question occurs at the end of the section in Byrhtnoth's last fight when Wulfmær the Young avenges the wounding of Byrhtnoth his lord by hurling back at the Viking the very same spear that had caused the wound.

To return to the story of Beowulf and the dragon and the flight of the retainers brings us to one of the closest of the various parallels we have been considering between *Beowulf* and *Maldon*. Wiglaf's first speech (lines 2631–60) exhorting the men to join him in the fight and rescue the beleaguered Beowulf uses similar tropes and rhetoric to the opening of Ælfwine's speech on the same theme after the death of Byrhtnoth in *Maldon* (see Chapter 6 earlier). Wiglaf begins as follows (2633–8):

> Ic ðæt mæl geman,　þær we medu þegun,
> þonne we geheton　ussum hlaforde
> in biorsele,　ðe us ðas beagas geaf,
> þæt we him ða guðgetawa　gyldan woldon
> gif him þyslicu　þearf gelumpe,
> helmas ond heard sweord.

[I remember the time when, as we drank mead there in the beer-hall, we would promise our lord, who gave us these treasures, that we would repay him for these battle-accoutrements, the helmets and the tough swords, if a need such as this should befall him.][7]

This passage should be compared with what seems to be its later reflex in *Maldon* (212–16):

> Gemunu þa mæla　þe we oft æt meodo spræcon,
> þonne we on bence　beot ahofon,
> hæleð on healle,　ymbe heard gewinn;
> nu mæg cunnian　hwa cene sy.
> Ic wylle mine æþelo　eallum gecyþan.

[I remember the times when we talked at the mead-drinking,
when as we sat on the benches we made our promises,
men in the hall, about the hard fighting ahead,
and now whoever claims to be brave may prove it.
I wish to declare my lineage to all.]

Here is the same appeal to the memory of times of gift-giving in the past, the use of mead-drinking as a metonym for the hall and the feast in the hall, on which occasion the various vows and promises of loyal service were made. Later, there is a similar refusal to go home (*Beowulf*, 2653–4) that clearly also resonated with the *Maldon* poet (for which, see the theme of hearth and home in Chapter 3).

The missing conclusion

What the details in this chapter have attempted to demonstrate is the cumulative effect of both stylistic effects and thematic parallels. These include the motif of the 'space of a foot', the warriors intent on mutual harm, the patterns of the verb 'to stand', the flight to the woods, the appeal to the vows in the mead hall and the similar uses of rhyme and rhythm and rhetorical structures. As the echoes and parallels mount up, the argument that the *Maldon* poet has been influenced by *Beowulf* becomes more compelling. The conclusion to be drawn from this, therefore, is that *The Battle of Maldon* is a poem that trades on the traditions of earlier Old English verse but also celebrates, in a Christian context, the life of the tenth-century nobility in all its aspects: the horsemanship and the falconry, the hall and the mead-bench, lordship and kinship, feud and friendship. What all this amounts to is that the poet of *Maldon* evokes or recreates a world that seems at first sight to belong to an older time and period. But this is the 'impression of depth' that Old English poets loved to create.[8] The allusions and echoes of *Beowulf* create a heroic tone that suits the purpose of the *Maldon* poet.

How might the poem *The Battle of Maldon* have concluded? As we will see in Chapter 12, *The Book of Ely* pictures Abbot Byrhtnoth, the ealdorman's namesake (and just possibly also his cousin), arriving with his men to bring Byrhtnoth's body home for stately burial at Ely. A similar set of events in a pagan setting occurs in the conclusion of *Beowulf*. Given the parallels with *Beowulf*, and the consequent heroic attitudes of the fighting men at the end of the text of *Maldon* as we have it, perhaps we have to imagine a similar chain of events in the concluding lines of *Maldon*. Accordingly, in *Beowulf* we have the aftermath on the field and the last words of farewell of the hero, who first presents his golden necklace, helmet, arm-ring and mailcoat to his thegn Wiglaf before he speaks (2813–16):

Þu eart endelaf   usses cynnes,
Wægmundinga.   Ealle wyrd forsweop
mine magas   to metodsceafte,
eorlas on elne;   ic him æfter sceal.

[You are the final remnant of our family, the Wægmundings; events have swept all my kin to their appointed end, men of valour; I shall go after them.][9]

In *Maldon* Byrhtnoth's arm-rings, mailcoat and decorated sword are mentioned at the end of his last fight, but we are not told whether the Viking and would-be robber was able to take them.

Next in *Beowulf*, after a speech of reproach to the men who fled comes Wiglaf's public announcement of the death of the hero (2892–7):

Heht ða þæt heaðoweorc   to hagan biodan
up ofer ecgclif,   þær þæt eorlweorod
morgenlongne dæg   modgiomor sæt,
bordhæbbende,   bega on wenum,
endedogores   ond eftcymes
leofes monnes.

[Then he directed that the results of the battle be announced to the
entrenchment up over the cliff's edge, where the host of men had sat
sorrowing the morning-long day, shield-bearers, in expectation both of a day
of finality and of the beloved man's return.][10]

The messenger as he rides predicts *orleghwile*, a time of war (2911a), which will
break out as soon as the Franks and the Frisians hear of Beowulf's fall; nor does
he expect *sibbe oððe treowe* (peace or good faith) from the Swedes (*Beowulf*,
2922–3). Such is the crisis caused by the fall of a great leader. A similar situation
is found in Byrhtferth of Ramsey's account of the run-up to the Maldon campaign
when the young prince Æthelred, bereft of help, with both his father Edgar and
his half-brother Edward the Martyr dead, succeeds to the throne, and the nation
of the Danes rises up against him:

Mox enim [. . .] surrexit contra eum princeps Beemoth, cum omni apparatu
suo, et satellibus suis, habens secum Cerethi (id est mortificantes): uenerunt
regnante illo nefandi Dani ad regnum Anglorum.

[Very soon, however [. . .] Prince Beelzebub rose up against him, with all his
engines of war, and his retinue, having with him the Cerethi (that is, 'the deadly
ones'): during his reign the accursed Danes came to England.][11]

According to *Beowulf*, line 2892a, the hero is *leof mon*, 'beloved man'. The
terms of affection in which the man Beowulf is held reminds us of expressions
of emotion in the speeches of Ælfwine and Byrhtwold with regard to Byrhtnoth
(see Chapter 7). And again it is Byrhtferth of Ramsey, who, while claiming that
the land is beleaguered by its enemies as a divine punishment, nevertheless
confirms the emotional attachment and widespread popularity that Byrhtnoth
enjoyed throughout the country:

When the aforesaid leader was killed, ealdormen and thegns, men and
women, everyone of either sex, were deeply moved.[12]

The story of Beowulf finishes with a funeral and a eulogy, and it is tempting to
imagine a similar end to the poem on Byrhtnoth at Maldon; perhaps the last word
in *The Battle of Maldon* is a eulogy for their friend from the 'hearth-companions'

in a traditional style, similar, but perhaps without the note of irony, to the well-known final lines of *Beowulf* (lines 3178–2):

Swa begnornodon   Geata leode
hlafordes hryre,   heorðgeneatas,
cwædon þæt he wære   wyruldcyninga
manna mildust   ond monðwærust,
leodum liðost   ond lofgeornost.

[So the people of the Geats mourned
the fall of their lord, the hearth-companions
declared that of the kings of the world he was
the gentlest of men and the most gracious,
kindest to people and most eager for praise.]

Translated, transferred, taken over into the language and culture of the tenth century, these 'hearth-companions' are a group of lesser thegns linked by ties of friendship and lordship, perhaps members of a Thegns' Guild united by their devotion to feud and friendship, pious and willing to pay the priests of Cambridge or the monks of Ely to dedicate their masses and recitals of the psalter to their late friend and lord. We can picture their meeting in a hall or guild-hall where they contemplate the actions of their fellow-thegns in Byrhtnoth's tapestry and celebrate his memory in a performance of the well-known poem.

PART II

After the battle

What really happened at Maldon in August 991? Is it possible to show 'how things actually were'? Given the paucity of sources, the temptation is to answer this question in the negative. However, in contrast to narratives of some early medieval battles, for which there is only one narrative source, there exists, in fact, a number of separate accounts of the battle at Maldon. Their details will be scrutinized in the three chapters that follow. We will attempt to work out the likely dates when these texts were written and assess their similarities and differences in content and literary style; connections with the poem will be discussed and attention will be paid to the larger context in which each writer presented the events at Maldon, for this also affects their message. As a result, a range of different perspectives emerges on 'Maldon', on how this event of national importance was viewed at the time.

Chapter 10

'And so to Maldon'

The account of the battle in the Anglo-Saxon Chronicle

we willaþ mid þam sceattum   us to scype gangan,
on flot feran,   and eow friþes healdan.

THE BATTLE OF MALDON (40–1)

[we will take ourselves off with the payments to our ships,
put to sea, and keep the peace with you.]

Chronicle A: 'And so to Maldon'

Apart from the poem itself, the earliest existing account of the battle at Maldon was probably copied in or around the year 1000, and presents the barest facts in a characteristically laconic form. This important text is manuscript A of the Anglo-Saxon Chronicle, otherwise known as the *Parker Chronicle* (after its first modern owner, Archbishop Matthew Parker, in the sixteenth century), or just simply as Chronicle A. The entry in question, assigned – perhaps by scribal error – to the year 993, reads as follows in its original wording [the symbol '7' is an abbreviation for *and*]:

Her on ðissum geare com Unlaf mid þrim 7 hund nigontigon scipum to Stane 7 forhergedon þær onytan 7 for ða ðanon to Sandwic 7 swa ðanon to Gipeswic 7 þæt eall ofereode 7 swa to Mældune; 7 him ðær com togeanes Byrhtnoð ealdorman mid his fyrde 7 him wið gefeaht, 7 hy þone ealdorman þær ofslogon, 7 wælstowe geweald ahtan.[1]

[Here in this year Olaf came with ninety-three ships to Folkestone and plundered the countryside there and moved thence to Sandwich and so thence to Ipswich and overran all that area, and so to Maldon. And Ealdorman Byrhtnoth encountered him there with his defence-force, and fought with him, and they killed the ealdorman there and had command of the battlefield.]

An extra sentence has been added somewhat later to this account, squeezed into half a line at the end and continuing in the margin: we will return to this quite significant addition in the discussion later.

What is clear from this main text of the annal for the year 993 is that the Vikings had attacked various ports and market towns along the south-east coast, including Sandwich in Kent. (Now landlocked, Sandwich in the Middle Ages was one of the Cinque Ports, and an important centre for shipping.) Perhaps these Vikings had come from the Duchy of Normandy, which gave shelter to Viking shipping (since the Normans, i.e. the 'Northmen', were originally Viking settlers). Alternatively, the Viking fleet may have hugged the continental coast south-westwards from Denmark and then crossed the Channel to strike England at Sandwich. From the text we can infer that they had then sailed up the coast past the mouths of the Medway, the Thames and the Blackwater. Probably put off by the formidable defences of the walled towns of Rochester, London and Maldon, they continued steering northwards. At the mouth of the Orwell they turned, sailed up the river estuary, and attacked and plundered Ipswich, a wealthy, tempting and easy target. Now, however, on their way back down the coast they had after all sailed up the Blackwater, as far as Maldon at the head of the estuary. Here Byrhtnoth encountered them with his *fyrd*, the local defence-force or standing army. The rest is clear: they killed the ealdorman and won the battle: these are the brute facts of the encounter as told by Chronicle A.

However, even in a factual objective chronicle style, there is scope for selectivity in the choice of word and phrase. The chronicler has an agenda. One could note the heavy emphasis on *there* and *thence* in his narrative style, which shifts the focus onto the significant itinerary of the Viking raiders, and the final sequencing effect of the formulation *and swa to Mældune*, 'and so to Maldon'. The meaning of *and so to* might be formulated as 'subsequent and eventual physical movement to a place where one is expected', with omission of the verb of movement. The phrasing is common in present-day English, as the following randomly selected examples show (taken from the online database of the British National Corpus at Brigham Young University):

And so to tea, and so to court, and so to bed, and so to Ascot, and so to Boggle Hole, and so to Shipley West Yorkshire, and so to Paradise, and so to the very gates of Revesby Abbey, and so to home.

The frequently occurring formula *and so to home* sums up this idiom. It was apparently less common in medieval English, but examples can be found. Here is a passage from Thomas Malory's *Morte Darthur* (c.1470), in which King Arthur holds a great festival and tournament on *Allhalowmasse* (All Saints' Day) but recalls all the knights from the field when the fighting becomes too fierce:

> Whan kynge Arthur and the two kynges saw hem begynne wex wroth on both partyes, they leped on smale hakeneyes and lette cry that all men sholde departe unto their lodgynge. And so they wente home and unarmed them, and so to evynsonge and souper.[2]

> [When King Arthur and the two kings saw them begin to grow angry on both sides, they leaped onto small hackneys [lesser, non-military horses] and had the order sent out that all the men should return to their lodgings. And so they went home and disarmed themselves, and so to evensong and supper.]

The same sequencing effect occurs in the phrase *and swa to* of Old English boundary clauses, describing the bounds and landmarks of the property that the new owner or tenant expects to see as he or she rides around its perimeter:

> Of holtwille to flyte and swa to þam dicum.[3]

> [From the forest well to the river, and so to the dyke.]

To return then to the *Parker Chronicle* for the year 993, we can see in this writer's style that Maldon is the expected destination, and the implied reader of this text already knows about 'Maldon' as an event. The chronicler, it should be remembered, was adding his entry to the manuscript in the early 1000s,[4] by which time 'Maldon' had acquired its distinct set of associations.

Additions to Chronicle A

In fact, Chronicle A tells an informative, if slightly garbled story of the battle at Maldon.[5] The suspicion is that this version of the events is coloured by the narrative that eventually became Chronicle C (for which, see further). But version A is the oldest of the seven surviving manuscripts of the Anglo-Saxon Chronicle (each is labelled chronologically in modern discussions with a *sigil* or letter ranging from A to G, A being the earliest and G the latest version of the Chronicle). For this reason alone, it deserves some credit. Manuscript A itself seems to be a copy of the Chronicle as it was first compiled in Alfred's reign. After the manuscript had been put together in the early 900s, new pages were later attached and material was then added in blocks, as and when consecutive owners of this book were induced to record the unfolding events of the tenth century. Certainly, the compilation of this Chronicle is subjective in what events it chooses to report: after a relatively 'full' coverage of the reigns of Alfred the Great (reigned 871–99) and of his son Edward the Elder (899–924), the reigns of the subsequent kings are rather more thinly treated, with only the really basic events of each reign being noted.

Appropriately for the politics of the day, the manuscript was kept during the tenth century at Winchester, essentially the chief city of England after the unification of the English kingdom under Edgar. Owners and users of this copy of the Chronicle are likely to have been churchmen, probably the clerics and later the monks of the Old Minster and/or the New Minster in Winchester, but lay people may also have had access to this book for consultation, and the royal court seems to have exercised some influence on its contents. In its perspective and sympathies, Chronicle A is 'West Saxon' and records the rise of the Wessex dynasty as the first rulers of a single united kingdom of England. For each reign, major events are selected for their importance (e.g. the death of a bishop, the accession of a new king) and recorded in brief, laconic prose. Occasionally, special moments are commemorated much more fully in the form of a poem inserted rather abruptly into the chronological format (e.g. Æthelstan's great victory at Brunanburh in 937 or Edgar's second 'imperial' coronation at Bath in 973, or 'The Death of Edgar' in 975).[6]

Perhaps surprisingly, the brief account of 'Maldon' in the year 991 in Chronicle A is given in prose. If the poem *The Battle of Maldon* was already available and circulating in oral performance or in writing, it was not chosen to serve as an annal in the Chronicle. The reason is not hard to see. At 325 lines (and this is lacking its beginning and end) *Maldon* is far too long: the nearest contender among the Chronicle poems is *The Battle of Brunanburh*, which is a mere 73 lines in length. And the two poems differ not only in length and but also in feeling and mood. *Brunanburh* is very definitely intended as a 'court' poem, celebrating the achievements of the West Saxon dynasty, while *Maldon* is more complex and more dramatic. Moreover, it seems unlikely that the scribes at Winchester had access to any account of 'Maldon', for if one looks at the manuscript itself we can see that they were not sure what to write for this annal. Quite simply, they lacked written information: changes in handwriting show that the original entry has been expanded by another scribe writing slightly later, who has added further text in the margins to complete the account of the battle and attach further significance to it. I will argue that this scribe was appealing to the lessons of history: he saw parallels in an earlier event recorded in the pages of the same chronicle.

The incident I have in mind in Chronicle A is the mustering at Egbert's Stone. This took place in the year 878, when Alfred, king of the West Saxons, later called Alfred the Great, gained his unexpected victory over the Danes under King

Guthrum at Eddington, two days after Alfred's men had gathered at 'Egbert's Stone', a local standing stone that seems to have been named (or renamed) after Alfred's royal grandfather.[7] The consequences of the West Saxon victory on that occasion were radical. A peace process was begun which involved Guthrum's conversion to Christianity, along with an exchange of gifts (note again that the symbol '7' means *and*, and note also that the Viking army is referred to generically as *se here* 'the Host'):

> 7 þær gefeaht wiþ alne þone here 7 hiene gefliemde, 7 him æfter rad oþ þæt geweorc 7 þær sæt .xiiii. niht; 7 þa salde se here him foregislas 7 micle aþas þæt hie of his rice uuoldon 7 him eac geheton þæt hiera kyning fulwihte onfon wolde, 7 hie þæt gelæston swa, 7 þæs ymb .iii. wiecan com se cyning to him Godrum þritiga sum þara monna þe in þam here weorþuste wæron æt Alre, 7 þæt is wiþ Eþelinggaeige; 7 his se cyning þær onfeng æt fulwihte, 7 his crismlising was æt Weþmor, 7 he was .xii. niht mid þam cyninge, 7 he hine miclum 7 his geferan mid feo weorðude.

> [And he fought there against all the Host and put it to flight; and rode after it as far as the fortification, and there besieged it for a fortnight. And then the Host gave him hostages and great oaths that they would depart from his kingdom, and they promised him that their king would receive baptism, and they fulfilled it so, and accordingly after three weeks the king Guthrum came to him, as one of thirty men in the Host who were most valued, at Alre, which is close to Athelney. And there the king received him in baptism, and his confirmation was at Wedmore, and he was twelve nights with the king, and Alfred greatly honoured him and his companions with remuneration.]

The Danes of the Host appear to negotiate with Alfred on Guthrum's behalf. Oddly juxtaposed and placed in parallel by the sentence structure are hostages and promises: these are what the Danes give Alfred. And once this negotiation by proxy is over, Guthrum becomes personally involved in the proceedings. He attends his confirmation at a new location: Wedmore (the present-day church is situated on raised ground in the middle of this valley settlement, from which you might see newcomers arriving and descending the valley slopes on all sides). For his part, Alfred in return gives the king and his companions *feo*, from the word *feoh*, a term which has a cognate in Old Norse (the language spoken by Vikings); *feoh* originally meant *cattle*, but was used to denote wealth, money and remuneration. With this money, Guthrum departed to found his own kingdom in East Anglia: that moment normally marks the beginning of what came to be known as the Danelaw, the area of eastern and north-eastern England with a mixed population, in which Danish laws and customs held sway.

It follows that the Peace of Wedmore as reported in the annal of 878 AD was an early medieval success story, at least from an English, Christian perspective: a heathen enemy threatens to invade and destroy the kingdom, but the king defeats him and converts him, bringing him into the fold of Christendom. There is evidence to suggest that this was the hope and aim of the Maldon campaign, at least in the eyes of a commentator such as the scribe of Chronicle A. It will be recalled that his original annal for the year 993 (rather than 991) reads as follows:

> Here in this year Olaf came with ninety-three ships to Folkestone and plundered the countryside there and moved thence to Sandwich and so thence to Ipswich and overran all that area, and so to Maldon. And Ealdorman Byrhtnoth encountered him there with his militia, and fought with him, and they killed the ealdorman there and had command of the battlefield.

This is the main text, but shortly afterwards the scribe added a further comment on the implications of the battle as he saw it. Lacking room on the page, which was already crowded with chronicle entries, he squeezed the extra text into a blank line and then continued in the left-hand margin, noting that the English 'made peace' with the Vikings, the word in question being *frith*, specifically a *truce* or *protection*:

> him man nam syððan frið wið, 7 hine nam se cing syððan to bisceopes handa.

> [And *with him* afterwards they made a truce and *him* the king received at the bishop's hands.]

The word order of the Old English emphasizes the personal pronoun *him* as the object of the two actions. In other words, the scribe states that the king 'received *him* at the bishop's hands': this is the Viking leader Olaf Tryggvasson, who converted to Christianity and for whom the king stood as sponsor in a ceremony with the bishop. Another scribe (hand 7a) then added further information, now using space in the margin of the page; this highlights the cooperation of two leading churchmen in the project:

> ðurh Sirices lare Cantware bisceopes 7 Ælfeages Wincæstre biscopes.

> [By the advice of Siric (traditionally spelled Sigeric), archbishop of Canterbury and that of Ælfeag (Ælfheah) the bishop of Winchester.]

In the view of Chronicle A, then, history was repeating itself, for this is basically the story of King Alfred and Guthrum. And like Guthrum, Olaf ratified the agreement and moved away to found his own kingdom, in this case in Norway. The much later Norse sagas tell the life of Olaf Tryggvason; their literary value is not disputed but their historicity is questionable. In the best known of these, *Heimskringla*, by the Icelander Snorri Sturluson (1179–1241), there is an account of Olaf's conversion after an encounter with a hermit in the Scilly Isles off the south-west coast of England. According to the saga, Olaf then spent some time peacefully in England after his conversion.[8]

The actual *frith* or peace agreement mentioned in the Anglo-Saxon Chronicle has survived as the legal text edited under the title II Æthelred, dated to the year 994.[9] What is clear is that the former enemies have been paid their *feoh* and the 'whole [Viking] Host' is now regarded as an ally who will fight alongside 'the English' against any further incursions by an incoming *sciphere* or 'Viking fleet':

> Ðæt ærost, þæt woroldfrið stande betweox Æthelrede cynge and eallum his leodscipe and eallum ðam here, ðe se cyng þæt feoh sealde, [. . .] And gif ænig sciphere on Englaland hergie, þæt we habban heora ealra fultum; and we him sculon mete findon, ða hwile ðe hy mid us beoð.
>
> [In the first place, a general truce [*woroldfrith*] shall be established between King Æthelred and all his subjects and the whole (Viking) fleet to which the king has paid tribute [*feoh*]. . . . And if any hostile fleet [*sciphere*] harry in England, we shall have the help of all of them; and we shall be under the obligation of finding provisions for them, as long as they remain with us.][10]

According to the scribe of version A, then, the battle at Maldon was a pyrrhic victory for the Danes, who won the battle but lost the war.

The conclusion to be drawn is that the writer of Chronicle A interpreted the Maldon campaign as both a spiritual success and a diplomatic achievement. In constructing his argument, he in fact conflates the stories of the Maldon campaign in 991 and the siege of London in 993 (at least as told in Chronicle C) but he regards the result as positive. The fact that the chronicler's interpretation may be historically inaccurate is not relevant: his 'mistake' reveals his attitude to the battle. As we will see shortly, the account in A differs from the more critical view by the later writer of Chronicle C, who attacks the payment of *gafol* ('tribute') to the Viking army and lays the blame on the churchmen who advised it. But both versions of the Chronicle agree that for three years there was a cessation of hostilities, and peace prevailed in the land. At least in the near-contemporary view of this early commentator, then, the battle at Maldon was instrumental in converting a major heathen leader and creating an effective peace in the kingdom of England. This is clearly a conversion narrative, a *religious* interpretation of the events of August 991.

Tribute and ill-advice: 'Maldon' in Chronicle C

Chronicle C is a manuscript written in the 1040s in the midland region of England, perhaps at Abingdon, or perhaps further north in Mercia.[11] It contains the earliest known version of what historians have come to call 'The Chronicle of the Reign of Æthelred', probably written in the aftermath of the Danish wars, which ended finally in 1016 when Cnut became king of England, initiating the first of the two conquests of England that took place in the eleventh century (the second, of course, being the Norman Conquest, which had more radical and longer lasting consequences).[12] Undoubtedly 1016 was a severe defeat, despite the heroic opposition of Edmund Ironside to the Danish invaders, and despite the fact that rule was briefly divided between the English king, Edmund, in the south and the Danish king, Cnut, in the north, just as it had been in 957, when Edwy and his younger brother Edgar had shared out the kingdom.

But Edmund Ironside died later in 1016, and Cnut became the sole ruler of the kingdom of England. On his accession there were reprisals against actual or potential opponents, and a huge tax, called a *gafol* in the text, was levied on the English nation.

Thereafter, Cnut and his wife Emma (Cnut had married the widow of his predecessor Æthelred) set about – with the advice of Archbishop Wulfstan, author of the *Sermo Lupi* in the reign of Æthelred – to establish and rule an Anglo-Danish kingdom on traditional English lines, as in the days of Edgar the great king. Despite the losses of land and wealth sustained by the English after the conquest, and despite all the new Danish men and women who flocked into the country to enjoy its delights as part of a new Anglo-Danish aristocracy, the emphasis of Cnut's reign was on continuity with the English past. In such a politically delicate situation, the author of the Anglo-Saxon Chronicle for the reign of Cnut becomes reticent: major events are recorded, but not in great detail, and there is no obvious aversion expressed towards the usurping king.

The same cannot be said however for the author of 'The Chronicle of the Reign of Æthelred', who now writes up his account of the war years from 983 through to 1016. In brief, his work has amplitude, especially in the years from 1012 to 1016; it is selectively detailed and indignant: his aim seems to be to show what went wrong in the war and to lay the blame squarely on the shoulders of some named individuals among the English nobility, who advised their king poorly and led their country astray. His work is well represented in manuscript C, so for convenience I will refer to his account of the Maldon campaign and its aftermath as it is given there. Where Chronicle A was rather untidily presented, Chronicle C is much more carefully organized and systematic. Where Chronicle A offers entries only for the years 978, 983, 984, 993, 994 and 1001 (with an addition in

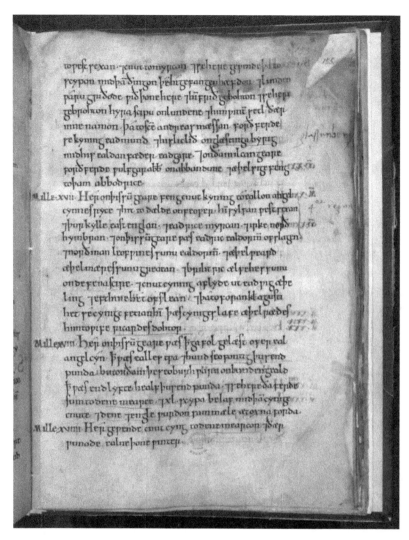

Figure 22 Folio 155r from Version C of the Anglo-Saxon Chronicle, London, British Library, Cotton Tiberius B. I. © The British Library.

Latin for 988 to mark the passing of Archbishop Dunstan), Chronicle C has no gaps, and no later additions or afterthoughts: over the same period it basically provides an annal for every year of Æthelred's reign. Moreover its chronology seems to be more accurate, so that the battle at Maldon is assigned squarely to the year 991 (note again that the symbol '7' means *and*):

Her wæs Gypeswic gehergod, 7 æfter þon swiðe raðe wæs Brihtnoð ealdorman ofslegen æt Mældune; 7 on þam geare man geræedde þæt man geald ærest gafol Denescum mannum for ðam miclan brogan þe hi worhton be ðam særiman; þæt wæs ærest .x. ðusend punda; þæne ræd gerædde ærest Syric arcebisceop.

[Here Ipswich was plundered, and very soon thereafter Ealdorman Byrhtnoth was killed at Maldon. And in that year it was advised that for the first time the tribute (*gafol*) should be paid to the Danish because of the great terror they were causing on the coast: at first this was ten thousand pounds. This advice was first advised by Archbishop Sigeric.]

Comparing this entry of C 991 with that of A 993 (quoted earlier) soon reveals the different perspectives of the two chroniclers. Both are writing at some time after the events, with accumulated oral and written knowledge of the battle available. But Chronicle A still feels more immediate: this is expressed in the mentions by name of Folkestone, Sandwich and Ipswich, its choice of the familiar temporal phrase 'and so to Maldon', and its focus on the *fyrd*, the 'defence-force' or standing army which Byrhtnoth was commanding when he made his fateful encounter with the Danes. Version C by contrast is (uncharacteristically) brief to the point of being laconic: it mentions the plundering of Ipswich, but more briefly than version A, and then reports the killing of Byrhtnoth without even troubling to inform the reader that his death was in battle.

All the adverbials suggest distance in time: the distancing effect of the demonstrative *that* in the phrase 'in *that* year' suggests that many years have since elapsed; and the C chronicler's repeated use of the adverb 'first' evinces hindsight, a knowledge of what has happened and what is to come, that the policy of paying *gafol*, 'tribute', was tried too many times, to no avail. In fact, as the later work of this chronicler for the period up to 1016 shows, the hated *gafol* is a recurrent theme. The mention of the price (10,000 pounds), one of the few extraneous details in the C text annal for 991, is significantly ominous, for the second occasion of a Viking invasion of southern England was in 994, the year 991 being only the first time, and now the payment rose to 16,000 pounds; and then on the third occasion when, according to Chronicle C, a truce was made in 1002, the *gafol* this time was 23,000 pounds (the figures continue to rise in later annals too). By this consciously repetitive and cumulative style, Chronicle C implies that the policy was a failure; and the author underlines his message by the repetition of the noun *ræd* and the related past tense verb *gerædde*, to suggest that Archbishop Sigeric wrongly 'advised this advice'. For the chronicler, *ræd* is an angry buzzword which he uses like *gafol* in his later annals to imply that these were poor policies and the king was literally 'ill-advised' in following them. And not for no reason did the wordplay on the king's name develop among later historians; the name *Æthelræd* means 'Noble Advice', but *Æthelræd Unræd* means 'Noble Advice, Bad Advice' or alternatively 'Æthelred the Ill-advised'.[13] These two keywords *gafol* and *ræd* are crucial, and emphatically cannot be ignored by students of *The Battle of Maldon*, for both terms also appear in the poem, suggesting that the poem in some way is responding to the same issues.

From the foregoing discussion an impression may have been created that the Chronicle of Æthelred's Reign is purely political and secular in its reporting of the events of the Danish wars. That is far from being the case, as a brief example will elucidate. It is all a question of emphasis and perspective. The story of the conversion of Olaf, for instance, is there in C, just as it is in A, but now it is assigned to the year 994 rather than to 991 and now it supplies further circumstantial detail on how Olaf and Æthelred met, how they arranged the christening ceremony and then came to their political agreement. The same annal has a passage worth quoting, because it further illustrates the religious sensibilities, and indeed also the local patriotism, of its author:

> Her on ðissum geare com Anlaf 7 Swegen to Lundenbyrig on Natiuitas Sanctę Marię mid .iiii. and hundnigontigum scypum, 7 hi ða on þa buruh fæstlice feohtende wæron 7 eac hi mid fyre ontendon woldan, ac hi þær geferdon maran hearm and yfel þonne hi æfre wendon þæt him ænig buruhwaru gedon sceolde. Ac seo halige Godes modor on þam dæge hire mildheortnesse þære buruhware gecydde 7 hi ahredde wið heora feondum;

> [Here in this year Olaf and Swegn came to London on the Feast of the Nativity of St Mary with ninety-three ships, and they attacked the city (*burh*) vigorously, intending also to burn it down with fire, but they experienced there more damage and harm than they ever supposed that any city-dwellers would cause them. Indeed, on that day, the Holy Mother of God demonstrated her mercy to the citizens and rescued them from their enemies.]

Writing in the early years of Cnut's reign, and not locally to Maldon, this chronicler is not well placed to remember, or attach any sympathy to, the figure of Byrhtnoth. For him 'Maldon' is the beginning of the bad policy of paying tribute. But when it comes to the *burh* – the still powerful, fortified city of London – his sympathies are roused (the same is true of the annal for 1013 when Swegn again tries to take the city), and these sympathies suggest that the man was himself a Londoner writing in London. But he is also a religious man, who believes in the power of the saints to intervene on their feast day on behalf of mortal humans in distress.

Chapter 11

Byrhtferth of Ramsey's *Life of St Oswald*

Se eorl wæs þe bliþra,
hloh þa, modi man,   sæde Metode þanc
ðæs dægweorces   þe him Drihten forgeaf.

THE BATTLE OF MALDON (146–8)

[The earl was all the happier,
he laughed, the courageous man, gave thanks to God
for the day's handiwork which the Lord had granted him.]

The monk Byrhtferth was a writer and teacher at Ramsey, a monastery situated in the former kingdom of East Anglia, about 80 miles to the north-west of Maldon. Among his prolific writings (in both Latin and Old English) is a biography in Latin of Oswald, archbishop of York, who had been one of the main figures of the Benedictine Reform movement that had dominated the politics of the reign of King Edgar, ruler of the English kingdom in the previous generation.[1] Towards the end of this work, Byrhtferth states that Oswald worked in collaboration with three figures. Foremost was Dunstan, the long-lived archbishop of Canterbury, a prominent figure in the politics of the tenth century.[2] Almost as important was the patronage of the lay magnate Æthelwine, the ealdorman of East Anglia, who (we learn elsewhere) had his princely hall and residence at Upwood, a few miles south-west of Ramsey.[3] In addition – and this is important for our study of 'Maldon' – Byrhtferth underlines the support of Ealdorman Æthelwine's friend and political ally, Byrhtnoth of Essex.

The prevailing character of Byrhtferth of Ramsey's *Life of St Oswald* is hagiographic, for although it is a biography, it adheres also to the conventions of a traditional saint's life in that it presents its subject as a man of sanctity and holiness. But it also gives us some insights into his character and how through

Figure 23 St Peter's Church, Upwood, Cambridgeshire, in the present day. © Mark Atherton.

sheer force of personality he exerted such a powerful influence on the lay people he encountered. The account of the first meeting of Ealdorman Æthelwine with Archbishop Oswald sets the tone appropriately. Following the Archbishop's blessing, the two men fall into conversation:

> When the blessing had been given, they spoke peaceably with each other, fulfilling the words of the prophet when he said: 'See how good and pleasing it is when brothers live together.' They said a good many things to each other concerning the salvation of their souls.[4]

The result of this meeting is that Æthelwine eventually offers Oswald land for a monastery at Ramsey, which of course he is delighted to accept, its remote beauty apparently part of the attraction to him (*Life of St Oswald*, III.15). As son of the famed Æthelstan Half-King and foster-brother to King Edgar, Æthelwine was a rich and powerful ally for Oswald in his programme of reform.

As Byrhtferth shows, Oswald was also a scholar, who attracted to him other men of a similar mind and temperament. Among these, Byrhtferth seems to have been particularly impressed by the French scholar, teacher and monk, Abbo of Fleury, who from 985 to 987 spent a two-year period of self-imposed exile in Ramsey and must have taught the young novice monk Byrhtferth while he was there. Abbo's spiritual home was the monastery at Fleury near Orléans in the Loire valley, a great centre of Benedictine learning and piety, where after his exile he returned to become abbot. Nowadays the place is known as St Benoît-sur-Loire, since the monastic church contains a shrine dedicated to the memory of Benedict of Nursia (480–c. 547), founder of the order – the Benedictines of course still base their everyday practice on the Rule of St Benedict. Fleury had played an influential role in the monastic revival in England in the middle years of the tenth century and, among other English monks and clerics, Bishop Oswald himself spent some time at Fleury in the 950s.[5] Oswald returned to England to become bishop of Worcester (961–92), archbishop of York (971–92) and indeed also the non-resident abbot of Ramsey, which he helped to found in the year 966.

In his *Life of St Oswald*, Byrhtferth describes the island of Ramsey in the marshes as a kind of *locus amoenus* or 'pleasant place', with its 'meadow, woodlands, fish pools, many kinds of fish, and a multitude of birds'. Interpreting Oswald's first journey there 'to the island replete with every kind of beauty', Byrhtferth refers to the large lake of Ramsey Mere to the north.[6] These waterways dominated this rural location in the Middle Ages right up the draining of the Fens in the mid-nineteenth century. After this description, Byrhtferth cites in full a fourteen-line Latin poem on Ramsey that his teacher Abbo wrote while in residence at the abbey.[7] Here is an extract (lines 5–8) in Lapidge's translation:

> For where the destroyer of the raven-bearing Hydra arises,
> There gleams an exquisite island with its woodland waters;
> And where the reins of gleaming Bootes sink,
> There is a land-bridge accessible to all the English.

In an enigmatic, allusive style which must have chimed well with the taste for riddles in his English readers, Abbo writes expansively of the great vistas of this landscape: the constellations seen from Ramsey in the broad night sky, the effect of the light on the water, and the 'land-bridge' (Latin *pons*), which is perhaps a causeway not unlike the 'bridge' that separates and connects the two warring armies in the poem *The Battle of Maldon*.

A second text directly relevant to *Maldon* is the work of hagiography that Abbo of Fleury composed during his two-year stay at Ramsey, *The Passion of St Edmund*. This celebrates the life and death of Edmund, king of the East Angles, during the first wave of Viking invasions a hundred years before (this was the period when Alfred the Great, king of Wessex, was first beginning to resist the Danish invaders). Edmund was killed by the Danes and later buried in a shrine at Bedericesworth (subsequently renamed as Bury St Edmunds). One scene in particular is reminiscent of *The Battle of Maldon*; in Abbo's account, the Danes, after sacking the town and massacring the inhabitants, send a messenger to order the king to surrender, in return for which he will be allowed to continue ruling as king. He consults his bishop, who urges him to flee, but this is Edmund's response:

> 'That', answered the king, 'is what I desire; that is my dearest wish, not to survive my loyal and dear subjects, who have been bereft of their lives and massacred with their children and their wives as they lay in bed, by a bloodthirsty brigand. And what do you advise? that in life's extremity, bereft of my comrades, I should besmirch my fair fame by taking to flight? I have always avoided the calumnious accusations of the informer; never have I endured the opprobrium of fleeing from the battlefield, realising how glorious it would be for me to die for my country; and now I will of my own free will surrender myself, for the loss of those dear to me has made light itself hateful. The Almighty disposer of events is present as my witness that, whether I live or die, nothing shall separate me from the love of Christ, the ring of whose faith I took on me in the sacrament of baptism, when I renounced Satan and all his vanities.'[8]

Edmund then confronts the messenger and dismisses him. Unlike Byrhtnoth in *Maldon*, Edmund dies the death of a pacifist and martyr for his people, but like Byrhtnoth he repudiates the Viking messenger.[9]

In the fifth and final part of *The Life of St Oswald*, Byrhtferth gives a short and intriguing account of 'Maldon'.[10] By that point in the chronology – essentially the early reign of Æthelred – Byrhtferth is taking stock, and drawing his narrative to an emotionally moving conclusion as he tells of the manner in which both Archbishop Oswald and Ealdorman Æthelwine reached the end of their lives. Although his style of writing is highly embellished, as we will see, the structure of the work as a whole is rather loose and flexible: Byrhtferth sometimes rather randomly includes episodes, anecdotes and digressions, and the reader is not always clear about the sequence and chronology of the events narrated. Of the twenty-two chapters in Part V, some of which are quite short (as in most early medieval biographies), the first is a kind of meditation on the order of creation and the waywardness of human beings, while the next two offer miraculous anecdotes from Oswald's time as archbishop at York; his chapters 4 and 5 then describe the coronation of King Æthelred and the early Viking attacks on his kingdom, including the fight at Maldon.

I will return to his 'Maldon' shortly, but to place it in context we should consider briefly the themes of the subsequent chapters. The story of the death of Byrhtnoth is followed by that of Archbishop Dunstan, passing 'triumphantly to the joys of eternal light'; there are stories from the life of Dunstan, and more poetry by Abbo in honour of Dunstan. A famous section of Part V (chs. 11–13) describes the lavish celebration, the playing of the merry organ, the flowing mead, the devout promises made on the great occasion of a dedication of a church tower at Ramsey. Byrhtferth makes much of the last visits by Oswald and Æthelwine to Ramsey before he describes the scenes of their passing from this life to the next.

In short, Part V of Byrhtferth's *Life of St Oswald* is concerned with the last years of four leading figures of the late tenth century, two laymen and two churchmen. The analogies are deliberate: the author turns a history and biography into a kind of typological narrative. As a narrative method, typology was used in the biblical art and literature of the Middle Ages to extract spiritual or allegorical meanings from the Old Testament, an example being the story of Abraham's near-sacrifice of his son Isaac, which is compared typologically to God's sacrifice of his son Jesus Christ. This approach to biblical interpretation is also used in hagiography, to draw parallels between the life of Christ or the lives of the Patriarchs and the lives of the saints. By employing this method, Byrhtferth seeks to uncover important spiritual analogies between spiritual and secular leaders of the country in the 990s. For example, he boldly compares Byrhtnoth and Dunstan. Paradoxically, the audacity of the comparison is so strong that it has been missed by many modern commentators, but the text is clear, the parallels being marked by juxtaposition of events at the beginning and end of chapters 4 to 6:[11]

> 4. Æthelred, the excellent prince, was consecrated to the summit of the realm by Dunstan, the apostle's representative, and by Oswald, his co-apostle. [. . .]
>
> [end of ch. 4] In fact one of our men, Stremwold, was killed along with several others who chose to end their lives by death in battle rather than to live on in shame.
>
> 5. After not many months had passed, another savage battle was fought in the east of this great country, in which Byrhtnoth, the distinguished ealdorman, alongside his personal retinue, held the military command. [. . .]
>
> [end of ch. 5] When the aforesaid leader was killed, ealdormen and thegns, men and women, everyone of either sex, were deeply moved.
>
> 6. Thereafter Dunstan, the excellent father and the glory of all this land, was taken from this world and conducted triumphantly to the joys of ethereal light.

As Archbishop of Canterbury, Dunstan had been King Edgar's right-hand man, and his career had spanned nearly all of the tenth century. At the end of chapter 5 and the beginning of chapter 6, Byrhtferth's typological juxtaposition of the deaths of Ealdorman Byrhtnoth and Archbishop Dunstan is striking, and it parallels the fuller account of the final days of Byrhtferth's two main figures, Archbishop Oswald and then Ealdorman Æthelwine, in the last few chapters of the *Life*.

This, then, is the context for Byrhtferth's narrative of the fight at Maldon. No doubt he had heard oral accounts of the battle, which had taken place up to ten years before his time of writing, but he certainly also used written sources. First and foremost is his use of a chronicle.[12] He is likely to have owned a manuscript of the Anglo-Saxon Chronicle which, like version A, told of a Viking attack in 988 at Watchet on the north coast of Devon and then a battle in 991 at Maldon. Byrhtferth's reading of the Chronicle is then combined with personal knowledge and local information. For example, he provides a description of Byrhtnoth as *statura procerus* 'tall of stature' which echoes, as Lapidge shows, that of the mighty leader Alboinus in the Carolingian author Paul the Deacon's *History of the Langobards*, which Byrhtferth knew and quoted elsewhere.[13] To all this he adds his knowledge of the Bible, of early medieval writers such as the eighth-century abbot and bishop Aldhelm, as well as the writings of his former teacher, Abbo of Fleury, drawing on all these works for the imagery and rhetoric that he needed in order to create his elaborate narrative.

He begins with a coronation. Æthelred is consecrated as king by the two archbishops of Canterbury and York: Dunstan and Oswald; the new monarch is praised for his handsome appearance and manner. But all is not well, for the devil Beelzebub has arisen, with his retinue of what Byrhtferth calls *Cerethi* 'the deadly ones'. Here Byrhtferth takes his idea from Aldhelm, and ultimately from the Bible.[14] The deadly ones are, of course, the Danes, depicted here with their shining swords, deadly arrows and helmets of bronze (rather than the expected iron), the bronze helmet being an allusion to Goliath of the Philistines; here is the relevant biblical passage, in which the beginning of the battle is determined partly by the geographical location, leading to a face-off between the armies arrayed on opposite slopes, with the valley between them:

(2) Porro Saul et filii Israël congregati venerunt in Vallem terebinthi, et direxerunt aciem ad pugnandum contra Philisthiim. (3) Et Philisthiim stabant super montem ex parte hac, et Israël stabat supra montem ex altera parte: vallisque erat inter eos. (4) Et egressus est vir spurius de castris Philisthinorum nomine Goliath, de Geth, altitudinis sex cubitorum et palmi: (5) et cassis ærea super caput ejus, et lorica squamata induebatur. Porro pondus loricæ ejus, quinque millia siclorum æris erat: (6) et ocreas æreas habebat in cruribus, et clypeus æreus tegebat humeros ejus. (7) Hastile autem hastæ ejus erat quasi liciatorium texentium: ipsum autem ferrum hastæ ejus sexcentos siclos habebat ferri: et armiger ejus antecedebat eum. (8) Stansque clamabat adversum phalangas Israël, et dicebat eis: Quare venistis parati ad prælium? numquid ego non sum Philisthæus, et vos servi Saul? eligite ex vobis virum, et descendat ad singulare certamen.

(2) And Saul and the children of Israel being gathered together came to the valley of Terebinth: and they set the army in array to fight against the Philistines.

(3) And the Philistines stood on a mountain on the one side, and Israel stood on a mountain on the other side: and there was a valley between them. (4) And there went out a man baseborn from the camp of the Philistines named Goliath, of Geth, whose height was six cubits and a span. (5) And he had a helmet of brass upon his head; and he was clothed with a coat of mail with scales. And the weight of his coat of mail was five thousand sicles of brass. (6) And he had greaves of brass on his legs; and a buckler of brass covered his shoulders. (7) And the staff of his spear was like a weaver's beam, and the head of his spear weighed six hundred sicles of iron. And his armourbearer went before him. (8) And standing he cried out to the bands of Israel, and said to them: Why are you come out prepared to fight? Am not I a Philistine, and you the servants of Saul? Choose out a man of you; and let him come down and fight hand to hand.[15]

The stand-off here between the two armies and the appearance of Goliath as a challenger bears a resemblance to the opening scenes of *Maldon*, and it is worth speculating whether Byrhtferth's use of the biblical imagery was influenced by the poem. The relevance of the David and Goliath imagery to this period of English history is highlighted by a large full-page illustration in a mid-eleventh-century book of the Psalms from Canterbury, which depicts Goliath in a helmet and chain mail, a sword at his hip and a great spear raised in his hand.[16] In this typology, the English are like the Israelites, and the Vikings are the Philistines.

Thinking symmetrically and geographically, Byrhtferth now tells of an affliction of 'all the kindreds of the north', with a battle in the west and a battle in the east. The battle in the west is a success for the Devonshiremen – Byrhtferth uses in his Latin text the Old English adjective *Deuinysce* (literally 'Devonish') to describe them – who gain 'uictoriam sancti triumphi . . . adquisita gloria' (the triumph of a sacred victory . . . and its accompanying glory): the word *sancti* (holy, sacred) hinting at a theme of a just or holy war. And there is a hero among the Devonshiremen named Stremwold, who is reminiscent of the character of the old retainer Byrhtwold in the Old English poem *Maldon*, in that he chooses 'uitam finire quam ignobiliter uiuere' (to 'end his life' in the battle rather than 'live in shame'). The *bellum*, the battle in the east, by contrast, is located 'in oriente huius inclite regionis' (in the east of this great region). The location is not named or identified any more specifically, but the wording suggests local patriotism, that the writer is thinking of *this* region where he lives and works, that is, East Anglia. But there is a general English perspective too, for in this eastern battle too it is a matter of '*us* against them', and in both west and east, the English are *nostrates* or *nostris* (our men) while the Vikings are *illis* (them); and later still there occurs the alliterative phrase 'pro patria pugnare' (to fight for his country). To preserve the typology of events on both the left-hand side and right-hand side of the country, Byrhtferth conflates the chronology by suggesting that this battle in the east took place only a few months later in the same year. This time the hero is 'gloriosus dux Byrihtnoðus' (the glorious *duke* Byrhtnoth) (i.e. *ealdorman* in a tenth-century English context), also described in Byrhtferth's Latin as *princeps belli* (battle-leader).

There are echoes of our poem here: *princeps belli* is reminiscent of Old English heroic attributes in *Maldon* such as *wigena hlaford* (lord of warriors [135]), *se guð-rinc* (the battle-warrior [138]) and *se fyrdrinc* (the army warrior [140]) – all referring to Ealdorman Byrhtnoth. In *The Life of St Oswald*, Byrhtnoth bravely exhorts his men *ad aciem*, the noun *acies* denoting the battle-order or line of battle, and again faintly recalling the beginning of the *Maldon* poem, where the ealdorman instructs his men how to stand and deploy their weapons. Ealdorman Byrhtnoth's old age, implied in the formula 'har hilderinc' (grey-haired battle-warrior) in the poem (169a), is signified here by his 'cygnea canities' (his 'swan-white hair), a phrase that Byrhtferth likes and reuses, drawing again on the writings of Aldhelm.[17] This suggests that Byrhtferth may well have known our poem *The Battle of Maldon*: at the very least the parallels are worth mentioning and show that he was familiar with the genre of heroic poetry, in Old English as well as in Latin.

References to the Old Testament continue to feature, for Byrhtferth now compares Byrhtnoth typologically to Moses with his two companions Aaron and Hur, who support him on either side as he surveys Joshua's battle against the Amalekites (Exod. 17. 12-14). Here again, one cannot help thinking of *The Battle of Maldon*: of Wulfstan Ceola's son on the bridge, with his two companions Ælfere and Maccus, or indeed of Byrhtnoth himself falling in battle with his two trusty companions Ælfnoth and Wulmær beside him. In Byrhtferth's *Life of St Oswald*, there is also the left-to-right symmetry when the hero fights to the right and protects himself on the left, his bravery recalling a similar hero in the Book of Maccabees, which was also regarded as a biblical model for behaviour in tenth-century England:

> And Judas and his army drew near for battle: and there fell of the king's army six hundred men. And Eleazar the son of Saura saw one of the beasts harnessed with the king's harness: and it was higher than the other beasts. And it seemed to him that the king was on it. And he exposed himself to deliver his people and to get himself an everlasting name. And he ran up to it boldly in the midst of the legion, killing on the right hand, and on the left, and they fell by him on this side and that side.[18]

But for Byrhtferth of Ramsey, Byrhtnoth demonstrates bravery in defeat, and the key phrase is 'et Byrihtnoðus cecidit, et reliqui fugerunt' (and Byrhtnoth fell, and the rest fled) suggesting that the writer chose not to glorify the last resistance of the brave retinue that we find in the poem *The Battle of Maldon*. Instead, for stylistic reasons, he chose to attach that part of the story to Stremwold and his men in the west.

Byrhtferth ends with an explanation for the Viking incursions: namely that the sea-borne invaders are the bearers of divine wrath. Reminiscent of the voice and rhetoric of the churchman and preacher Wulfstan, archbishop of York, who was to become an active preacher and writer in Old English from early years of the eleventh century to his death in 1023, Byrhtferth cites the Old Testament prophet Jeremiah (25. 8-9) and he writes of the 'kindreds of the north' as an instrument of the Lord's judgement. This prophetic element is typical of post-millennial writers such as Wulfstan, whose 'famous *Sermo Lupi ad Anglos* or *Sermon of Wolf to the English*' (subtitled 'When the Danes Persecuted Them Most') expresses very fittingly the mood of the 1010s.[19] In this way, Byrhtferth's perspective on the battle is very different to that of Chronicle A and prefigures that of Archbishop Wulfstan, who pictures the Vikings as a punishment sent by God. But in the end, Byrhtferth of Ramsey returns to eulogy. For him, Byrhtnoth is a symbol of spiritual resistance, for he is sustained in his last fight by 'the Lord's manifold mercy'; 'alms and holy Masses gave him consolation'; 'prayers and good deeds uplifted him';[20] by no means does Byrhtferth see him as a scapegoat for the sins of the English, as has been argued.[21] The monk Byrhtferth's last word on the battle is a general emotional response, for he declares that all are moved, all the ealdormen and thegns, all the men and women in the country, by the death of Byrhtnoth, the secular leader who in terms of spiritual status is to be seen typologically as the equivalent of Dunstan, archbishop of Canterbury, the great spiritual leader of the country.

Figure 24 Monastic walls at Ramsey Abbey. © Mark Atherton.

Chapter 12

Memories of a golden age
'Maldon' in *The Book of Ely*

Gemunu þa mæla þe we oft æt meodo spræcon . . .
THE BATTLE OF MALDON (212)

[I remember the times when we often talked at the mead-drinking . . .]

The Book of Ely

The Book of Ely is technically speaking a cartulary-chronicle, that is to say, a compilation of documents and charters recording landholdings and conveyances, mixed with historical anecdotes and biographical facts. It was compiled in stages at the monastery of Ely in East Anglia during the period 1131–74. Ely has a significant role in the story of the battle at Maldon, since Byrhtnoth was a generous patron of the Abbey of Ely, and after his death in the battle his body was taken there for burial. Despite its late date, *The Book of Ely* preserves a large number of charters and other information translated into Latin from the original Old English. One section in particular includes a work called the *Libellus Æthelwoldi episcopi* ('The Little Book of Bishop Æthelwold'), written in the early twelfth century on the basis of Old English accounts of the refoundation and development of Ely Abbey: of how the politically active monastic reformer Bishop Æthelwold had refounded the abbey in the 970s and protected it from depredations after the death of Edgar in 975. As with all these documents, but especially because of its mixed sources and traditions, considerable critical judgement needs to be exercised by the reader wishing to unravel the likely truth from embroidered legend in the version of events presented here.

Figure 25 Ely Cathedral in its present-day setting. © Mark Atherton.

From close scrutiny of his account of Byrhtnoth and the battle, however, which is found in Book II, ch. 62 of the work, it seems likely that the author of *The Book of Ely* was familiar with the text of *The Battle of Maldon* or had heard performances of the poem, details of which he retained in his memory. One specific parallel is the assertion in *The Book of Ely* that Byrhtnoth hurried to the battle 'lest the enemy army should occupy so much as one foot of land in his absence', the detail about 'one foot' echoing in the poem *Maldon* in the refusal of both Leofsunu of Sturmer and Edward the Tall to flee 'even by the space of one foot' (lines 247 and 275). Not all such details appear to have been correctly understood. One feature of *The Battle of Maldon* as we know it is that the fight divides into two stages. First, there is the fight on the causeway, when the thegn Wulfstan and his two brave companions hold back the might of the Viking army and prevent them from crossing to the mainland. In the poem the noun used is *brycg* (literally 'bridge), which appears to refer to the causeway of hard stones that still connects Northey island to the mainland at low tide. In *The Book of Ely*, this episode becomes the first battle, taking place also on a 'bridge' (Latin *pons*), specifically on the *pontem aque* (literally 'bridge of water'). It results in the utter defeat of the Vikings, and only a few escape to their home country. But the Vikings then return after considerable time, eager for revenge, in order to fight a second battle at Maldon, from which they emerge victorious. The oddity of this narrative may be explained perhaps as a memory of hearing the poem performed, or perhaps simply that the archaic poetic diction of the poem caused difficulties of comprehension to the later writer. Or was the Ely writer writing an expansion or amplification of the poem?[1]

One considerable difference between the early poem and the later chronicle is seen in the Ely writer's claim that this main battle lasted fourteen days, almost certainly an exaggeration.[2] It is tempting to explain this as the influence of the twelfth-century romance, a genre in which the hero, though human and not god-like, is nevertheless superior in kind to ordinary people and capable of almost superhuman feats of endurance.[3] On the other hand, some details seem to correspond to the historical truth of 'what really happened': the Ely writer reports that the Vikings finally killed Byrhtnoth by forming a kind of phalanx, charging the English ranks and decapitating the hero. The body was then recovered by the abbot of Ely and taken for burial. The detail is missing in the poem *The Battle of Maldon* as we have it, but the fact of the decapitation was confirmed in the eighteenth century when Byrhtnoth's tomb was opened and a tall, headless skeleton was uncovered.[4] Such concrete evidence is salutary: we are not simply dealing with texts, but with reports that reflect actual events.

For his story of Byrhtnoth in Book II, ch. 62 of *The Book of Ely*, the chronicler writes a short preface in which he employs the conventional modesty topos to which many monastic chroniclers paid lip service in their writings. But behind this modesty lies the conviction that Byrhtnoth's fame was still celebrated in the writer's own day:

> De Brithnodo viro singulari et glorioso succedit memoranda relatio, cuius vitamet gesta non parvis preconiis Anglice commandant historie, de quibus pauca qualicumque stilo cum venia lectoris excepimus.

> [What follows is a noteworthy account concerning Byrhtnoth, an outstanding and famous man whose righteous life and deeds English histories commend with no small praises. From these, begging the reader's pardon, we have extracted a few items, irrespective of the character of our style.][5]

A good deal of time has of course elapsed, along with many cultural changes, and the chronicler feels compelled to add a linguistic explanation of the term 'ealdorman':

> Itaque vir iste nobilissimus Northanimbrourum dux fortissimus fuit, qui ob mirabilem sapientiam et corporis fortitudinem, qua se suosque viriliter protegebat, Anglica lingua alderman id est senior vel dux, ab omnibus cognominabitur.

[This most noble man was indeed a very valiant leader of the Northumbrians who, on account of the marvellous wisdom and physical fortitude with which he manfully defended himself and his people, was given by everyone the title of *ealdorman*, in the English language, that is, 'elder' or 'leader'.]

Oddly, the Ely writer makes Byrhtnoth an ealdorman of *Northumbria*. At first sight this seems a gross error, for the ascription contradicts all earlier documents, which imply that Byrhtnoth was the governor of *Essex*. In the poem, however,

Figure 26 Byrhtnoth's eighteenth-century shrine in Ely Cathedral. © Mark Atherton.

there is the presence of the 'Northumbrian hostage' fighting on the side of the East Saxons (*Maldon*, 268–72). Throughout the eleventh century, the people of Northumbria maintained a sense of autonomy and independence, a resistance to rule from the West Saxon south, and indeed (after 1066) from the Norman south.[6] It may be that Byrhtnoth had been involved in some peace-keeping mission or expedition to Northumbria shortly before he returned to Essex in August 991 to deal with the Viking threat. Also, as Cyril Hart has pointed out, it is possible that Byrhtnoth's jurisdiction extended into Northumbria rather than simply being confined to the borders of Essex.[7]

Following his insistence on the rank and rule of his hero, the Ely chronicler now turns to Byrhtnoth's qualities as a man. These are a mixture of the heroic and the saintly. He tells us that Byrhtnoth was 'fluent in speech' (*sermone facundus*), 'powerful in strength' (*viribus robustus*) and 'of huge physical stature' (*corpore maximus*), all of which can be inferred from the way Byrhtnoth is presented by the *Maldon* poet. The chronicler adds that Byrhtnoth was tireless in his fight against the 'enemies of the kingdom' (i.e. the Vikings), demonstrating great courage, without fear of death. Byrhtnoth is also presented as showing honour to bishops, priests and monks, and as being a generous patron who gave great gifts of land for the use of the church. In addition we are told that he honoured Holy Church and the servants of God everywhere and 'bequeathed the whole of his patrimony to their use'. Like Byrhtferth in his *Life of St Oswald*, the author of *The Book of Ely* honours Byrhtnoth as defender of the monastic movement in the English Church. This became a crucial issue in the period after King Edgar's death, when some secular nobles had sought to seize and recover lands given to the monasteries, but at a great synod Byrhtnoth rose to their defence:

> On behalf of the religious communities, too, he used always to place himself as a bulwark against those who attempted to disturb holy places. For that religious man (*vir iste religiosus*), while present at a synod (*in sinodo constitutus*), resisted with great firmness the greed and madness of certain prominent men, who wanted to expel the monks and recall to the churches those who had previously been ejected by Edgar and Saint Æthelwold. He said that he could in no way tolerate the expulsion from the kingdom of the monks who upheld all religion in the kingdom.[8]

Byrhtnoth's support for the monastic movement is seen as closely tied to his commitment to 'defending the freedom of his native land' (*ad defendendam patrie libertatem*), for which 'he would rather die than tolerate an unavenged injury to his country'. According to *The Book of Ely* too, in the face of the Danish raids and devastations all the principal men of the country 'bound themselves loyally' to him *fideliter alligabant*. Evidently, Ealdorman Byrhtnoth inspired loyalty 'because of his great worth and reliability, so that under his protection they might defend themselves against the enemy more confidently'. Such passages indicate that the Ely chronicler may well have known or recalled from memory the words and themes of the poem *The Battle of Maldon*.[9]

Equally, there are passages which intrigue us because they are not present in the text of the poem as we have it today, which lacks the beginning and end of the narrative. So the beginning of the Ely account tells of Byrhtnoth's ride from the north and his attempts to billet his men at Ramsey Abbey and Ely Abbey on the way southwards. This makes sense if Byrhtnoth really had been on an expedition to the north shortly before the battle. The conclusion of the Ely account may also supply material that featured in the poem. The story has it that the abbot of Ely came to the field to recover the body and take it for honourable burial at the abbey church.

The next, very short, chapter (*Book of Ely*, II. 63) provides further matter to ponder. It concerns Byrhtnoth's widow and her actions following her husband's death and burial:

> Uxor quippe eius, nomine Ælfleda domina, eo tempore, quo vir idem suus interfectus est et humatus, manerium de Ratendune, quod erat de dote sua, et terram de Saham, que est ad stagnum iuxta Ely, et Dittune, et unam hidam in Chefle, et torquem auream et cortinam gestis viri sui intextam atque depictam in memoriam probitatis eius huic ecclesie donavit.

> [This man's wife, indeed, the Lady Ælfflæd by name, at the time when her husband was killed and buried, gave to this church an estate at Rettendon, which formed part of her marriage-portion, and land at Soham, which is by a mere adjoining Ely, and Ditton, and a hide at Cheveley, and a golden torque, and a hanging woven upon and embroidered with the deeds of her husband, in memory of his probity.]

This 'cortina . . . intexta' (hanging woven upon and embroidered) poses several questions. Certainly such wall-hangings were to be found in the halls of the tenth-century English elite.[10] For example, in her surviving will, a certain lady named Wulfwaru grants to her first son a *heallwahrift* (hall tapestry) and a *beddreaf* (bed-cover), and to her second son a *heallreaf* (tapestry for a hall), a *burreaf* (tapestry for a chamber) and a *beodreaf* (table-cover).[11] Such fine textiles of various sizes needed to be preserved for posterity. As to Byrhtnoth's widow, what were the 'deeds of her husband' pictured on this wall-hanging? Some scholars, such as Dodwell, dismiss it as not relevant to the events of the poem *Maldon*, since the text indicates an immediate gift to Ely Abbey.[12] Mildred Budny and Ute Schwab, by contrast, suggest that the tapestry was concerned solely with the events at Maldon.[13] As we will see shortly, the text indicates that some time may have elapsed before the gift was made. Andrew Wareham has even made the interesting suggestion that the tapestry was completed by Byrhtnoth's granddaughter, Æthelswyth, whom *The Book of Ely* (ll. 88) records as choosing a monastic life at Coveney 'where in great seclusion she used to devote her time to gold-embroidery and tapestry-weaving'.[14]

Arguably, Byrhtnoth's widow Ælfflæd continued to live seven miles to the south-west of Maldon, in the princely hall on her estate on the hill at Rettendon, which commands fine views towards the estuaries of the Blackwater and the Crouch. Rettendon had after all been given to her by Byrhtnoth as her morning-gift on the day after their wedding. We know about the morning-gift from Ælfflæd's will, composed in her own voice in Old English, which survives in an early eleventh-century scribal hand on a single sheet of parchment, along with that of her sister. Probably the will was composed in the year 1002.[15] Where *The Book of Ely* states that 'at the time when her husband was killed and buried, [she] gave to this church an estate at Rettendon', the will suggests that Rettendon was granted to the saints of Ely as a promise for the future:

And I grant to St Peter and St Etheldreda and St Wihtburg and St Sexburg and St Eormenhild, at Ely, where my lord's body lies buried, the three estates which we both promised to God and his saints; namely, Rettendon, which was my marriage gift, Soham and Ditton, just as my lord and my sister have

Figure 27 View across the fields from All Saints Church, Rettendon. © Mark Atherton.

granted it; and the one hide at Cheveley, which my sister obtained, and the pair to the ring which was given as burial fee for my lord.

In this context, her 'lord' (Old English *hlaford*) is the respectful way Ælfflæd refers to her husband; by then his death was eleven years in the past and his tomb, as the Old English text puts it, is at Ely: *þer mines hlafordes lichoma rest* (literally where my lord's body rests).[16] The passage implies that Byrhtnoth's burial-fee – the phrase in Old English is more spiritually expressed by *to sawlescæatte* (as soul-payment) – was paid at the time of his passing, but these other gifts and grants of land came later. If that is so, then there was ample time for Ælfflæd to commission a commemorative hall tapestry to celebrate her husband's deeds at Maldon.

What might the Byrhtnoth Tapestry have looked like? The obvious point of comparison is the Bayeux Tapestry, a work of secular pictorial narrative which celebrates the deeds of Harold II, highlights his failure, and narrates the preparations, invasion, battle and conquest of England by Duke William of Normandy in 1066; this was probably an Anglo-Saxon work of embroidery commissioned by a Norman patron such as Odo of Bayeux.[17] Various illustrated manuscripts that predate the Bayeux Tapestry (1066–86) include calendars, psalters, the Old English Hexateuch and the illustrations to *Psychomachia*, a textbook used in the schools or for private reading. Like the Bayeux Tapestry, all the illustrations in these books employ the techniques of linear pictorial narrative, where one scene follows on from the other with recognizable characters that recur from one picture to the next (for those unfamiliar with the style of these manuscript illustrations the comparison with a graphic novel is appropriate). In the illustrated manuscripts of Prudentius's poem *Psychomachia*, there are many narrative scenes that merit consideration, despite the subject matter being an allegorical battle that differs considerably from *Maldon*. The text of the *Psychomachia* was studied intensely and annotated with glosses in the tenth-century schools, and these manuscripts seem to have been made in the 990s, which makes their illustrations doubly relevant.[18] The poem itself, written by the late Roman author Aurelius Clemens Prudentius (348–413), is an allegory, narrating a series of battles, or rather individual fights, between women warriors, personifications of virtue and vice such as Patience and Anger. The tenth-century English-illustrated manuscripts give an impression of what the illustrative frieze of the Byrhtnoth Tapestry looked like. Though the dress of the women is fantastical, the weapons and equipment, and other objects depicted such as buildings, are relevant to the period, as they reflect contemporary tenth-century artefacts.[19] And Prudentius's Preface, on the story of one of the biblical Abraham's battles in Genesis, is furnished with particularly appropriate illustrations of authentically looking Anglo-Saxon soldiers, horses and equipment. The point is that, like the tenth-century illustrations of biblical books and the Psalms, the figures in the illustrations are largely modernized, as though they represented contemporary tenth-century people rather than figures from antiquity.

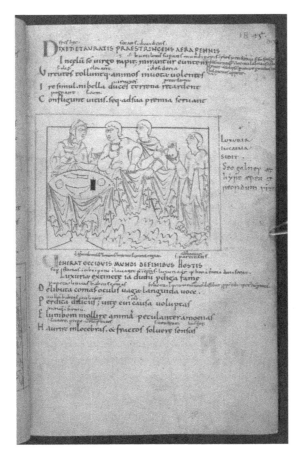

Figure 28 Feast scene from Prudentius, *Psychomachia*; London, British Library, Cotton Cleopatra C. VIII, folio 18r. © The British Library.

Arrivals, challenges, scenes of feasting and ceremonial drinking – these are familiar to us from the preliminary episodes of the Bayeux Tapestry. It seems reasonable to speculate that such scenes also featured in the Byrhtnoth Tapestry. A likely episode is the arrival at the abbey of Ramsey, as reported in *The Book of Ely*, where Abbot Wulfsige tells the unexpected guests that his abbey lacks the resources for such a large army and can only symbolically offer board and lodging, for Byrhtnoth and just seven of his men:

Ad quod fertur eleganter respondisse: 'Sciat dominus abbas, quod solus sine istis nolo prandere, quia solus sine illis nequeo pugnare.'

[To this, Byrhtnoth is said to have made the elegantly phrased response, 'Let the lord Abbot know that I will not dine alone without the men you refer to, because I cannot fight alone without them.']

The sentiment of loyalty and companionship expressed here would not be out of place in the lost beginning of the poem *The Battle of Maldon* or, indeed, in the lost tapestry of the life and deeds of Ealdorman Byrhtnoth.

Perspectives on the poem *The Battle of Maldon*

In the last three chapters I have presented sources which reflect, in varying ways, what happened at Maldon in August of the year 991. It will be seen that they sometimes share common features, such as the idea that the battle took place in two stages, the question of *gafol* (tribute) and *ræd* (advice), the 'bridge' across the water, or the bravery of the East Saxon leader and his inspirational leadership. But more illuminating, perhaps, than these details is the way the four texts reflect attitudes to the battle that were current in or around the year 1000. On the evidence presented here, it seems likely that the battle at Maldon was viewed as an event in the religious as well as in the political life of the country. The sources closest in time to the battle bear this out. In Chronicle A, the focus is Christian apologetics: the conversion of the Viking leader. In Byrhtferth of Ramsey, who is writing contemporaneously or slightly later, that conversion is ignored, and his text is made prophetic: the Vikings are seen as the Philistines, bearing divine punishment upon the English, though Byrhtnoth himself is portrayed in pious and positive terms. A major theme is the role of Byrhtnoth as a secular defender of the monastic churches, a view borne out by the details recorded in our fourth source, *The Book of Ely*, which, though it is much later in date, preserves traditions from the late tenth century quite closely. These sources represent contemporary attitudes to the events and principal actors in the drama that was played out in August 991. What is striking is their favourable responses to the character of Byrhtnoth, and their views cannot be ignored by interpreters of *The Battle of Maldon*, for such attitudes were current when the poet put pen to parchment and composed his poem.

PART III

Appendices

Appendix 1 *The Battle of Maldon*

Text and translation

In the text that follows, the capital letters from Casley's transcript are taken as scribal or even authorial, and a text is offered that divides into sections or verse-paragraphs of varying length that seem to reflect the medieval scribe's conception of the structure of the poem. The modern English translation then follows on from the relevant section or 'stanza'. One difficulty is that the paragraph-initial capitals fade away later in the text; in such cases, I treat the beginning of a speech as a new paragraph and indent accordingly. In the translation I aim to be fairly literal, keeping to the rhetoric and word order of the original where possible.

[. . .] brocen wurde.

Het þa hyssa hwæne   hors forlætan,
feor afysan,   and forð gangan,
hicgan to handum   and to hige godum.
Þa þæt Offan mæg   ærest onfunde   5
þæt se eorl nolde   yrhðo geþolian,
he let him þa of handon   leofne fleogan
hafoc wið þæs holtes,   and to þære hilde stop;
be þam man mihte oncnawan   þæt se cniht nolde
wacian æt þam wige,   þa he to wæpnum feng.   10
Eac him wolde Eadric   his ealdre gelæstan,
frean to gefeohte,   ongan þa forð beran
gar to guþe.   He hæfde god geþanc
þa hwile þe he mid handum   healdan mihte
bord and bradswurd;   beot he gelæste   15
þa he ætforan his frean   feohtan sceolde.

[. . .] was broken.
Then he commanded each of his men to release their horses,
drive them far away, and go forth,
to think on the work at hand and on their firm resolve.
So when Offa's kinsman first realized   5
that the earl would not tolerate any cowardice,
he let his favourite fly from his hands
 – his falcon to the forest – and stepped forward to the fight;
by this it could be seen that the young man
would not weaken in the battle, when he took up his weapons.   10
Also Eadric wished to support his prince,
his leader in the fight, and so he took up his spear
and bore it to the battle. He kept his firm resolve
for as long as he could hold in his hands
shield and broad sword; he fulfilled his vow   15
that he would fight in the forefront, in the presence of his lord and leader.

    Ða þær Byrhtnoð ongan   beornas trymian,
    rad and rædde,   rincum tæhte
    hu hi sceoldon standan   and þone stede healdan,
    and bæd þæt hyra randas   rihte heoldon   20
    fæste mid folman,   and ne forhtedon na.
    Þa he hæfde þæt folc   fægere getrymmed,
    he lihte þa mid leodon   þær him leofost wæs,
    þær he his heorðwerod   holdost wiste.

By now Byrhtnoth had begun arranging the troops:
he rode and gave counsel, instructing the men
how they should stand and hold their position,
and he commanded that they hold their shields correctly   20
and firmly in their hands, that they should not be afraid.
When he had deployed the people appropriately,
he dismounted among his own men, where it was dearest to him,
where he knew his hearth-troop to be most loyal.

    Þa stod on stæðe,   stiðlice clypode   25
    wicinga ar,   wordum mælde,
    se on beot abead   brimliþendra
    ærænde to þam eorle,   þær he on ofre stod:
    'Me sendon to þe   sæmen snelle,
    heton ðe secgan   þæt þu most sendan raðe   30
    beagas wið gebeorge;   and eow betere is
    þæt ge þisne garræs   mid gafole forgyldon,

þon we swa hearde   hilde dælon.
Ne þurfe we us spillan,   gif ge spedaþ to þam;
we willað wið þam golde   grið fæstnian.   35
Gyf þu þat geræ dest,   þe her ricost eart,
þæt þu þine leoda   lysan wille,
syllan sæmannum   on hyra sylfra dom
feoh wið freode,   and niman frið æt us,
we willaþ mid þam sceattum   us to scype gangan,   40
on flot feran,   and eow friþes healdan.'

THERE STOOD ON THE BEACH and called out sternly –   25
the messenger from the Vikings – spoke these words –
declaring in a boast the seafarers'
message to the earl where he stood on the shore:
'I was sent to you by hardened seamen,
who commanded me to say to you that you are quite permitted to hand over   30
rings in exchange for protection; and that it is better for you
that you buy out of this battle, by payment of tribute,
rather than we wage war so fiercely.
There is no need for us to destroy each other, if you are sufficiently wealthy;
we will, in return for the gold, establish a truce.   35
And if you, sir, counsel this, who are the richest here,
that you will redeem your people,
give the seamen, on their terms,
money in exchange for friendship, and make peace with us,
we will take ourselves off with the payments to our ships,   40
put to sea, and keep the peace with you.'

Byrhtnoð maþelode,   bord hafenode,
wand wacne æsc,   wordum mælde,
yrre and anræd   ageaf him andsware:
'Gehyrst þu, sæ lida,   hwæt þis folc segeð?   45
Hi willað eow to gafole   garas syllan,
æ ttrynne ord   and ealde swurd,
þa heregeatu   þe eow æt hilde ne deah.
Brimmanna boda,   abeod eft ongean,
sege þinum leodum   miccle laþre spell,   50
þæt her stynt unforcuð   eorl mid his werode,
þe wile gealgean   eþel þysne,
Æþelredes eard,   ealdres mines,
folc and foldan.   Feallan sceolon
hæþene æt hilde.   To heanlic me þinceð   55

> þæt ge mid urum sceattum   to scype gangon
> unbefohtene,   nu ge þus feor hider
> on urne eard   in becomon.
> Ne sceole ge swa softe   sinc gegangan:
> us sceal ord and ecg   ær geseman,   60
> grim guðplega,   ær we gofol syllon.'

BYRHTNOTH MADE A SPEECH, raised his shield,
brandished his slender ash, declared in words,
angry and resolute, he gave him an answer:
'Do you hear, sea traveller, what this people are saying?   45
They will give you all spears as tribute,
deadly spear-point and heirloom sword,
the heriot that will not aid you in the battle.
Viking messenger, take back this response
and deliver to your men a much more pointed reply,   50
that here stands undiminished an earl with his troop:
one who intends to defend this homeland,
my lord King Æthelred's country,
land and people. Pagans must fall in battle!
It seems to me too shameful   55
that you will take our money and return to your ships,
without a fight, now that you have come in so far
onto this our land.
You should not acquire our treasure so easily:
point of spear and edge of sword must reconcile us first,   60
the grim play of battle, rather than we pay tribute.'

> Het þa bord beran,   beornas gangan,
> þæt hi on þam easteðe   ealle stodon.
> Ne mihte þær for wætere   werod to þam oðrum;
> þær com flowende   flod æfter ebban,   65
> lucon lagustreamas.   To lang hit him þuhte,
> hwænne hi togædere   garas beron.

HE ORDERED SHIELDS TO BE CARRIED, men to advance,
until they all stood on the riverbank.
Because of the water the one army could not reach the other.
Then came flowing the flood-tide after the ebb,   65
ocean-streams locked together. Too long, it seemed to them,
before they would bear their spears together.

Hi þær Pantan stream   mid prasse bestodon,
Eastseaxena ord   and se æschere.
Ne mihte hyra ænig   oþrum derian,   70
buton hwa þurh flanes   flyht fyl genam.

THERE BY PANTA STREAM they stood in force,
the vanguard of the East Saxons and the Viking army:
neither of them could harm the other,   70
except if death took them through the flight of an arrow.

Se flod ut gewat;   þa flotan stodon gearowe,
wicinga fela,   wiges georne.

THE TIDE WENT OUT: the men of the sea stood ready,
many Vikings, eager for war.

Het þa hæleða hleo   healdan þa bricge
wigan wigheardne,   se wæs haten Wulfstan,   75
cafne mid his cynne,   þæt wæs Ceolan sunu,
þe ðone forman man   mid his francan ofsceat
þe þær baldlicost   on þa bricge stop.
þær stodon mid Wulfstane   wigan unforhte,
Ælfere and Maccus,   modige twegen,   80
þa noldon æt þam forda   fleam gewyrcan,
ac hi fæstlice   wið ða fynd weredon,
þa hwile þe hi wæpna   wealdan moston.
Þa hi þæt ongeaton   and georne gesawon
þæt hi þær bricgweardas   bitere fundon,   85
ongunnon lytegian   þa laðe gystas,
bædon þæt hi upgang   agan moston,
ofer þone ford faran,   feþan lædan.

THEN THE PROTECTOR OF HEROES ordered the bridge to be held
by a veteran warrior, whose name was Wulfstan,   75
bold in war as were many of his kindred, this was Ceola's son,
who shot down with his spear the foremost man
who was bold enough to step onto the bridge.
There with Wulfstan stood the fearless fighters
Ælfere and Maccus, two brave men   80
who refused to take flight at the ford
and instead doggedly defended themselves against their enemies
for the time that they were permitted to wield weapons.

When they acknowledged this and clearly realized
that they found the guardians there on the bridge too fierce   85
then the hostile guests devised a plan:
they asked that they be allowed access,
to lead their men over and to cross the ford.

Ða se eorl ongan   for his ofermode
alyfan landes to fela   laþere ðeode.   90
Ongan ceallian þa   ofer cald wæter
Byrhtelmes bearn,   beornas gehlyston:
'Nu eow is gerymed,   gað ricene to us,
guman to guþe;   God ana wat
wa þære wælstowe wealdan mote.'   95

THEN BECAUSE OF HIS PRIDE, the earl granted
too much land to that hostile nation.   90
He called out across the cold water,
Byrhthelm's son, and the men listened:
'Now the way is open to you, come quickly to us,
as men to battle; God alone knows
who will control this battlefield.'   95

Wodon þa wælwulfas,   for wætere ne murnon,
wicinga werod,   west ofer Pantan,
ofer scir wæter   scyldas wegon,
lidmen to lande   linde bæron,
þær ongean gramum   gearowe stodon –   100

THE WOLVES OF BATTLE CAME ON, caring little for the water,
the troop of Vikings, west over Panta,
over the bright water they carried their shields,
the men of the sea bore their linden wood to land,
where against the hostile men stood –   100

Byrhtnoð mid beornum;   he mid bordum het
wyrcan þone wihagan   and þæt werod healdan
fæste wið feondum.   Þa wæs feohte neh,
tir æt getohte.   Wæs seo tid cumen
þæt þær fæge men   feallan sceoldon.   105
Þær wearð hream ahafen,   hremmas wundon,
earn æses georn;   wæs on eorþan cyrm.

BYRHTNOTH AND HIS MEN, ready and waiting: he ordered them
to make the 'battle fence' formation with their shields and hold it
firmly against their enemies. Then it was near to fighting,
glory in battle. The time had come
when fated men must fall.   105
A clamour was raised, ravens circled,
eagle ready for carrion; on earth there was noise.

> Hi leton þa of folman feolhearde speru,
> gegrundene garas fleogan;
> bogan wæron bysige, bord ord onfeng.   110
> Biter wæs se beaduræs, beornas feollon
> on gehwæðere hand, hyssas lagon.

THEY LET FLY FROM THEIR HANDS the file-hardened spears,
the sharpened javelins;
bows were busy, shield received spear-point.   110
The rush of battle was fierce, fighting men fell,
warriors lay on either side.

> Wund wearð Wulfmær, wælræste geceas,
> Byrhtnoðes mæg; he mid billum wearð,
> his swuster sunu, swiðe forheawen.   115
> Þær wearð wicingum wiþerlean agyfen.
> Gehyrde ic þæt Eadweard anne sloge
> swiðe mid his swurde, swenges ne wyrnde,
> þæt him æt fotum feoll fæge cempa;
> þæs him his ðeoden þanc gesæde,   120
> þam burþene, þa he byre hæfde.

WULFMÆR WAS WOUNDED, chose his resting-place in the battle,
Byrhtnoth's kinsman, his sister's son;
the swords cut him down fiercely,   115
but the Vikings were given requital.
I heard that Edward struck one of them
fiercely with his sword, nor did he withhold the blow,
so that the fated warrior fell at his feet;
for which his prince declared his thanks   120
to his chamberlain, when he had the opportunity.

> Swa stemnetton stiðhicgende
> hysas æt hilde, hogodon georne
> hwa þær mid orde ærost mihte

on fægean men   feorh gewinnan,   125
wigan mid wæpnum;   wæl feol on eorðan.
Stodon stædefæste;   stihte hi Byrhtnoð,
bæd þæt hyssa gehwylc   hogode to wige
þe on Denon wolde   dom gefeohtan.

So THEY PREVAILED, sternly determined,
the men in battle, they directed their thoughts eagerly
as to who first at weapon point
would win a life from fated warriors,   125
men at arms; the dead fell to the earth.
Steadfast they stood, Byrhtnoth encouraged them,
commanded that all his men direct their thoughts to the fight
if they wished to gain glory against the Danes.

Wod þa wiges heard,   wæpen up ahof,
bord to gebeorge,   and wið þæs beornes stop.
Eode swa anræd   eorl to þam ceorle,
ægþer hyra oðrum   yfeles hogode.
Sende ða se særinc   suþerne gar,
þæt gewundod wearð   wigena hlaford;   135
he sceaf þa mid ðam scylde,   þæt se sceaft tobærst,
and þæt spere sprengde,   þæt hit sprang ongean.
Gegremod wearð se guðrinc;   he mid gare stang
wlancne wicing,   þe him þa wunde forgeaf.
Frod wæs se fyrdrinc;   he let his francan wadan   140
þurh ðæs hysses hals,   hand wisode
þæt he on þam færsceaðan   feorh geræhte.

THEN A BATTLE-HARDENED WARRIOR CAME ON, raised his weapon,   130
his shield for protection, and advanced toward the nobleman.
Just as resolute the earl advanced on this churl
each intended evil to the other.
Then the sea-warrior sent out his spear of southern design
so that the lord of men was wounded,   135
but he pushed with his shield so that the shaft broke,
and the spear vibrated so that it sprang out again.
The battle-warrior became enraged; with his spear he stabbed
the proud Viking who had given him the wound.
The *fyrd*-warrior was experienced; he caused his spear   140
to go through the man's neck, his hand guided him
so that he reached the life of the sudden assailant.

Ða he oþerne   ofstlice sceat,
þæt seo byrne tobærst;   he wæs on breostum wund
þurh ða hringlocan,   him æt heortan stod   145
ætterne ord.   Se eorl wæs þe bliþra,
hloh þa, modi man,   sæde Metode þanc
ðæs dægweorces   þe him Drihten forgeaf.

THEN HE STABBED ANOTHER quickly,
so that his coat of mail burst apart; he was wounded in the breast
through the interlocking rings, the deadly point stood at his heart. 145
The earl was all the happier,
he laughed, the courageous man, gave thanks to God
for the day's handiwork which the Lord had granted him.

Forlet þa drenga sum   daroð of handa,
fleogan of folman,   þæt se to forð gewat   150
þurh ðone æþelan   Æþelredes þegen.
Him be healfe stod   hyse unweaxen,
cniht on gecampe,   se full caflice
bræd of þam beorne   blodigne gar,
Wulfstanes bearn, Wulfmær se geonga,   155
forlet forheardne   faran eft ongean;
ord in gewod,   þæt se on eorþan læg
þe his þeoden ær   þearle geræhte.
Eode þa gesyrwed   secg to þam eorle;
he wolde þæs beornes   beagas gefecgan,   160
reaf and hringas   and gerenod swurd.

THEN ONE OF THE VIKINGS launched a javelin,
flying from his hands, which advanced too far   150
through Æþelred's noble thegn.
At his side in the battle stood a youth not fully grown,
a retainer in the household, who most bravely
drew out the bloody spear from the nobleman;
this was Wulfstan's son, Wulfmær the Young,   155
who sent the hard weapon flying back,
the point went in, so that he lay on the earth,
the one who had so grievously wounded his prince.
Then an armed man moved towards the earl;
he intended to carry off the prince's arm-bands,   160
garment and rings and embellished sword.

Þa Byrhtnoð bræd   bill of sceðe,
brad and bruneccg,   and on þa byrnan sloh.
To raþe hine gelette   lidmanna sum,
þa he þæs eorles   earm amyrde.   165
Feoll þa to foldan   fealohilte swurd;
ne mihte he gehealdan   heardne mece,
wæpnes wealdan.   Þa gyt þæt word gecwæð
har hilderinc,   hyssas bylde,
bæd gangan forð   gode geferan;   170
ne mihte þa on fotum leng   fæste gestandan.
He to heofenum wlat:
'Geþancie þe,   ðeoda waldend,
ealra þæra wynna   þe ic on worulde gebad.
Nu ic ah, milde Metod,   mæste þearfe   175
þæt þu minum gaste   godes geunne,
þæt min sawul to ðe   siðian mote
on þin geweald,   þeoden engla,
mid friþe ferian.   Ic eom frymdi to þe
þæt hi helsceaðan   hynan ne moton.'   180

THEN BYRHTNOTH DREW HIS SWORD from its sheath,
broad and bright-edged, and struck at the man's mailcoat.
Too easily he was hindered by one of the seamen,
when he wounded the earl in the arm.   165
It fell to the earth – the golden-hilted sword;
he could no longer hold the fierce blade,
or wield any weapon. But still he spoke this speech,
the grey-haired warrior, encouraged the men,
commanded the good companions to advance,   170
but he could no longer stand firmly on his feet,
and he looked to the heavens:
'I thank you, Ruler of nations,
for all the joys that I have experienced in this world.
Now, gracious God, I have great need   175
that you might grant my spirit bliss,
so that my soul may make its journey to you,
into your power, O King of Angels,
that it may journey in peace [i.e. with *frith*, protection],
that the assailants of hell, I beseech you, may not harm it.   180

Ða hine heowon   hæðene scealcas
and begen þa beornas   þe him big stodon,

Ælfnoð and Wulmær begen lagon,
ða onemn hyra frean feorh gesealdon.

THEN THEY SLEW HIM – the heathen warriors –
and with him the two men who stood by him:
there lay both Ælfnoth and Wulmær,
who gave up their lives alongside their lord.

Hi bugon þa fram beaduwe   þe þær beon noldon,   185
þær wearð Oddan bearn   ærest on fleame,
Godric fram guþe,   and þone godan forlet
þe him mænigne oft   mear gesealde.
he gehleop þone eoh   þe ahte his hlaford,
on þam geræedum   þe hit riht ne wæs,   190
and his broðru mid him   begen ærndon,
Godwine and Godwig,   guþe ne gymdon,
ac wendon fram þam wige   and þone wudu sohton,
flugon on þæt fæsten   and hyra feore burgon,
and manna ma   þonne hit ænig mæð wære,   195
gyf hi þa geearnunga   ealle gemundon
þe he him to duguþe   gedon hæfde.
Swa him Offa on dæg   ær asæde
on þam meþelstede,   þa he gemot hæfde,
þæt þær modiglice   manega spræcon   200
þe eft æt þearfe   þolian noldon.

THEN THEY TURNED FROM THE BATTLE – those who did not want to be
    there –   185
Odda's son was the first in flight –
Godric fled the battle and abandoned the good prince
who had often given him many a horse:
he mounted the steed that his lord had owned,
with all its harness and trappings, though it was not a just action,   190
and his brothers both ran off with him,
Godwine and Godwig, who did not care for battle
but turned from the war and sought the woods,
flew to safety and protected their lives,
and many more of them than was in any way fitting,   195
if they had remembered all the favours
that he had done for their benefit.
So Offa had declared that day
at the place of parley, when they had had their council,

that many there spoke boldly   200
who afterwards in time of need would be unwilling to endure.

    Þa wearð afeallen   þæs folces ealdor,
    Æþelredes eorl;   ealle gesawon
    heorðgeneatas   þæt hyra heorra læg.
    Þa ðær wendon forð   wlance þegenas,   205
    unearge men   efston georne;
    hi woldon þa ealle   oðer twega,
    lif forlætan oððe   leofne gewrecan.

So the leader of the people had now fallen,
Æthelred's earl; all the hearth companions
saw that their leader lay there.
And so the proud thegns went forward,   205
undaunted men, they hastened eagerly:
they all wanted one of two things:
to relinquish their lives or avenge the man who was dear to them.

    Swa hi bylde forð   bearn Ælfrices,
    wiga wintrum geong,   wordum mælde,   210
    Ælfwine þa cwæð,   he on ellen spræc.
    'Gemunu þa mæla   þe we oft æt meodo spræcon,
    þonne we on bence   beot ahofon,
    hæleð on healle,   ymbe heard gewinn;
    nu mæg cunnian   hwa cene sy.   215
    Ic wylle mine æþelo   eallum gecyþan,
    þæt ic wæs on Myrcon   miccles cynnes;
    wæs min ealda fæder   Ealhelm haten,
    wis ealdorman,   woruldgesælig.
    Ne sceolon me on þære þeode   þegenas ætwitan   220
    þæt ic of ðisse fyrde   feran wille,
    eard gesecan,   nu min ealdor ligeð
    forheawen æt hilde.   Me is þæt hearma mæst;
    he wæs ægðer min mæg   and min hlaford.'
    Þa he forð eode,   fæhðe gemunde   225
    þæt he mid orde   anne geræhte
    flotan on þam folce,   þæt se on foldan læg
    forwegen mid his wæpne.   Ongan þa winas manian,
    frynd and geferan,   þæt hi forð eodon.

So he encouraged them, the son of Ælfric,
[he was] a warrior young in winters, these words he declared,   210
Ælfwine then said – speaking boldly:
'I remember the times when we often talked at the mead-drinking,
when as we sat on the benches we made our promises,
men in the hall, about the hard fighting ahead,
and now whoever claims to be brave may prove it to the test.   215
I wish to declare my lineage to all:
that I was from a great kindred in Mercia.
My grandfather was called Ealhhelm,
a wise ealdorman and prosperous in the world.
and none of the thegns in that nation may reproach me   220
with wanting to desert this army
or seek out my own country, now that my prince lies
slain in battle. For me it is the greatest of sorrows,
for he was both my kinsman and my lord.'
Then he went forward – directing his mind to the feud,   225
so that with his spear he wounded
a seaman in the crowd, who lay there on the earth,
killed by this weapon. He urged his fellows,
friends and companions that they move forward.

    Offa gemælde,   æscholt asceoc: 230
    'Hwæt þu, Ælfwine,   hafast ealle gemanode
    þegenas to þearfe.   Nu ure þeoden lið,
    eorl on eorðan,   us is eallum þearf
    þæt ure æghwylc   oþerne bylde
    wigan to wige,   þa hwile þe he wæpen mæge   235
    habban and healdan,   heardne mece,
    gar and god swurd.   Us Godric hæfð,
    earh Oddan bearn,   ealle beswicene.
    Wende þæs formoni man,   þa he on meare rad,
    on wlancan þam wicge,   þæt wære hit ure hlaford;   240
    forþan wearð her on felda   folc totwæmed,
    scyldburh tobrocen.   Abreoðe his angin,
    þæt he her swa manigne   man aflymde!'

Offa made a speech, brandishing his ash-wood: 230
'So, Ælfwine, you have exhorted
all the thegns for our good now that our prince lies there,

the earl on the earth, it is good for us all
that each encourage the other
as warriors in war, for as long as we are able   235
to have and hold our weapons,
the hard sword, the spear and the trusty blade: Godric,
cowardly son of Odda, has betrayed us all.
Many men supposed, when he rode off on the horse,
on the proud steed, that it was our prince [who fled],   240
and so the people in the field were divided
and the shield wall was broken. May all his enterprise fail,
that he caused so many men to flee!'

    Leofsunu gemælde   and his linde ahof,
    bord to gebeorge;   he þam beorne oncwæð   245
    'Ic þæt gehate,   þæt ic heonon nelle
    fleon fotes trym,   ac wille furðor gan,
    wrecan on gewinne   minne winedrihten.
    Ne þurfon me embe Sturmere   stedefæste hælæð
    wordum ætwitan,   nu min wine gecranc,   250
    þæt ic hlafordleas   ham siðie,
    wende fram wige,   ac me sceal wæpen niman,
    ord and iren.'   He ful yrre wod,
    feaht fæstlice,   fleam he forhogode.

Leofsunu made a speech, and raised his linden wood
shield for protection, he replied to the nobleman: 245
'I promise this: that I will not flee from here,
not even a footstep, but will advance further,
avenge in the fight my friend-and-lord.
The steadfast warriors of Sturmer will not be able
to utter accusing words, now that my friend has fallen,   250
that I would return home lordless, desert the battle;
instead weapon must take me,
point and iron.' He advanced in anger,
fought firmly, disdained flight.

    Dunnere þa cwæð,   daroð acwehte,   255
    unorne ceorl, ofer eall clypode,
    bæd þæt beorna gehwylc   Byrhtnoð wræce:
    'Ne mæg na wandian   se þe wrecan þenceð
    frean on folce, ne for feore murnan.'

Þa hi forð eodon,   feores hi ne rohton;   260
ongunnon þa hiredmen   heardlice feohtan,
grame garberend,   and God bædon
þæt hi moston gewrecan   hyra winedrihten
and on hyra feondum   fyl gewyrcan.

Dunnere then spoke, shook his spear,   255
a simple landowner, called out over all,
and demanded that each of the men should avenge Byrhtnoth,
'A man must not flinch, if he intends to avenge
his lord among the people, nor must he worry about his life.'
Then they advanced forward, they did not care for their lives;   260
the household men fought hard,
the fierce spear-bearers, and they prayed to God
that they might be able to avenge their lord
and bring about the fall of their enemies.

Him se gysel ongan   geornlice fylstan;   265
he wæs on Norðhymbron   heardes cynnes,
Ecglafes bearn,   him wæs Æscferð nama.
He ne wandode na   æt þam wigplegan,
ac he fysde forð   flan genehe;
hwilon he on bord sceat,   hwilon beorn tæsde,   270
æfre embe stunde   he sealde sume wunde,
þa hwile ðe he wæpna   wealdan moste.

As for the hostage, he helped them eagerly;   265
he was from a fierce hard kindred in Northumbria,
Ecglaf's son, his name was Æscferth:
he did not flinch from the play of battle,
but shot forth frequent arrows;
at times he struck a shield, at times he hit a man;   270
repeatedly he dealt out wounds
for as long as he was permitted to wield his weapons.

Þa gyt on orde stod   Eadweard se langa,
gearo and geornful,   gylpwordum spræc
þæt he nolde fleogan   fotmæl landes,   275
ofer bæc bugan,   þa his betera leg.
He bræc þone bordweall   and wið þa beornas feaht,
oðþæt he his sincgyfan   on þam sæmannum
wurðlice wrec,   ær he on wæle læge.

STILL THERE STOOD IN THE VANGUARD Edward the Tall,
ready and waiting, he spoke with boastful words
that he would not flee, not the space of a foot of land,   275
nor would he turn back now that his lord lay there.
He broke the Viking shield wall and fought with the warriors
until he had avenged his treasure-giver on the men of the sea,
worthily, before he too lay among the dead.

    Swa dyde Æþeric,   æþele gefera,   280
    fus and forðgeorn,   feaht eornoste.
    Sibyrhtes broðor   and swiðe mænig oþer
    clufon cellod bord,   cene hi weredon;
    bærst bordes lærig,   and seo byrne sang
    gryreleoða sum.   Þa æt guðe sloh   285
    Offa þone sælidan,   þæt he on eorðan feoll.
    And ðær Gaddes mæg   grund gesohte:
    raðe wearð æt hilde   Offa forheawen;
    he hæfde ðeah geforþod   þæt he his frean gehet,
    swa he beotode ær   wið his beahgifan
    þæt hi sceoldon begen   on burh ridan,
    hale to hame,   oððe on here crincgan,
    on wælstowe   wundum sweltan;
    he læg ðegenlice   ðeodne gehende.

LIKEWISE ÆTHERIC, a noble companion,   280
ready and eager to go forth, fought doggedly.
Sibyrht's brother and many another
cleaved the decorated shield; they defended bravely,
the rim of the shield burst, and the mailcoat sang
a terrifying song. Then in the battle   285
Offa struck the seaman so that he fell to the earth.
And there Gadd's kinsman went to ground:
quickly in the battle Offa was cut down;
nevertheless he had accomplished what he had promised his lord,
what he had vowed to his ring-giver: 290
that they would both either ride back to the *burh*,
safe to their home, or fall in the conflict
on the battlefield and die of their wounds;
he lay there in a thegnly manner close to his *theoden*.

    Ða wearð borda gebræc.   Brimmen wodon   295
    guðe gegremode;   gar oft þurhwod

fæges feorhhus.   Forð þa eode Wistan,
Þurstanes sunu,   wið þas secgas feaht;
he wæs on geþrange   hyra þreora bana,
ær him Wigelmes bearn   on þam wæle læge.   300
Þær wæs stið gemot;   stodon fæste
wigan on gewinne,   wigend cruncon,
wundum werige.   Wæl feol on eorþan.

Then there was a breaking of shields. The seamen came on,   295
enraged by the battle. Spear often passed
through fated house-of-life. Then Wigstan went forth
[while] Thurstan's son was fighting against those warriors.
In the press Wighelm's son was the destroyer of three
before he too lay among the dead.   300
That was a stern council there. They stood firm,
soldiers in battle. Warriors fell,
weary with wounds. The dead fell to the earth.

Oswold and Eadwold   ealle hwile,
begen þa gebroþru,   beornas trymedon,   305
hyra winemagas   wordon bædon
þæt hi þær æt ðearfe   þolian sceoldon,
unwaclice   wæpna neotan.

Oswold and Eadwold all the time,
the two brothers, arranged the men,   305
their friends and kinsmen, issued words of command
that in this moment of need they would have to endure,
using their weapons with courage.

Byrhtwold maþelode,   bord hafenode
(se wæs eald geneat),   æsc acwehte;   310
he ful baldlice   beornas lærde:
'Hige sceal þe heardra,   heorte þe cenre,
mod sceal þe mare,   þe ure mægen lytlað.
Her lið ure ealdor   eall forheawen,
god on greote.   A mæg gnornian   315
se ðe nu fram þis wigplegan   wendan þenceð.
Ic eom frod feores;   fram ic ne wille,
ac ic me be healfe   minum hlaforde,
be swa leofan men,   licgan þence.'
Swa hi Æþelgares bearn   ealle bylde,   320

Godric to guþe.   Oft he gar forlet,
wælspere windan   on þa wicingas,
swa he on þam folce   fyrmest eode,
heow and hynde,   oðþæt he on hilde gecranc.
Næs þæt na se Godric   þe ða guðe forbeah.   325

BYRHTWOLD MADE A SPEECH, raised his shield,
(he was an old retainer), brandished his ash-wood;   310
very bravely he exhorted the men:
'Thought must be harder, heart the keener,
courage the greater, as our strength diminishes.
Here lies our prince, cut down by swords,
a good man on the ground. A man will regret it forever   315
if he means to turn from the battle-play now.
I have some experience in life. And I will not go from here,
instead I mean to lie next to my lord,
a man who we held in such great affection.'
Æthelgar's son Godric encouraged them all   320
in the battle. He often sent his javelin
and deadly spear flying at the Vikings,
and advanced foremost among the people,
struck and slew until he fell in the fighting.
This was not the Godric who deserted the battle.   325

Appendix 2 'The Battle of the Holme'

Text and translation

From version B of the Anglo-Saxon Chronicle (London, British Library, Cotton Tiberius A. vi). The punctuation of the text has been modernized, and abbreviations have been expanded.

The year 901

Her gefor Ælfred Aþulfing syx nihtum ær Ealra Haligra mæssan, se wæs cing ofer eall Angelcynn butan þam dæle ðe under Dene anwealde wæs, and he heold þæt rice oþrum healfum geare læs þe þritig wintra. And þa feng Eadweard his sunu to rice. And þa gerad Æþelwold æþeling his fædran sunu þone ham æt Winburnan, and æt Tweoxneam, þæs cinges unþances and his witena. Þa rad se cing mid fyrde þæt he gewicode æt Baddanbyrig wiþ Winburnan. And Aþolwold sæt binnan þam ham mid þam mannum þe him to gebugan, and hæfde ealle þa gatu forworhte inn to him, and sæde þæt he wolde oþþe þær lybban oþþe þær licggean. Þa under ðam þa rad se æþeling on niht aweg and gesohte þone here on Norðhymbrum, and hie hine underfengon heom to cinge and him to bugan. Þa berad man þæt wif þæt he hæfde ær genumen butan ðæs cinges leafe and ofer þara bisceopa gebodu, forðon þe heo wæs nunne ær gehalgod. And on þys ilcan geare forðferde Æþered, se wæs on Defnum ealdormann, feower wucan ær Ælfred cing.

[Here Alfred Æthewulfing departed this life, six nights before the Feast of All Hallows, who was king over all the English nation except for the part that was under Danish dominion, and he ruled that kingdom for thirty winters less half a year.[1] And so Edward his son succeeded to the kingdom. And then the ætheling Æthelwold, Alfred's nephew, occupied the residence at Wimbourne and Twinnam, against the permission of the king and his counsellors.[2] And then the king rode with the defence-force and duly camped at Badbury opposite Wimbourne. Æthelwold remained in the residence with the men who had commended themselves to him, and he secured all the gates against them, and said that he would do one of two things: live there or lie there. But in the meanwhile, the atheling rode away by night and met with the Viking army in Northumbria, and they received him as king and became his commended men. But his wife was captured whom he had taken without the king's permission and against the command of the bishop, because she had been consecrated as a nun. And in this same year Æthelred died, who was ealdorman in Devon, four weeks before King Alfred.]

The year 903

Her gefor Aþulf ealdorman, Ealhswiþe broðor, Eadweardes modor cinges, 7 Uirgilius abbud on Scottum ond Grimbold mæssepreost.

[Here Ealdorman Athulf died, brother of Ealhswith, King Edward's mother, and Abbot Virgil in Scotland, and Grimbold the mass-priest.]

The year 904

Her com Aþelwold hider ofer sæ mid eallum þam flotan þe he begitan mihte, and him to gebogen wæs on Eastsexum.

[Here Æthelwold arrived by sea with all the ships he was able to obtain, and they submitted to him in Essex.][3]

The year 905

Her gelædde Æþelwold þone here on Eastenglum to unfriþe, þæt hie hergodan ofer eall Myrcna land þæt hie coman to Cracgelade, and foran þær ofer Temese and naman ægþer ge on Bradene ge þær onbutan eal þæt hie gehentan mihtan, ond wendon þa eft hamweard. Ða for Eadweard cing æfter, swa he raðost mihte his fyrde gegaderian, and oferhergode eall heora land betuh dicon and Wusan eall oþ fennas norð. Ða he eft þonon faran wolde, þa het he beodan ofer ealle ða fyrd, þæt hie foran ealle ut ætsamne. Ða ætsætan ða Centiscan þær beæftan ofer his bebod and seofon ærendracan he him hæfde to onsend. Þa befor se here hie þær, and hie þær gefuhtan, and þær wearð Sigulf ealdormann ofslegen and Sigelm ealdormann and Eadwold cinges þegn and Cenulf abbud and Sigebriht Sigulfes sunu and Eadwold Accan sunu and manige eac to him, þeah ic þa geþungenestan nemde. And on ðara Deniscra healfe wæs ofslegen Eohric cing and Aþelwold æþeling, þe hie him to cinge gecuron, and Byrhsige, Byrhtnoðes sunu æþelinges, and Ysopo hold and Oscytel hold and swiþe manig eac mid him, þe we nu genemnan ne magon. And þær wæs on gehweþere hand mycel wæl geslegen, and þara Deniscra wearð ma ofslegen, þeah hi wælstowe geweald ahton. And Ealhswiþ gefor þy ilcan geare.

[Here Æthelwold led the Host to war in Essex, so that they plundered all the way through Mercia until they came to Cricklade, and there they crossed the Thames and seized all that they could in Braydon and the surrounding area, and then turned for home. Edward then pursued them, as quickly as he could gather his defence force, and he plundered all their land between the dykes and all the Ouse as far as the northern Fens. When he (Edward) wanted to retreat from there, he sent out orders throughout all the defence force that they should all retire together. But the Kentishmen remained in their rearguard position in defiance of his order, though he had sent seven messengers to them. Then the Host came upon them there, and there they fought. And there Ealdorman Sigulf was slain, and Ealdorman Sigelm and Eadwold the king's thegn, and Abbot Cenulf (Cenwulf) and Sigebriht Sigewulf's son, and Eadwold Acca's son, and many others with them, though I have named only the most distinguished. And on the Danish side King Eohric, the ætheling Æthelwold that they had elected as their king, and Byrhtsige, the son of the ætheling Byrhtnoth, and Ysopo the *holdr*, and Oscytel the *holdr*, and many others with them, though we cannot name them all now. And there was slain there a great number on each side, and more of the Danes were slain, although they held possession of the battlefield.]

Appendix 3 The case of Æthelric of Bocking

Text and translation

The evidence for the historical Byrhtnoth's landholdings has been intensely studied: we do not have all the information, but various charters, the three wills of his wife's family, and the evidence of *The Life of St Oswald* and *The Book of Ely* give a representative picture.[1] For those interested in the historical Byrhtnoth, the story of his estates is illuminating, for we are given a view of the chain of lands that Byrhtnoth and his wife held in the 970s and 980s in south-eastern Suffolk and north-eastern Essex, all very close together, many of them barely four miles apart. Starting at the mouth of the Stour estuary, at what is now the seaport of Harwich, a walker or rider could travel westwards through Byrhtnoth's family lands, through Dovercourt (in his wife Ælfflæd's will named in OE as Douorcort) and Beaumont (Fulanpettæ) then up the river Stour as far as Stratford St Mary (Stredfordæ) and Stoke-by-Nayland, site of the family church. Striking north then across the river, the traveller would pass through the estates of Withermarsh (Wifærmyrsc), Polstead (Polstyde) and so on through a number of now picturesque rural villages on the route northwards to Bury St Edmunds: Elmsett (Ylmesætun), Chelsworth (Cæorlesweorthæ), Monks Eleigh (Illanlege), Lavenham (Lauanham), Balsdon Hall (Byliesdyne), Cockfield (Cochanfelde).[2] The latter village is now on the road to the A1141, about 6 miles south of Bury St Edmunds.

The couple held further land elsewhere in Essex. There is a cluster of properties south of Colchester moving southwards through Peldon, Fingringhoe and Alresford to the (already mentioned) island of Mersea, which was strategically located for defending both the mouth of the Colne estuary leading upstream to the port of Colchester and the Blackwater leading up to Maldon. Moving westwards from Colchester, the family owned more land. Broadly along the old Roman road of Stane Street that connected Colchester to Ermine Street near Hertford, a rider would have passed through another line of connected estates belonging to Byrhtnoth and his family: Lexden, Stanway, Tey and Colne. Just west of Braintree, further along the Roman road – and past the estate of Baythorn (Babbingþyrnan), also held by Ælfflæd – is Bocking, the manorial seat of the famous, or rather perhaps infamous, Æthelric of Bocking, a local thegn who was accused posthumously of treason and treachery, plotting to receive Swegn, king of the Danes, in Essex in the early 990s, around the time of the Maldon campaign.

The case concerning Æthelric (spelled in the texts without the 'l' as Æþeric) was recorded in two documents, and the man's widow eventually managed to persuade the king to drop the 'terrible accusation'.[3] The case illustrates the

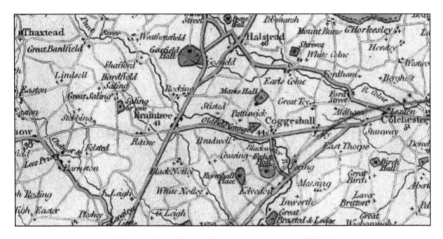

Map 5 Estates and villages along Stane Street to the west of Colchester.

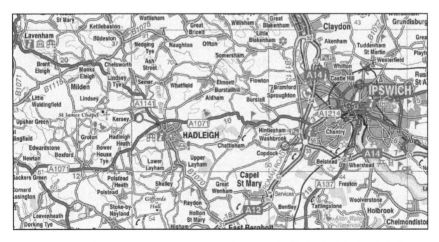

Map 6 Map of Suffolk, including Lavenham, Chelsworth, Stoke-by-Nayland. Ordnance Survey. © Crown Copyright.

mixed motives of the men of East Anglia, some of whom had distant family connections with the Danes, and it also serves to explain further the betrayal of Godric and the sons of Odda, as told in *Maldon*. Men fighting for their land in Essex or East Anglia did not necessarily want to resist the Danes if they felt they had cultural connections or kinship with them. There is of course also an Æthelric in the poem, described as a 'noble companion' who 'fought eagerly' (*Maldon*, 280–1), but there is nothing to indicate that this could be the same Æthelric. The *Maldon* Æthelric (also spelled without the 'l' as Æþeric) fights alongside his brother, a certain Sibyrht (282a). It may or may not be significant, but coincidentally, Byrhtnoth's sister-in-law Æthelflæd also had a kinsman of the same name, Sibriht, to whom she granted ten hides of land at Wickford, situated just south of Rettendon.[4]

The will of Æthelric of Bocking[5]

Her cyð Æþeric on þissum gewrite hwam he geann ofor his dæig þæra æhta þe him god alæned hæfð; þæt is ærest sona minum hlaforde, syxti mancusa goldes, and mines swyrdes mid fetele, and þarto twa hors, and twa targan, and twegen francan.

[Here Æthelric makes known in this document whom he will grant after his day the possessions that God has loaned him: that is, first, immediately, to my lord: sixty mancuses of gold, and my sword with the belt, and in addition to that: two horses, two shields and two spears.]

And ic geann Leofwynne minan wife ealles þæs þe ic læfe hire dæig; and ofor hire dæg, gange þæt land on Boccinge into Cristes circean þam hirede for uncera saule and for mines fæder þe hit ær begeat; eall buton anre hide ic gean into þære cyrcean þam preoste þe þar Gode þeowaþ.[6]

[And I grant to Leofwynn my wife everything that I leave, for her lifetime; and after her day the land at Bocking is to go to Christ Church, to the community, for our souls and for the soul of my father who previously acquired it; all except one hide which I grant to the church to the priest who serves God there.][7]

And ic geann þæs landes æt Rægene be westan. into sancte Paule þam bisceope to to geleohtenne. and þar on godes folce cristendom to dælenne. and ic geann þarto twegra hida þe Eadric gafelaþ ælce geare mid healfum punde and mid anre garan. and ic geann be eastan stræte ægþer ge wudas ge feldas Ælfstane bisceope into Coppanforde. and þæs heges on Glæsne.

[And I grant the land at Rayne – westwards along Stane Street[8] – to St Paul's for the Bishop, to provide lighting and to deliver Christianity to God's people there; and besides this I grant the two hides that Eadric rents every year for half a pound and one gore.[9] And I grant – eastwards along Stane Street – both the woods and the fields – to Copford for Bishop Ælfstan, along with the enclosure at Glazen.]

And ic geann þæs landes æt Norðho, healf into sancte Gregorie, on Suþbyrig, and healf into sancte Eadmunde on Bedericeswyrþe.

[And I grant the estate at Northho: half to St Gregory's at Sudbury, and half to St Edmund's at Bedericesworth.][10]

Nu bidde ic þone bisceop Ælfstan. þæt he amundige mine lafe and þa þincg þe ic hyre læfe. and gif him God lifes geunne lencg þonne unc þæt he gefultumige þæt ælc þara þinga stande þe ic gecweden hæbbe.

[Now I pray Bishop Ælfstan that he will protect my widow and the things which I leave to her, and, if God grants longer life to him than to us, that he will help so that each of the bequests may stand which I have made.]

King Æthelred's confirmation of the will of Æthelric of Bocking[11]

Her swutelað on þison gewrite hu Æðelred kyning geuðe þæt Æþerices cwyde æt Boccinge standan moste.

[Here is declared in this document how king Æthelred granted that Æthelric's will should be allowed to stand.]

Hit wæs manegon earon ær Æðeric forðferde þæt ðam kincge wæs gesæd þæt he wære on þam unræde þæt man sceolde on Eastsexon Swegen underfon ða he ærest þyder mid flotan com. and se cincg hit on mycele gewitnysse Sigerice arcebiscope cyðde þe his forespeca þa wæs for ðæs landes þingon æt Boccinge ðe he into Cristes cyrcean becweden hæfde.

[It was many years before Æthelric passed away that the king was told that he had been in the plot to receive Swegn in Essex when he first came there with a fleet. And in the presence of many witnesses the king made it known to Archbishop Sigeric, who at the time was Æthelric's advocate on the matter of the land at Bocking which he had left to Christchurch.]

Þa wæs he þisse spæce ægþer ge on life. ge æfter ungeladod ge ungebétt oð his laf his hergeatu þam cincge to Cócham brohte þær he his witan widan gesomnod hæfde.

[But then, during his life or afterwards, he was neither acquitted nor did he atone for the crime, until his widow brought his heriot to the king at Cookham, where he had summoned his counsellors from far and wide.]

Þa wolde se cing ða spæce beforan eallon his witan uphebban. and cwæð þæt Leofsige ealdorman. and mænige men þære spæce gecnæwe wæron.

[Then the king wished to raise the matter before all his counsellors, and he said that Ealdorman Leofsige and many men were familiar with the terms of the charge.]

Þa bad seo wuduwe Ælfric arcebisceop, ðe hire forespeca wæs, and Æðelmær þæt hig þone cincg bædon þæt heo moste gesyllan hire morgengyfe into Christes cyrcean for ðone cincg, and ealne his leodscype wið ðam ðe se cing ða egeslican onspæce alete. and his cwyde standan moste þæt is swa hit herbeforan cwyð, þæt land æt Boccinge into Christes cyrcean, and his oðre landare into oðran halgan stowan swa his cwyde swutelað.

[Then the widow asked Archbishop Ælfric, who was her advocate, and Æthelmær, that they might petition the king that she could give her morning-gift to Christ Church for the sake of the king and all his people, in return for which the king would withdraw the terrible accusation, and his will might stand, that is, as is said before, the estate at Bocking to Christ Church and his other property to the other holy places, as his will declares.]

Þa God forgylde þam cincge getiðode he ðæs for Christes lufan, and sancta Marian, and sancte Dunstanes, and ealra þæra haligra ðe æt Christes cyrcean restað, þæs costes ðe heo þis gelæste, and his cwyde fæste stode.

[Then (God reward the king!) he granted this, for the love of Christ and saint Mary, and saint Dunstan and all the saints who rest at Christchurch, on condition that she carry this out and that his will might stand firm.]

Þeos swutelung wæs þærrihte gewriten, and beforan þam cincge and þam witon ge)rædd.

[This declaration was immediately written and read out before the king and the counsellors.]

Þis syndon ðæra manna naman ðe ðises to gewittnesse wæron:

[These are the names of the men who are witness to this:]

Ælfric arcebiscop, and Ælfheh biscop on Wintaceastre, and Wulfsige biscop on Dorsæton, and Godwine biscop on Hrofeceastre, and Leofsige ealdorman,[12] and Leofwine ealdorman, and Ælfsige abbod, and Wulfgar abbod, and Byrhtelm abbod, and Lyfincg abbod, and Alfwold abbod, and Æðelmær, and Ordulf, and Wulfget, and Fræna, and Wulfric Wulfrune sunu,[13]

and ealle ða ðegnas ðe þær widan gegæderode wæron ægðer ge of Westsexan, ge of Myrcean, ge of Denon, ge of Englon, þissa gewrita syndon þreo: an is æt Christes cyrcean, oðer æt þæs cinges haligdome, þridde hæfð seo widuwe.

[and all the thegns who had assembled there from far and wide, both West Saxons and Mercians, both Danish and English. There are three of these copies, one is at Christ Church, the other in the king's sanctuary; the widow has the third.][14]

Appendix 4 'The will of Leofwine'

Text and translation

Of all the coincidences and connections that have been found between the poem *The Battle of Maldon*, the likely battle site(s) and the charter evidence, perhaps the most intriguing is the one uncovered by the editors of the so-called *Crawford Charters* and promoted by E. V. Gordon in his edition of the poem.[1] The character in question from the poem is Wulfstan, son of Ceola, whom Byrhtnoth commanded to 'stand and hold' the bridge against all comers (*Maldon*, 74–5). The textual parallel appears in a short will and testament of the year 998, composed by Leofwine, son of Wulfstan, who grants '*of Purlea in to Hnutlea healfere hide landes on easthealf stræte for mine sawle þam Godes þeowan. & minre faþan Leofware þæs heafodbotles on Purlea & ealles þæs þe me þær to locaþ*' (from Purleigh into Notley, to God's servants, half a hide of land on the east side of the paved road, for the sake of my soul. And to my paternal aunt, Leofwaru, the chief building in Purleigh, and all that belongs to me there). Etymologically the name Purleigh itself is made up of the elements *pur* and *leah* and is interpreted by both Watts and Reaney as meaning 'bittern or snipe wood or clearing'.[2] As Watts points out, the element *pur* may refer either to the long-necked bittern, a large bird similar to a heron, or to the snipe, a much smaller bird with a long straight bill, both breeds of bird being common in water margins and marshes.[3] Purleigh was clearly a piece of woodland just above the salt marsh, and this fact is reflected in its name.

Of note is the noun *botl* in the compound *heafodbotl*, which is a prose variant of the more poetic term *bold* meaning 'hall, dwelling-place' that occurs in *Beowulf*, famously describing Hrothgar's hall as *fæger foldbold*, 'fair dwelling on the earth' (773) or Beowulf's own royal hall as his *sylfes ham, bolda selest* 'his own home, best of halls' (2325–6).[4] Also worthy of note is the word *stræt*, which I have translated here as 'paved road' – the term often refers to the long, straight, paved Roman roads that were still essential thoroughfares in the world

Figure 29 The Street at Purleigh, on the edge of the Dengie Peninsula. © Mark Atherton.

of the early middle ages.[5] There is still a road named The Street in Purleigh, which approaches the village from the low-lying salt marsh to the east and ascends the hill to the main village centre and the church at the top of the hill.

The intriguing idea has been raised that the Wulfstan who stood and fought on the bridge, as reported in the poem, is the same as Leofwine's father, who is mentioned in the will. And the house and home which they apparently succeeded in defending came eventually into the possession of Leofwaru, who, according to this interpretation, is the heroic Wulfstan's sister. The sceptic may object that there are too many Wulfstans in the records of the time (there even appear to be two Wulfstans in the poem). Nevertheless the interest lies in the fact that a *heafodbotl* existed in the settlement at Purleigh, only seven years after 'Maldon' was fought, and that this hearth and home can be connected with the families of the kind of men who were present and took part in the battle.

The will of Leofwine

+ In nomine domini nostri Ihesu Cristi. þys is Leofwines cwide Wulfstanes suna . þæt is þonne ærest þæt ic gean Criste 7 sancte Petre for minre saule in to Westmynster ealra þara þinga þe me Crist to gefultumian wyle æt þam

lande æt Cynlaue dyne . 7 æt Mearcyncg seollan on wuda 7 on felda . 7 ic
gean of Purlea in to Hnutlea healfere hide landes on easthealf stræte for mine
sawle þam Godes þeowan . 7 minre faþan Leofware þæs heafodbotles on
Purlea . 7 ealles þæs þe me þær to locaþ . 7 gif Eadwold længc libbe hire
suna þonne heo . fo he þærto . gif heo þonne læng beo 7 þæt God wille sylle
hit on þa hand þe hire æfre betst gehyre on uncer bega cynne . 7 ic gean
minum hlaforde Wulfstane bisceope þæs landes æt Bærlingum. Þys wæs
gedon þæs geares fram ures Drihtnes gebyrdtide. DCCCCXCVIII

[*In the name of our Lord Jesus Christ.* This is Leofwine's will, Wulfstan's son.
That is first, then, that I grant to Christ and to St Peter, for the sake of my
soul, to Westminster: all of the things that Christ may wish to help me to on
the estate at Kelvedon and at Mearcyncg seollan, in wood and in field. And I
grant from Purleigh into Notley, to God's servants, half a hide of land on the
east side of the paved road, for the sake of my soul. And to my paternal aunt,
Leofwaru, the chief building in Purleigh, and all that belongs to me there. And
if her son Eadwold lives longer than she does, let him succeed to it. But if she
should be longer living, and God wills it, then let her give it to whoever obeys
her best among our two kindreds. And I grant to my lord, Bishop Wulfstan, the
estate at Barling. This was done in the year 998 from the birth of our Lord.]

Notes

Introduction

1 Figures in parentheses refer to the line numbers of the poem in the following standard editions: E. V. Gordon, ed., *The Battle of Maldon* (London, 1937); D. G. Scragg, ed., *The Battle of Maldon* (Manchester, 1981); Bill Griffiths, ed., *The Battle of Maldon: Text and Translation* (Pinner, 1993); John C. Pope, ed., *Eight Old English Poems*, 3rd edn, revised by R. D. Fulk (New York and London, 2001). Dr Mark Griffith is working on a new critical edition.

2 Levi Roach, *Æthelred the Unready* (New Haven and London, 2016), pp. 112–67.

3 Simon Keynes, 'The Declining Reputation of King Ethelred the Unready', in David Hill, ed., *Ethelred the Unready*, B.A.R. British Series 59 (Oxford, 1978), pp. 227–53.

4 Gillian R. Overing and Marijane Osborn, *Landscape of Desire: Partial Stories of the Medieval Scandinavian World* (Minneapolis, 1994), p. xv; the notion of 'thicken' is derived from the anthropology of Clifford Geertz – see his 'Thick Description: Toward an Interpretive Theory of Culture', in *The Interpretation of Cultures: Selected Essays* (New York, 1973), pp. 3–30.

5 Cyril Hart, 'The Battle of Maldon', in his *The Danelaw* (London, 1992), pp. 533–51, at p. 535, note 5.

6 P. H. Reaney, *The Place-names of Essex*, English Place-name Society (Cambridge, 1935), pp. 9–10 and 282.

7 For a text, translation and commentary of the West Mersea charter see Hart, *The Danelaw*, pp. 495–508.

8 P. J. Drury and N. P. Wickenden, 'An Early Anglo-Saxon Settlement within the Romano-British Small Town at Heybridge, Essex', *Medieval Archaeology* 26 (1982): 1–40.

9 John Chapman and Peter André, *Map of the County of Essex* (1777). See 'Map of Essex 1777', based on *A Reproduction of a Map of the County of Essex 1777 by John Chapman & Peter André* (Chelmsford, 1950). This is an open access resource produced by Tim Fransen with digitized assets from the Virtual Library of Bibliographical Heritage (BVPB) collection and the Essex Record Office (ERO) (accessed 23 January 2020).

10 Edward A. Freeman, *The History of the Norman Conquest of England, Its Causes and Results*, vol. I (Oxford, 1867), pp. 296–303, esp. at p. 298. For the idea that

Byrhtnoth had been in the north before the battle, see my discussion of *The Book of Ely* in Chapter 12 .

11 Reaney, *The Place-names of Essex*, pp. 303–4.

12 Hart, *The Danelaw*, pp. 535–7.

13 George Petty and Susan Petty, 'A Geological Reconstruction of the Site of the Battle of Maldon', in Janet Cooper, ed., *The Battle of Maldon: Fiction and Fact* (London and Rio Grande, 1993), pp. 159–69.

14 E. D. Laborde, 'The Site of the Battle of Maldon', *English Historical Review* 40 (1925): 161–73.

15 The arguments in favour of Laborde's location of the site are rehearsed and extended by John McN. Dodgson, 'The Site of the Battle of Maldon', in Donald Scragg, ed., *The Battle of Maldon, AD 991* (Oxford, 1991), pp. 170–9.

16 Daniel Thomas, '*Landes to fela*: Geography, Topography and Place in *The Battle of Maldon*', *English Studies* 98 (2017): 781–801. This essay is a valuable corrective to assumptions some critics have made in the many articles written on the poem. On the positive side, Thomas's article presents a reading of the poem's structure in the context of disputes over land ownership and anxieties about land tenure in tenth-century society, which will be seen to be highly relevant to the discussion in Chapters 1, 3 and 4.

17 In the published version of 'The Homecoming of Beorhtnoth, Beorhthelm's Son', in Christopher Tolkien, ed., *Tree and Leaf* (London, 2001), pp. 143–50, Tolkien adds a short essay 'Ofermod' discussing the Old English term *ofermod*, that is, 'pride', which the poet uses apparently to criticize Byrhtnoth's decision to grant the Vikings 'too much land'.

18 This view is confirmed by Stuart Lee, '*lagustreamas*: The Changing Waters Surrounding J.R.R. Tolkien and *The Battle of Maldon*', in *Festschrift for Patrick Conner* (WVU Press, forthcoming), who maps Tolkien's developing views of the poem and shows that 'Tolkien's criticism of Byrhtnoth was far from evident at first and seemed to develop as the years went on'.

19 Tolkien, 'The Homecoming of Beorhtnoth', pp. 121–42, at p. 141.

20 Arguing that Tolkien has a positive attitude to the heroic in 'The Homecoming of Beorhtnoth', Peter Grybauskas, 'Dialogic War: From the *Battle of Maldon* to the War of the Ring', *Mythlore: A Journal of J.R.R. Tolkien, C.S. Lewis, Charles Williams, and Mythopoeic Literature* 29, no. 3 (2011), article 5, takes issue with Tom Shippey, 'Tolkien and "The Homecoming of Beorhtnoth"', in *Roots and Branches: Selected Papers on Tolkien* (Zollikofen, 2007), pp. 323–39.

21 Tolkien, 'Ofermod', in *Tree and Leaf*, pp. 143 and 147.

22 Tolkien, *Tree and Leaf*, p. 150.

23 John D. Niles, 'Maldon and Mythopoesis', *Mediaevalia* 17 (1994): 89–121, repr. in R. M. Liuzza, ed., *Old English Literature: Critical Essays* (New Haven, 2002), pp. 445–74. Niles makes a revisionist case for the poem as a plea for appeasement of the Vikings, because the fighting of battles serves no useful purpose and leads only to heavy losses. Notably, two prominent critics regard the poem as a critique of poor leadership: T. D. Hill, 'History and Heroic Ethic in *Maldon*', *Neophilologus* 54 (1969): 291–6 and Heather Stuart, 'The Meaning of Maldon', *Neophilologus*

66 (1982): 126–39. A recent approach of this kind is to be found in Laura Ashe, *Conquest and Transformation: The Oxford English Literary History, Volume I, 1000-1350* (Oxford, 2017), pp. 52–63. Her argument touches on the notion of the warrior braving the salvation of his soul for the good of the nation, but ultimately she sees *Maldon* as heavy social critique.

24 Ashe, *Conquest and Transformation*, pp. 60–1.

25 See Eric G. Stanley, *The Search for Anglo-Saxon Paganism* (Cambridge, 1975) for a critical exploration of the neo-Romantic legacy of the study of Old English poetry.

26 John D. Niles, 'Old English Studies 1901–1975', in his *Old English Literature: A Guide to Criticism with Selected Readings* (Oxford, Malden and Chichester, 2016), pp. 3–39.

27 Menzies McKillop, *The Battle of Maldon: A Play for Radio* (London, 1991).

28 Ian Rodger, 'Glory and Grief'; a review in *The Listener* (1 March 1982).

29 The text of 'The Will of Ælfflæd' is printed in *Anglo-Saxon Wills*, ed. Dorothy Whitelock (Cambridge, 1930), p. 39.

30 Cyril Hart, 'The Earliest Suffolk Charter', in his *The Danelaw* (London, 1992), p. 479.

31 For a survey of the secondary literature on the poem see John D. Niles, '*Brunanburh*, *Maldon*, and the Critics', in his *Old English Literature: A Guide to Criticism*, pp. 142–9.

32 The millennial celebration produced two volumes of studies: Donald Scragg, ed., *The Battle of Maldon, AD 991* (Oxford, 1991) and Janet Cooper, ed., *The Battle of Maldon: Fiction and Fact* (London and Rio Grande, 1993).

33 Helmut Gneuss and Michael Lapidge, *Anglo-Saxon Manuscripts: A Bibliographical Handlist of Manuscripts and Manuscript Fragments Written or Owned in England up to 1100* (Toronto, 2014).

34 H. L. Rogers, '*The Battle of Maldon*: David Casley's Transcript', *Notes and Queries*, new series, 32 (1985): 147–55.

35 For the text of *Maldon* with facing-page translation, see, for example, Richard F. S. Hamer, ed. and trans., *A Choice of Anglo-Saxon Verse* (London, 2006) or Elaine Treharne, ed. and trans., *Old and Middle English c.890-c.1450: An Anthology*, 3rd edn (Oxford, 2010). For an introduction to the language of the poem see Mark Atherton, *Complete Old English*, 3rd edn (London, 2019), unit 21.

36 Jun Terasawa, *Old English Metre: An Introduction* (Toronto and London, 2011).

Chapter 1

1 M. O. H. Carver, *Sutton Hoo: Burial Ground of Kings?* (London, 1998); and *Sutton Hoo: A Seventh-Century Princely Burial Ground and Its Context* (London, 2005).

2 Robert Macfarlane, *The Wild Places* (London, 2007), p. 285.

3 Sarah Perry's novel *The Essex Serpent* (London, 2016), p. 305, or the quest of the nature writer J. A. Baker for the elusive wild falcon in his autobiographical *The Peregrine* (London, 1967).

4   For the text of the Peterborough manuscript, see *The Anglo-Saxon Chronicle: A Collaborative Edition, Manuscript E*, ed. Susan Irvine (Cambridge, 2004).

5   Bede, *Ecclesiastical History of the English People*, bk II, ch. 22; ed. and trans. Bertram Colgrave and R. A. B. Mynors (Oxford, 1969), pp. 282–3.

6   On Mersea and its relevance, see discussion in Introduction, note 4, and Hart, *The Danelaw*, pp. 495–508.

7   N. A. M. Rodger, *Command of the Ocean: A Naval History of Britain, 1649–1815* (London, 2006), p. 244.

8   Nicholas Brooks, 'Treason in Essex in the 990s: The Case of Æthelric of Bocking', in Gale Owen-Crocker and Brian W. Schneider, eds, *Royal Authority in Anglo-Saxon England*, BAR British Series 584 (Oxford, 2013), pp. 17–27. For the text, see Appendix 3.

9   Norman Longmate, *Island Fortress: The Defence of Great Britain, 1603–1945* (London, 1993), pp. 148–9.

10 According to the Oxford English Dictionary (accessed 13 December 2019), a vill is 'a territorial unit or division under the feudal system, consisting of a number of houses or buildings with their adjacent lands, more or less contiguous and having a common organization; corresponding to the Anglo-Saxon tithing and to the modern township or civil parish'. For further definition and discussion, see W. L. Warren, *The Governance of Norman and Angevin England 1086–1272* (London, 1987), pp. 2–3.

11 Owen Bewin, 'Early Iron Age Settlement at Maldon and the Maldon "Burh": Excavations at Beacon Green 1987', *Essex Archaeology and History*, 23 third series (1992): 10–24; see especially the map of the *burh* at 11 with discussion at 18–22.

12 David Hill and Alexander R. Rumble, eds, *The Defence of Wessex: The Burghal Hidage and Anglo-Saxon Fortifications* (Manchester, 1996).

13 For a detailed study of this monarch's reign see Nicholas J. Higham and David H. Hill, eds, *Edward the Elder, 899–924* (London, 2001).

14 Whitelock, ed., *Anglo-Saxon Wills*, nos. I, II, XIV, XV.

15 Ryan Lavelle, *Alfred's Wars: Sources and Interpretations of Anglo-Saxon Warfare in the Viking Age* (Woodbridge, 2010), p. 251.

16 Janet Bately, ed., *The Old English Orosius*, Early English Text Society, supplementary series 6 (London, 1980).

17 Thomas J. T. Williams, 'The Place of Slaughter', in Ryan Lavelle and Simon Roffey, eds, *Danes in Wessex: The Scandinavian Impact on Southern England,* c.800–c.1100 (Oxford, 2016), pp. 35–55, at p. 42.

18 Williams, 'The Place of Slaughter', p. 36.

19 C. Tilley, *A Phenomenology of Landscape: Places, Paths and Monuments* (Oxford, 1994), pp. 18–19.

20 Philip Morgan, 'The Naming of Medieval Battlefields', in D. Dunn, ed., *War and Society in Medieval and Early Modern Britain* (Liverpool, 2000), pp. 34–52.

21 Guy Halsall, 'Anthropology and the Study of Pre-Conquest Warfare and Society', in S. C. Hawkes, ed., *Weapons and Warfare in Anglo-Saxon England* (Oxford, 1989), pp. 155–78.

22 For the names of the region, see Reaney, *The Place-names of Essex*.

23 For reflections on this topic, see Scott T. Smith, 'Marking Boundaries: Charters and the *Anglo-Saxon Chronicle*', in Alice Jorgensen, ed., *Reading the Anglo-Saxon Chronicle: Language, Literature, History* (Turnhout, 2010), pp. 167–85; and the same scholar's *Land and Book: Literature and Land Tenure in Anglo-Saxon England* (Toronto, 2012).

24 The text and bibliography for S 714 is available online in the Electronic Sawyer, an updated version of the printed catalogue by Peter Sawyer, *Anglo-Saxon Charters: An Annotated List and Bibliography* (London, 1968); the text of the charter and a translation is printed in E. E. Barker, 'Sussex Anglo-Saxon Charters, III', *Sussex Archaeological Collections* 88 (1949): 51–113; the recent critical edition is found in S. E. Kelly, ed., *The Charters of Abingdon Abbey*, Anglo-Saxon Charters, 2 vols (Oxford, 2000–2001), no. 98.

25 The mentions of heathen burial mounds are discussed in Andrew Reynolds, *Later Anglo-Saxon England: Life & Landscape* (Stroud, 2002), pp. 176, 193. For the topographical names see A. Mawer, F. M. Stenton and J. E. B. Gover, *The Place-names of Sussex*, English Place-name Society (Cambridge, 1929–1930), pp. 6–7, p. 240n; on the bounds see R. Forsberg, *A Contribution to a Dictionary of Old English Place-Names* (Uppsala, 1950), p. 110.

26 Edgar's older brother Edwy (Old English spelling Eadwig), who came to the throne in 955, had married this particular lady, Ælfgifu, a descendant of another branch of the West Saxon royal family, but the marriage was later annulled on the grounds of consanguinity.

27 The Newnham Murren charter is S 738 in Sawyer's catalogue.

28 John Blair, *Anglo-Saxon Oxfordshire* (Stroud, 1994), pp. 125–6.

29 T. Miller, ed., *The Old English Version of Bede's Ecclesiastical History of the English People*, Early English Text Society, original series 95–6, 110–11 (London, 1890–8).

Chapter 2

1 See glossary entry for *hicgan* in Scragg, *The Battle of Maldon*, p. 97; also *hicgan* and *hogian* in Dictionary of Old English.

2 'Ne þurfon ge no *hogian* on þam anwealde, ne him æfter þringan gif ge wise bið and gode. He wile folgian eow þeah ge his no ne wilnian.' [You must not *direct your thoughts* to power, nor rush to it, if you are wise and honest. It will follow you even if you do not wish for it.] See Malcolm Godden and Susan Irvine, eds, *The Old English Boethius: An Edition of the Old English Versions of Boethius's De Consolatione Philosophiae*, 2 vols (Oxford, 2009), vol. 1, B Text, ch. 16, lines 37–9.

3 'Se *higode* symble þurh fæsten and forhæfdnesse of his cnihthade to þære lufan þæs heofenlican eðles.' [From his childhood he *directed his thoughts* through fasting and abstinence to love of the heavenly homeland.] See H. Hecht, ed., *Bischof Waerferths von Worcester Uebersetzung der Dialoge Gregors des Grossen*, Bib. ags. Prosa 5 (Leipzig, 1907) [repr. Darmstadt 1965], 1.11, 5.

4 Compare the text and translation of *Exodus* in Daniel Anlezark, ed., *Old Testament Narratives* (Cambridge, MA, 2011).

5   Hawkes, *Weapons and Warfare in Anglo-Saxon England*, pp. 141–4.

6   Gale Owen-Crocker, 'Hawks and Horse-Trappings', in Scragg, ed., *The Battle of Maldon, AD 991*, pp. 220–37.

7   The pictures from the copy of *Psychomachia* illustrated in London, British Library, Cotton Cleopatra C viii, folios 4–37, can be viewed online at the Digitized Manuscripts website of the British Library (accessed 24 August 2019). For the pictures of Abram see ff. 4v and 5r. Black and white reproductions and descriptions are found in Thomas Ohlgren, ed., *Anglo-Saxon Textual Illustration: Photographs of Sixteen Manuscripts with Descriptions and Index* (Kalamazoo, 1992), figs. 15.2 and 15.3.

8   Nicholas Brooks, 'Weapons and Armour', in Scragg, ed., *The Battle of Maldon, AD 991*, pp. 208–19, at pp. 210–12. For more information on military equipment, see Tuchard Underwood, *Anglo-Saxon Weapons and Warfare* (Stroud, 2000); I. P. Stephenson, *The Late Anglo-Saxon Army* (Stroud, 2007); Matthew Strickland, *Anglo-Norman Warfare: Studies in Late Anglo-Saxon and Anglo-Norman Warfare* (Woodbridge, 1992).

9   For issues involved in interpreting 'semiotic dress' in manuscript illustrations see Gale Owen-Crocker, *Dress in Anglo-Saxon England* (Woodbridge, 2004), pp. 327–31; she discusses women's and men's dress in the tenth and eleventh centuries at pp. 202–71.

10 W. A. Seaby and P. Woodfield, 'Viking Stirrups from England and their Background', *Medieval Archaeology* 24 (1980): 87–122.

11 Owen-Crocker, 'Hawks and Horse-Trappings', pp. 230–3.

12 *Beowulf*, line 138; trans. Bradley, *Anglo-Saxon Poetry* (London, 1982), p. 439.

13 Rafael Pascual, 'A Possible Emendation in *Beowulf* 1042a', *Notes and Queries* 66, no. 2 (2019): 166–8.

14 For text and translation see Whitelock, ed., *Anglo-Saxon Wills*, no. 34, pp. 88–91.

15 For example in Tom Shippey, *Old English Verse* (London, 1976), pp. 19 and 35.

16 For similar reflections on word order, see Helen Phillips, 'The Order of Words and Patterns of Opposition in *The Battle of Maldon*', *Neophilologus* 81(1997): 117–28.

17 For the text, see G. M. Garmonsway, ed., *Ælfric's Colloquy* (London, 1939; reprinted Exeter, 1983). For the use of such texts, see David W. Porter, 'The Latin Syllabus in the Anglo-Saxon Monastic Schools', *Neophilologus* 78, no. 3 (1994): 463–82.

18 'The Will of Brihtric and Ælfswith', in Whitelock, ed. and trans., *Anglo-Saxon Wills*, no. xi, pp. 26–9, at p. 26, lines 19–20.

19 The noblemen appear to be hunting a variety of birds, including cranes; see London, British Library, Cotton, Julius A.VI, folio 7v; the image may also be viewed online at the British Library Manuscript website. For brief discussion see Owen-Crocker, 'Hawks and Horse-Trappings', p. 222.

20 David M. Wilson, ed., *The Bayeux Tapestry* (London, 1985), plate 2, and commentary at pp. 174–5; Owen-Crocker, 'Hawks and Horse-Trappings', p. 228.

21 For the full poem, see 'The Fortunes of Mortals', in Robert E. Bjork, ed., *Old English Shorter Poems, Volume II: Wisdom and Lyric* (Cambridge MA, 2014), pp. 56–63.

22 Bradley, *Anglo-Saxon Poetry*, p. 343.

23 Helen Macdonald, *H is for Hawk* (London, 2014), pp. 74–5, responding to T. H. White, *The Goshawk* (1951).

24 Macdonald, *H is for Hawk*, p. 67.

25 See the Old English poem *The Gifts of Men*, line 81, in *The Exeter Book*, ed. George Philip Krapp and Elliot Van Kirk Dobbie, The Anglo-Saxon Poetic Records 3 (New York, 1936).

26 *Beowulf*, ed. F. Klaeber, 4th edn, revised by R. D. Fulk, Robert E. Bjork and John D. Niles, *Klaeber's Beowulf and the Fight at Finnsburg* (Toronto, 2008); Bradley, *Anglo-Saxon Poetry*, p. 471.

27 *King Alfred's Old English version of Boethius De consolatione philosophiae*, ed. and trans. Walter J. Sedgefield (Oxford, 1899) [repr. Darmstadt, 1968], ch. 35, p. 97, line 32.

28 Wulfstan, Sermon on Baptism, Homily 8b, in Dorothy Bethurum, ed., *The Homilies of Wulfstan* (Oxford, 1957), pp. 172–4, at lines 63–6.

29 Richard Dance sees evidence of extensive word play in the poem in '"þær wearð hream ahafen": A Note on Old English Spelling and the Sound of *The Battle of Maldon*', in Hugh Magennis and Jonathan Wilcox, eds, *The Power of Words: Anglo-Saxon Studies Presented to Donald G. Scragg on his Seventieth Birthday* (Morgantown, 2006), pp. 278–317.

30 *The Old English Prose Life of Guthlac*, 5.107–111. The text is edited by P. Gonser, *Das angelsächsische Prosa-Leben des heiligen Guthlac* (Heidelberg, 1909).

31 Trans. Bradley, *Anglo-Saxon Poetry*, p. 272. For the text, see *The Exeter Anthology of Old English Poetry: An Edition of Exeter Dean and Chapter Manuscript 3501*, ed. Bernard J. Muir, 2nd edn (Exeter, 2000), or Mary Clayton, ed. and trans., *Old English Poems of Christ and His Saints* (Cambridge, MA, 2013).

32 For example, in Riddle 8 ('The nightingale') and Riddle 57 ('Swallows and/or swifts').

33 For reflections on 'how human speech and its spatio-temporal movement is bound up with non-human sound', see James Paz, *Nonhuman Voices in Anglo-Saxon Literature and Material Culture* (Manchester, 2017), pp. 83–92. In his PhD thesis, Eric Lacey discusses the internconnections of sound and communication in Old English 'beasts of battle' scenes. See Mohamed Eric Rahman Lacey, 'Birds and Bird-lore in the Literature of Anglo-Saxon England', submitted for the degree of PhD, University College London (2014), at pp. 123–9.

34 For the two versions of the text, with translations, see *The Battle of Brunanburh: A Casebook*, ed. Michael Livingston (Exeter, 2011), pp. 40–9.

35 Trans. Bradley, *Anglo-Saxon Poetry*, p. 517.

36 Della Hooke, *Trees in Anglo-Saxon England: Literature, Lore and Landscape* (Woodbridge, 2010).

Chapter 3

1 On the duties of a man of Byrhtnoth's rank, see Pauline Stafford, 'Ealdorman', in Michael Lapidge, John Blair, Simon Keynes and Donald Scragg, eds, *The Wiley Blackwell Encyclopedia of Anglo-Saxon England*, 2nd edn (Oxford, 2014).

2 Nicholas Brooks, 'Weapons and Armour', pp. 208–19, at pp. 214–17.

3 In Chronicle C for the period up to 1016, the following annals use *folc* to mean 'people': 894, 896, 913, 982, 999, 1010, 1011, 1013, 1014, 1015, 1016; whereas in entries for the years 879, 894, 999, 1001, 1003, 1004, 1009, 1013, there are more ambiguous instances where *folc* may denote either 'people' or 'army'. For the meaning 'army, body of troops' see 'folc', sense 12, in Angus Cameron, Ashley Crandell Amos, Antonette diPaolo Healey et al., ed., *Dictionary of Old English: A to I online* (Toronto, 2018) (accessed 28 August 2019).

4 For the text see Anglo-Saxon Chronicle, Version C. *The Anglo-Saxon Chronicle: A Collaborative Edition, Volume 5, Manuscript C*, ed. Katherine O'Brien O'Keeffe (Cambridge, 2001).

5 Translation slightly adapted from Michael Swanton, trans., *The Anglo-Saxon Chronicle* (London, 1996), p. 135. As Swanton suggests at p. 135, note 14, the poetic formula *yðhengestas* may be a translation of the Old Norse *uðhestir*. If so it suggests the poet/chronicler knew Old Norse poems, perhaps war poetry on the subject of the Anglo-Danish wars.

6 For a discussion of *Maldon* in the context of the Chronicle, see John Scattergood, 'The Battle of Maldon and History', in John Scattergood, ed., *Literature and Learning in Medieval and Renaissance England: Essays Presented to Fitzroy Pyle* (Dublin, 1984), pp. 11–24; Courtney Konshuh, in her article '*Anræd* in their *Unræd*', also highlights the chronicler's ironic choice of words.

7 The literary historian Eric Weiskott regards this text as a poem in its own right, and he has given it the modern title *Sweyn Forkbeard Razes Wilton*. For his edition, an arrangement of the text into fourteen lines, see his *English Alliterative Verse: Poetic Tradition and Literary History* (Cambridge, 2016), p. 177.

8 Clayton, ed. and trans., *Old English Poems of Christ and His Saints*.

9 Robert E. Bjork, ed. and trans., *The Old English Poems of Cynewulf* (Cambridge, MA and London, 2013).

10 F. W. Maitland, *Domesday Book and Beyond: Three Essays in the Early History of England*, new edition with foreword by J. C. Holt (Cambridge, 1987), p. 67. Cited in Stephen Baxter, *The Earls of Mercia* (Oxford, 2007), p. 204.

11 Baxter gives a lucid explanation and analysis of the practice of commendation; see his *The Earls of Mercia*, pp. 204–8.

12 Harold Godwinesson swears an oath on two altars containing relics; see Wilson, ed., *The Bayeux Tapestry*, plate 26, commentary at pp. 180–1.

13 Liebermann, ed., *Die Gesetze der Angelsachsen*, vol. I, pp. 396–7.

14 Trans. Dorothy Whitelock, *The Beginnings of English Society* (London, 1953), p. 33; cited in Baxter, *Earls of Mercia*, p. 205

15 Bjork, ed., *Old English Shorter Poems. Volume II: Wisdom and Lyric*, pp. 4–5.

16 'Bugan', in *The Dictionary of Old English* (accessed 20 October 2019).

17 John Blair, *Building Anglo-Saxon England* (Princeton and Oxford, 2018), p. 356.

18 Blair, *Building Anglo-Saxon England*, ch. 10, pp. 354–80.

19 Pauline Stafford, 'Kinship and Women in the World of *Maldon*: Byrhtnoth and his Family', in Cooper, ed., *The Battle of Maldon: Fiction and Fact*, pp. 225–35, at p. 227.

20 Sawyer, *Catalogue*, S 1539; Whitelock, ed., *Anglo-Saxon Wills*, no. III; Blair, *Building Anglo-Saxon England*, pp. 365–7; K. Weikert, 'The Biography of a Place: Faccombe Netherton, Hampshire, c. 900-1200', *Anglo-Norman Studies* 37 (2015): 253–79.

21 Gale R. Owen, 'Wynflæd's Wardrobe', *Anglo-Saxon England* 8 (1979): 195–222; Gale Owen-Crocker, *Dress in Anglo-Saxon England*, pp. 211–12; Blair, *Building Anglo-Saxon England*, pp. 62, 65.

22 For a translation of *Geþyncðo* see Dorothy Whitelock, trans., *English Historical Documents I: c. 500–1042*, 2nd edn (London, 1979), no. 51.

23 The thegnly dwellings are considered by Andrew Reynolds, *Later Anglo-Saxon England: Life and Landscape* (Stroud, 1999), pp. 123–35. See also Blair, *Building Anglo-Saxon England*, pp. 372–6, 390–5.

24 Rumours of the fall of a leader are found in other battle accounts of the period. A scene in the Bayeux Tapestry shows some Norman knights retreating until Duke William, lifting his helmet, shows his men that he is still alive; the Normans regroup and continue the fight. See Wilson, *Bayeux Tapestry*, plates 67–8 and commentary at p. 194.

25 As Don Scragg noted in his edition of *Maldon*, p. 84, the *burh* must be Byrhtnoth's manor rather than the fortified town or *burh* of Maldon itself.

26 For Byrhtnoth's landholdings, see Whitelock, ed., *Anglo-Saxon Wills*, pp. 106–7; Locherbie-Cameron, 'Byrhtnoth and his Family', in Scragg, ed., *The Battle of Maldon, AD 991*, pp. 255 and 257–60; Hart, *The Danelaw*, pp. 131–5.

27 See the lawcode *II Æthelstan* in Felix Liebermann, ed., *Die Gesetze der Angelsachsen* (Halle, 1903–16), pp. 150–64, esp. paragraphs 2 and 2.1.

28 Trans. F. L. Attenborough, *The Laws of the Earliest English Kings* (Cambridge, 1922; reprinted Felinfach, 2000).

29 Stephen Pewsey and Andrew Brooks, *East Saxon Heritage: An Essex Gazetteer* (Stroud, 1993), pp. 78–9. The site at Sturmer Hall is pre-Conquest; it has not yet been excavated, but is listed as a scheduled monument by Historic England under the heading 'Sturmer Hall moated site and mill complex', list entry number 1012094; see historicengland.org.uk (accessed 31 January 2020).

30 *Domesday: A Complete Translation*, ed. Ann Williams and G. H. Martin (London, 2002), p. 1032.

Chapter 4

1 B. Danet and B. Bogoch, 'From Oral Ceremony to Written Document: The Transitional Language of Anglo-Saxon Wills', *Language and Communication* 12 (1992): 95–122. Linda Tollerton, *Wills and Will-Making in Anglo-Saxon England* (York, 2011).

2 For Beowulf's arming, see *Klaeber's Beowulf*, lines 1441–72.

3 'The Will of the Ætheling Æthelstan', in Whitelock, ed. and trans., *Anglo-Saxon Wills*, no. XX, pp. 56–63. There is discussion of Offa's sword in Mark Atherton, 'Mentions of Offa in the Anglo-Saxon Chronicle, *Beowulf*, and *Widsith*', in David Hill and Margaret Worthington, eds, *Æthelbald and Offa: Two Eighth-Century Kings of Mercia*, BAR British Series, 383 (Oxford, 2005), pp. 65–73, at p. 65.

4 Whitelock, ed. and trans., *Anglo-Saxon Wills*, p. 7. For comments on this will see Hart, 'The Ealdordom of Essex', in *The Danelaw*, p. 129.

5   Richard Abels, 'Heriot', in Lapidge, et al., eds, *The Wiley Blackwell*.

6   'The Will of the Ealdorman Ælfheah', in Whitelock, ed. and trans., *Anglo-Saxon Wills*, no. IX, pp. 22–5.

7   Anthony Faulkes and Michael Barnes, *A New Introduction to Old Norse, Part III: Glossary and Index of Names* (London, 2007), p. 125.

8   Cecily Clark, 'On Dating *The Battle of Maldon*: Certain Evidence Revisited', in her *Words, Names and History: Selected Papers*, ed. Peter Jackson (Cambridge, 1995), pp. 20–36, at pp. 30–6.

9   'Dreng', in *Dictionary of Old English* (accessed 6 November 2019).

10   Leonard Neidorf, 'II Æthelred and the Politics of The Battle of Maldon', *Journal of English and Germanic Philology* 111, no. 4 (2012): 451–73.

11   'A Compilation on Status', in Whitelock, *English Historical Documents*, no. 51 (b).

12   Brooks, 'Weapons and Armour', pp. 215–17.

13   'Alyfan', in *Dictionary of Old English* (accessed 21 September 2019).

14   For a perceptive literary-critical discussion of land in the poem see Thomas, '*Landes to fela*'.

15   Alan Kennedy, 'Law and Litigation in the *Libellus Æthelwoldi Episcopi*', *Anglo-Saxon England* 14 (1995): 131.

16   *Libellus Æthelwoldi*, ch. 38; in Janet Fairweather, *Liber Eliensis: A History of the Isle of Ely* (Woodbridge, 2005), II.27.

17   Byrhtferth of Ramsey, *Life of St Oswald*, iv.12, in *The Lives of St Oswald and St Ecgwine*, ed. and trans. Michael Lapidge (Oxford, 2009), pp. 124–5.

18   Sawyer, S1216; Kelly, *Charters of Abingdon*, no. 115; the document records the sale of twenty hides at Kingston Bagpuize, Berkshire, while the meeting itself took place at Alderbury, Wiltshire, at some point in the period 971–80.

19   *Libellus Æthelwoldi*, ch. 35 and *Liber Eliensis*, II.25; Patrick Wormald, 'A Handlist of Anglo-Saxon Lawsuits', *Anglo-Saxon England* 17 (1988): 247–81, no. 121.

20   *Libellus Æthelwoldi*, ch. 35; in Fairweather, *Liber Eliensis*, II.25. The summary here ignores some of the complexities of the case.

21   Roland Bainton, *Here I Stand: A Life of Martin Luther* ([1950] Nashville, 1980).

22   The term 'collocation' denotes a linguistically predictable co-occurrence of words such as *dry wine*, *staple diet*, *wield a weapon*, *have and hold*. A useful introduction is David Crystal, *The Cambridge Encyclopedia of the English Language*, 3rd edn (Cambridge, 2019), pp. 172–5.

23   Bradley, *Anglo-Saxon Poetry*, p. 287.

24   For the text, see *King Alfred's Old English Prose Translation of the First Fifty Psalms*, ed. Patrick P. O'Neill (Cambridge, MA, 2001).

Chapter 5

1   The origins of Old English poetic diction are explored in Richard North, *Pagan Words and Christian Meanings* (Amsterdam, 1991).

2   The Latin background is surveyed by Patrick McBrine, *Biblical Epics in Late Antiquity and Anglo-Saxon England: divina in laude voluntas* (Toronto, 2017).

3   For a list of the manuscripts see Catherine E. Karkov, 'Broken Bodies and Singing Tongues: Gender and Voice in the Cambridge, Corpus Christi College 23 *Psychomachia*', *Anglo-Saxon England* 30 (2001): 115–36, at p. 115, note 3.

4   Griffiths, ed., *The Battle of Maldon: Text and Translation*, p. 41.

5   The Dictionary of Old English Corpus online (accessed 21 August 2019). Of the sixty hits for *geunne*, which is either the subjunctive form of *geann* or the imperative, fifty-three refer to God or Christ as the agent and the subject of the verb, while six refer to the king or authority figure in the Old English laws; it is clear that *geunne* belongs within the discourse of prayer.

6   A similar motif occurs in a homily by Ælfric, *Dominica XII Post Pentecosten*, in Malcolm Godden, ed., *Ælfric, Catholic Homilies*, 2nd Series, p. 253, where God grants to the heathen king Nebuchadnezzar the restoration of his wits, and Nebuchadnezzar looks to the heavens and praises God.

7   Mary Clayton and Hugh Magennis, eds, *The Old English Lives of St. Margaret* (Cambridge, 1994), 18.4.

8   J. E. Cross argues for a non-saintly Byrhtnoth in his 'Oswald and Byrhtnoth – A Christian Saint and a Hero who is Christian', *English Studies* 46 (1965): 93–109. For another approach see Laura Ashe's lively *Conquest and Transformation*, pp. 206–7, where she compares what she sees as doubtful attitudes to Christian warriors and their salvation in *Maldon* with the more positive assertions of the later Old French *Chanson de Roland*.

9   Byrhtferth, *Life of St Oswald*, V.21, pp. 200–1.

10 Scragg, ed., *The Battle of Maldon*, p. 79. The prayer is printed by H. Logeman, 'Anglo-Saxon Minora', in the journal *Anglia* (1889): 497–518.

11 Some late Anglo-Saxon prayers are discussed by Ananya Jahanara Kabir, *Paradise, Death and Doomsday in Anglo-Saxon Literature* (Cambridge, 2001), pp. 132–40; for a discussion of the genre of devotional prayer, see D. G. Bzdyl, 'Prayer in Old English Narrative', *Medium Ævum* 51 (1982): 135–51.

12 The manuscript of the Regius Psalter is London, British Library, Royal 2 B. V.

13 For an account of the Glastonbury school, with further bibliography, see Mark Atherton, *The Making of England: A New History of the Anglo-Saxon World* (London, 2017), pp. 192–205.

14 The already classic study of the glossing of the Regius Psalter under Æthelwold's tutelage is Mechthild Gretsch, *The Intellectual Foundations of the English Benedictine Reform* (Cambridge, 1999).

15 For some orientation in the medieval use of the Psalter, see Nancy van Deusen, *The Place of the Psalms in the Intellectual Culture of the Middle Ages* (Albany, 1999); also now Tamara Atkin and Francis Leneghan, eds, *The Psalms and Medieval English Literature: From the Conversion to the Reformation* (Cambridge, 2017).

16 M. J. Toswell, *The Anglo-Saxon Psalter* (Turnhout, 2014). See also the chapter by Jane Roberts, 'Some Anglo-Saxon Psalters and their Glosses', in Atkin and Leneghan, *The Psalms and Medieval English Literature*.

17 *Der altenglische Regius Psalter* [*The Old English Regius Psalter*], ed. Fritz Roeder (Halle, 1904).

18 For the illustrated psalters see, for example, Koert van der Horst, et al., eds, *The Utrecht Psalter in Medieval Art: Picturing the Psalms of David* (Utrecht, 1996).

19 Here Margaret is described using the masculine demonstrative *se* rather than the feminine form *seo*.

20 Jean Leclercq, *The Love of Learning and the Desire for God* (New York, 1974 and London, 1978).

21 For the idea that the hero experiences 'cosmic uncertainty', and so seems all the more heroic, see Fred C. Robinson, 'God, Death, and Loyalty in *The Battle of Maldon*', in Mary Salu and Robert T. Farrell, eds, *J.R.R. Tolkien, Scholar and Storyteller: Essays in Memoriam* (Ithaca, NY, 1979), pp. 76–98; reprinted in his *The Tomb of Beowulf and Other Essays*; also in Liuzza, ed., *Old English Literature: Critical Essays*, pp. 425–44.

22 *Liber Eliensis: A History of the Isle of Ely*, trans. Janet Fairweather (Woodbridge, 2005).

23 *Liber Eliensis*, II.63, trans. Fairweather, pp. 162–3.

24 Byrhtferth, *Life of St Oswald*, IV.13, pp. 128–9.

Chapter 6

1 Pauline Stafford, 'Byrhtnoth and his Family', in Cooper, ed., *The Battle of Maldon: Fiction and Fact*, pp. 225–35, at p. 226. For kindred relations in the poem I have relied heavily on Margaret Locherbie-Cameron, 'Ælfwine's Kinsmen and *The Battle of Maldon*', *Notes & Queries* 25 (1978): 486–7, and also her 'Byrhtnoth, his Noble Companion and his Sister's Son', *Medium Ævum* 57 (1988): 159–71.

2 Other examples are *bearn Ælfrices* (209b), *Ecglafes bearn* (267a), *Þurstanes sunu* (298a), *Wigelmes bearn* (300a), *Æþelgares bearn* (320a).

3 Cameron, et al., eds, *Dictionary of Old English* (accessed 10 August 2019).

4 The latest study assigns the copying of the manuscript to the reign of Cnut, that is, post-1016; see Simon C. Thomson, *Communal Creativity in the Making of the 'Beowulf' Manuscript: Towards a History of Reception for the Nowell Codex* (Leiden, 2018).

5 The larger theme of dynasty is treated in Francis Leneghan, *The Dynastic Drama of Beowulf* (Cambridge, 2020).

6 Whitelock, ed., *Anglo-Saxon Wills*, no. IX, pp. 22–3.

7 Ealhhelm, the ealdorman of Mercia appointed by King Edmund, is known from mentions in administrative documents: he witnesses a number of charters in the period 940–51; discussion may be found in Ann Williams, '*Princeps Merciorum gentis*: The Family, Career and Connections of Ælfhere, Ealdorman of Mercia, 956–83', *Anglo-Saxon England* 10 (1982): 143–72, at pp. 143–6.

8 Ælfric Cild is mentioned as a prominent thegn at a meeting that took place between 971 and 980 at Alderbury, Wiltshire; for the text see my Chapter 5 and also Sawyer S 1216 and Kelly, *Charters of Abingdon*, no. 115.

9 Grant by King Æthelred; Whitelock, *English Historical Documents*, no. 123, pp. 582–4, at p. 583. Sawyer, S 937; Kelly, *Charters of Abingdon*, no. 129.

10 Roach, *Æthelred the Unready*, pp. 91, 106.

Chapter 7

1 Stafford, 'Byrhtnoth and his Family', p. 227.

2 W. G. Busse and R. Holtei, 'The Battle of Maldon: A Historical, Heroic and Political Poem', *Neophilologus* 65 (1981): 614–21; the article is reprinted in Katherine O'Brien O'Keeffe, ed., *Old English Shorter Poems: Basic Readings* (New York, 1994), pp. 185–97.

3 'Gyld', in *Old English Dictionary* (accessed 22 September 2019).

4 Gervase Rosser, 'Anglo-Saxon Gilds', in John Blair, ed., *Minsters and Parish Churches: The Local Church in Transition. 950-1200* (Oxford, 1988), pp. 31–4. Victoria Thompson discusses the function of the various Old English guilds in *Dying and Death in Later Anglo-Saxon England* (Woodbridge, 2004), pp. 112–15.

5 Whitelock, *English Historical Documents*, p. 606, n. 4.

6 The abbey ruin of St Peter's, Abbotsbury, founded by Urki in 1044, is still visible today on the shore below the steep-sided hill on which stands the imposing tower of St Catherine's Chapel.

7 'The Abbotsbury Guild Statutes', in Whitelock, *English Historical Documents*, no. 139, pp. 606–7.

8 Whitelock, *English Historical Documents*, no. 139, p. 607.

9 Benjamin Thorpe, ed., *Diplomatarium Anglicum ævi Saxonici* (London, 1865), pp. 605–8, at p. 608.

10 Whitelock, *English Historical Documents*, no. 138, pp. 605–6. The statues of the Bedwyn guild are copied in Bern, Stadtbibliothek, manuscript 671, ff. 75v–76r, edited by Max Förster in his *Der Flussname Themse und seine Sippe: Studien zur Anglisierung keltischer Eigennamen und zur Lautchronologie des Altbritischen* (Munich, 1941), pp. 791–2.

11 The page from the Exeter gospel book is now bound in the manuscript in London, British Library, Cotton, Tiberius B. v, folio 75; for the date see Neil Ker, *Catalogue of Manuscripts Containing Anglo-Saxon* (Oxford, 1957), no. 194.

12 Patrick Conner, 'The Old English Elegy: A Historicization', in David Johnson and Elaine Treharne, eds, *Readings in Medieval Texts* (Oxford, 2005), pp. 30–45, at p. 32; for his edition and translation of the Exeter Guild Statutes, see p. 33; for another translation see Whitelock, *English Historical Documents*, no. 137, p. 605.

13 Conner, 'The Old English Elegy', p. 34.

14 Conner, 'The Old English Elegy', p. 37.

15 Conner, 'The Old English Elegy', p. 44.

16 Patrick W. Conner, *Anglo-Saxon Exeter: A Tenth-Century Cultural History* (Woodbridge, 1993); Richard Gameson, 'The Origin of the Exeter Book of Old English Poetry', *Anglo-Saxon England* 25 (1996): 135–85.

17 Ker, Catalogue, no. 22. The eighth-century Latin gospel-book from Ely is now Cambridge, University Library Kk. I. 24; the loose leaf with the late-tenth-century additions is now in London, British Library, Cotton Tiberius B. V, f. 74; the grant of land was written first and then the Cambridge Guild Statutes were added later, before and after it on both sides of the page.

18   Locherbie-Cameron, 'Byrhtnoth and his Family', pp. 253–62, at pp. 253–4.

19   For Byrhtnoth's landholdings, see Locherbie-Cameron, 'Byrhtnoth and his Family',
     pp. 255 and 257–60; Hart, *The Danelaw*, pp. 131–5.

20   'The Thegns' Guild in Cambridge', in Whitelock, *English Historical Documents*, no.
     136.

21   The character Offa is in focus at lines 198, 230, 286, 288 of *Maldon*, and there is
     one mention of 'Offa's kinsman' at line 5.

22   *Oxford English Dictionary* (accessed 11 August 2019).

23   The text, with translation and explanatory commentary, is printed in Atherton,
     Complete Old English, unit 19.

24   The phrase *grimme guðgemot* occurs in the Old English biblical epic *Genesis*,
     2056b, in the scene where Abraham leads an army to rescue his kinsman Lot.
     Perhaps because of the confrontational aspect of *gemot* as a council or meeting,
     the noun could function as a synonym for battle. So for example Riddle 5, which
     seems to deal with the subject of a shield in battle, speaks of *abidan sceal laþran
     gemotes* 'having to await a more hostile encounter', and a similar phrase appears
     in *Guthlac A*, line 236, during Guthlac's exchanges with the demons that come to
     afflict him in his fenland hermitage.

25   'The Thegns' Guild in Cambridge', in Whitelock, *English Historical Documents*, no.
     136, pp. 603–5, at p. 604.

Chapter 8

1   *Pace* Rosemary Woolf and others, who envisaged that the heroic attitude was
    revived in the 990s, perhaps inspired by writers deliberately fostering the study of
    Tacitus's *Germania*; Rosemary Woolf, 'The Ideal of Men Dying with their Lord in the
    Germania and in *The Battle of Maldon*', *Anglo-Saxon England* 5 (1976): 63–81.
    There is a response to Woolf's theory in Roberta Frank, 'The Ideal of Men Dying with
    their Lord in *The Battle of Maldon*: Anachronism or *Nouvelle Vague*?', in Ian Wood
    and Niels Lund, eds, *People and Places in Northern Europe 500-1600: Essays in
    Honour of Peter Hayes Sawyer* (Woodbridge, 1991), pp. 95–106; see also Niles,
    '*Brunanburh*, *Maldon*, and the Critics', pp. 142–9, at pp. 144–5.

2   For a discussion of this story, with bibliography, see Francis Leneghan, 'Royal
    Wisdom and the Alfredian Context of *Cynewulf and Cyneheard*', *Anglo-Saxon
    England* 39 (2010): 71–104.

3   *The Chronicle of Æthelweard*, ed. and trans. Alistair Campbell (London, 1962).

4   Patrick Wormald, 'Æthelweard [Ethelwerd] (d. 998?)', in *Oxford Dictionary of
    National Biography* (online, 2004) (accessed 20 August 2019).

5   See the Alfredian Preface to the *Pastoral Care* in *King Alfred's West Saxon Version
    of Gregory's Pastoral Care*, ed. Henry Sweet (London, 1871); the apparently
    grudging comment occurs in the Anglo-Saxon Chronicle, Version A, annal for 901.
    A useful primer is Simon Keynes and Michael Lapidge, trans., *Alfred the Great:
    Asser's Life of King Alfred and Other Contemporary Sources* (Harmondsworth,
    1983).

6 I discuss the dramatic confrontation at Wimborne in Atherton, *Making of England*, esp. pp. 113–15.

7 Examples of the parley before battle are found in the 'Cynewulf and Cyneheard' story (annal 755 of the Chronicle); the St Edmund Story; the Old High German poem *Hildebrandslied* [The Lay of Hildebrand]. For the latter poem see text in W. Braune, K. Helm and E. A. Ebbinghaus, eds, *Althochdeutsches Lesebuch*, 17th edn (Tübingen 1994); discussion in J. Knight Bostock, *A Handbook on Old High German Literature*, 2nd edn (Oxford, 1976).

8 The verb *licgan* also occurs in *Beowulf* with the same basic meaning of 'to lie bereft of life'; see Fulk et al., *Klaeber's Beowulf*, p. 406; examples include 2051, 2201.

9 Tolkien, 'The Homecoming of Beorhtnoth', p. 124; for more discussion see my Introduction.

10 *Waldere*, lines 8–11; modern English version adapted from the translation by S. A. J. Bradley; for a critical edition see *Waldere*, ed. A. Zettersten (Manchester, 1979) or Joyce Hill, ed., *Old English Minor Heroic Poems* (Durham, 1994).

11 Hart, *The Danelaw*, pp. 118, 513.

12 For discussion of the events and location of The Holme, see Cyril Hart, 'The Battles of the Holme, Brunanburh, and Ringmere', in his *The Danelaw* (London, 1992), pp. 511–32, at pp. 511–15.

13 Alice Oswald, *Memorial* (London, 2011), p. 14.

14 Ute Schwab, '*The Battle of Maldon*: A Memorial Poem', in Cooper, ed., *The Battle of Maldon: Fiction and Fact*, pp. 63–85. For further insights into the genre, see J. A. Burrow, *The Poetry of Praise* (Cambridge, 2009).

15 Locherbie-Cameron, 'Byrhtnoth and his Family', pp. 253–62.

Chapter 9

1 For a study of such phrases, see Ward Parks, 'The Traditional Narrator and the "I heard" Formulas in Old English Poetry', *Anglo-Saxon England* 16 (1987): 45–66.

2 Gordon, ed., *Battle of Maldon*, p. 23.

3 The classic study is Francis Peabody Magoun, Jr., 'The Oral-Formulaic Character of Anglo-Saxon Narrative Poetry', *Speculum* 28 (1953): 446–67, reprinted in R. D. Fulk, *Interpretations of Beowulf: A Critical Anthology* (Bloomington, 1991), pp. 45–65.

4 Andy Orchard, 'Oral Tradition', in Katherine O'Brien O'Keeffe, ed., *Reading Old English Texts* (Cambridge, 1997), pp. 101–23; also his *A Critical Companion to Beowulf* (Cambridge, 2003), pp. 130–68; Niles, 'Orality', in his *Old English Literature: A Guide to Criticism with Selected Readings*, pp. 112–35.

5 I am grateful to Andy Orchard for pointing out these four examples to me.

6 Translation adapted from R. D. Fulk, *The Beowulf Manuscript* (Cambridge, MA and London, 2010), p. 257.

7 Trans. Bradley, *Anglo-Saxon Poetry*, p. 480.

8   The literary quality of 'depth' is discussed by T. A. Shippey, *The Road to Middle-earth*, 2nd edn (London, 1992), pp. 272–81.

9   Trans. Fulk, *Beowulf Manuscript*, p. 271.

10 Trans. Fulk, *Beowulf Manuscript*, p. 277.

11 Byrhtferth, *Life of St Oswald*, V.4, pp. 154–5.

12 Byrhtferth, *Life of St Oswald*, V.5, pp. 158–9.

Chapter 10

1   Janet Bately, ed., *The Anglo-Saxon Chronicle: A Collaborative Edition, Volume 3, Manuscript A* (Cambridge, 1986), p. 79.

2   Malory *Works*, Bk I.11, in Eugene Vinaver, ed., *The Works of Sir Thomas Malory*, revised P. J. C. Field, 3 vols (Oxford, 1990), p. 23, I.35–p. 24, I.6.

3   Sawyer S 595. Other examples may be found in the following charters: S 141 *And swa to weohles heale. And swa to Antan hlawe*; S 417 *And swa to weawan hocan*; S 424 *And swa to wodnes dic. . . . And swa to meos leage*.

4   'The main hand of 993 A is that of scribe 5, working in the first decade of the eleventh century'. See Janet M. Bately, ed., 'The *Anglo-Saxon Chronicle*', in Scragg, ed., *The Battle of Maldon, AD 991*, pp. 37–50, at p. 42.

5   I follow here the analysis by Bately, 'The *Anglo-Saxon Chronicle*', pp. 37–50.

6   For an account of the politics and poetry of the tenth century, see generally Atherton, *The Making of England*.

7   Discussion in Atherton, *Making of England*, pp. 54–5.

8   For the story of Olaf's conversion in the Scilly Isles and his peaceful presence in England, including his marriage to 'Gyða, sister of Óláfr kváran who was king in Ireland in Dublin' see Snorri Sturluson, *Óláfs saga Tryggvasonar*, chs 31 and 32 in *Heimskringla, Vol. 1, The Beginnings to Óláfr Tryggvason*, 2nd edn, trans. Alison Finlay and Anthony Faulkes (London, 2016), pp. 165–6 (online version accessed 30 January 2020); discussion of these sources in Sverre Bagge, 'The Making of a Missionary King: The Medieval Accounts of Olaf Tryggvason and the Conversion of Norway', *Journal of English and Germanic Philology* 105 (2006): 473–513.

9   Discussed by Neidorf, 'II Æthelred and the Politics of *The Battle of Maldon*', pp. 451–73.

10 II Æthelred, 1–1.1. For the text and translation see A. J. Robertson, *The Laws of the Kings of England from Edmund to Henry I* (Cambridge, 1925), pp. 56–63.

11 Stephen Baxter, 'MS C of the Anglo-Saxon Chronicle and the Politics of Mid-Eleventh-Century England', *The English Historical Review* 122, no. 499 (2007): 1189–227.

12 Simon Keynes, 'The Declining Reputation of Æthelred the Unready' (1978), rev. and repr. in David Pelteret, ed., *Anglo-Saxon History: Basic Readings* (New York, 2000), pp. 157–90, at pp. 158–68.

13 Courtney Konshuh, '*Anræd* in their *Unræd*: The Æthelredian Annals (983–1016) and their Presentation of King and Advisors', *English Studies* 97 (2016): 140–62.

Chapter 11

1   Byrhtferth of Ramsey, *The Lives of St Oswald and St Ecgwine*, ed. and trans.
    Michael Lapidge (Oxford, 2009). There is a brief assessment of *The Life of St
    Oswald* in Karen A. Winstead, *The Oxford History of Life-Writing. Volume I: The
    Middle Ages* (Oxford, 2018), pp. 17–18. For background studies on Oswald, see
    Nicholas Brooks and Catherine Cubitt, eds, *Oswald of Worcester: Life and Influence*
    (Leicester, 1996).

2   Atherton, *The Making of England, passim.*

3   W. D. Macray, ed., *Chronicon Abbatiae Rameseiensis* (London, 1886), p. 52.

4   Byrhtferth, *Life of St Oswald*, III.13, p. 83; the biblical quotation is from Ps. 133. 1.

5   Æthelwold, abbot of Abingdon and later Bishop of Winchester, was another of
    the tenth-century Benedictine reformers; he also sent his supporters to Fleury
    to complete their Benedictine education. See Atherton, *Making of England*,
    pp. 225–37.

6   Byrhtferth, *Life of St Oswald*, pp. 89 and 91.

7   For a discussion of this poem in the context of other fenland poetry from the period,
    see Catherine A. M. Clarke, *Literary Landscapes and the Idea of England, 700–
    1400* (Cambridge, 2006), pp. 85–9.

8   Abbo, *Passio Sancti Eadmundi*, ch. viii. For a full translation, see Francis Hervey,
    ed. and trans., *Corolla Sancti Eadmundi* (New York, 1907), pp. 7–59. For a history
    of the veneration of St Edmund, see Rebecca Pinner, *The Cult of St Edmund
    in Medieval East Anglia* (Woodbridge, 2015).

9   The Latin text of Abbo's *Passio Sancti Eadmundi* is edited by Michael Winterbottom,
    Three Lives of English Saints (Toronto, 1982), pp. 67–87.

10 Byrhtferth of Ramsey, *The Lives of St Oswald and St Ecgwine*; Part V of *The Life of
    St Oswald* is on pp. 146–203.

11 Lapidge, *Lives of St Oswald and St Ecgwine*, pp. 154–9.

12 Byrhtferth may also have written, in Latin, his own chronicle of tenth-century history;
    see Lapidge, *Lives of St Oswald and St Ecgwine*, pp. xlii–xliii.

13 Byrhtferth, *Life of St Oswald*, pp. 156–7, n. 52, and pp. 54–5, n. 10 where Lapidge
    shows that Byrhtferth was particularly interested in Paul the Deacon's account of St
    Benedict, founder of the Benedictines.

14 For the sources of word and image and the allusions in Byrhtferth's text, see the
    notes and commentary in *Life of St Oswald*, pp. 154–9.

15 Translation of the Latin Vulgate from the Douay Bible; 1 Samuel (1 Kings) 17. 2-8.
    See *The Holy Bible: Douay Version* (London, 1956).

16 The two-page image of David and Goliath may be seen in manuscript in London,
    British Library, Cotton, Tiberius C. VI.

17 Byrhtferth, *Life of St Oswald*, pp. 156–7, n. 56.

18 1 Maccabees 6. 42-5. There is an Old English version of Maccabees written by
    Ælfric of Eynsham. See *Ælfric's Lives of Saints*, ed. W. W. Skeat, 4 vols, EETS os
    76, 82, 94, and 114 (London, 1881–1900; repr. as 2 vols, 1966).

19   For a text and translation of Wulfstan's *Sermo Lupi*, see Treharne, ed. and trans., *Old and Middle English c.890–c.1450*.

20   Byrhtferth, *Life of St Oswald*, bk 5, ch. 5, 156–7.

21   Ashe, *Conquest and Transformation*, pp. 52–63, at p. 55.

Chapter 12

1   This is the 'auxetic mode' as expounded by J. A. Burrow in his *The Poetry of Praise* (Cambridge, 2008).

2   The relevant section of the standard edition is E. O. Blake, ed., *Liber Eliensis*, Camden third series xcii (London, Royal Historical Society, 1962), pp. 133–6; the Latin original may be compared with the useful translation by Fairweather, *Liber Eliensis*, pp. 160–3; see also C. E. Wright, *The Cultivation of Saga in Anglo-Saxon England* (Edinburgh, 1939), pp. 23–4.

3   For definitions of the genres of myth, romance, epic and novel in terms of the differing qualities and capabilities of the hero, see the classic study by Northrop Frye, *Anatomy of Criticism: Four Essays* (Princeton, 1957).

4   Marilyn Deegan and Stanley Rubin, 'Byrhtnoth's Remains: A Reassessment of his Stature', in Scragg, ed., *The Battle of Maldon, AD 991*, pp. 289–93.

5   Blake, ed., *Liber Eliensis*, pp. 133–6; Fairweather, *Liber Eliensis*, pp. 160–3.

6   William E. Kapelle, *The Norman Conquest of the North: The Region and its Transformation, 1000–1135* (Chapel Hill, 1979) and Ann Williams, *The English and the Norman Conquest* (Woodbridge, 1995).

7   Cyril Hart, in 'Byrhtnoth and the Northumbrian Eorldom', in his *The Danelaw*, pp. 138–40, argues that Byrhtnoth held Northamptonshire, which at the time was accounted as part of Northumbria.

8   *Book of Ely*, II.62. In Fairweather, *Liber Eliensis*, pp. 160–1.

9   For another approach to *The Book of Ely* and its relevance to the poem, see Thomas D. Hill, 'The *Liber Eliensis* "Historical Selections" and the Old English *Battle of Maldon*', *Journal of English and Germanic Philology* 96 (1997): 1–25.

10   There is a survey of the documentary evidence for wall-hangings and tapestries in C. R. Dodwell, *Anglo-Saxon Art: A New Perspective* (Manchester, 1982), pp. 129–45.

11   Whitelock, ed., *Anglo-Saxon Wills*, no. xxi, pp. 64–5.

12   Dodwell, *Anglo-Saxon Art*, pp. 134–6, argues vigorously for an immediate gift to Ely Abbey of a tapestry celebrating earlier deeds in Byrhtnoth's life.

13   Schwab, '*The Battle of Maldon*: A Memorial Poem', pp. 63–85.

14   Trans. Janet Fairweather. For discussion see Andrew Wareham, *Lords and Communities in Early Medieval East Anglia* (Woodbridge, 2005), pp. 74–7.

15   Sawyer charter, S 1486. The manuscript, from the archive at Bury St Edmunds, is British Library, Harley Charter 43, C. 4; see Whitelock, ed., *Anglo-Saxon Wills*, no. xiv, 'The Will of Æthelflæd' [Byrhtnoth's sister-in-law], and no. xv, 'The Will of Ælfflæd' [Byrhtnoth's widow].

16 Whitelock, ed., *Anglo-Saxon Wills*, no. xv, p. 40, lines 6–7.

17 Gale Owen-Crocker, ed., *King Harold II and the Bayeux Tapestry* (Woodbridge, 2005).

18 Gernot R. Wieland, 'The Origin and Development of the Anglo-Saxon *Psychomachia* Illustrations', *Anglo-Saxon England* 26 (1997): 169–86.

19 See the discussion in Mark Atherton, 'The Image of the Temple in the *Psychomachia* and Late Anglo-Saxon Literature', *Bulletin of the John Rylands University Library of Manchester* 79 (1997): 263–85.

Appendix 2 'The Battle of the Holme'

1 Alfred Æthewulfing is a formal, poetic way of expressing in plainer English, Alfred son of Æthewulf.

2 Twinnam is present-day Christchurch, Dorset. Note also the emphasis in this text on Alfred's kindred, in which the pronoun *his* refers to Alfred; first we have *Eadweard his sunu* that is, 'Edward his son' and then *Æþelwold æþeling his fædran sunu* 'the ætheling [i.e. prince] Æthelwold, his paternal nephew'.

3 For commentary see Chapter 8. Note the southern English perspective of *com . . . hider* (literally came hither), that is, 'arrived here', in this part of the country.

Appendix 3 The case of Æthelric of Bocking

1 For Byrhtnoth's landholdings, see Whitelock, ed., *Anglo-Saxon Wills*, pp. 106–7; Locherbie-Cameron, 'Byrhtnoth and his Family', pp. 255 and 257–60; Hart, *The Danelaw*, pp. 131–5.

2 All these place-names occur in the will of Byrhtnoth's widow Ælfflæd, compiled around the year 1002, and preserved originally in the archives at Bury St Edmunds; the manuscript is now London, British Library, Harley Charter 43, C. 4. For the text see Whitelock, ed., *Anglo-Saxon Wills*, no. XV, pp. 38–43, with notes at pp. 141–6.

3 For text, translation and discussion, see Brooks, 'Treason in Essex', pp. 17–27.

4 Whitelock, ed., *Anglo-Saxon Wills*, no. XIV, pp. 36–7.

5 Sawyer, *Catalogue*, S 1501. Text from Whitelock, ed., *Anglo-Saxon Wills*, VI (1), pp. 42–3, 146–8; text and discussion also in Brooks, 'Treason in Essex', and in Nicholas Brooks and Susan Kelly, eds, *Charters of Christ Church Canterbury* (Oxford, 2013), no. 136.

6 Whitelock notes that the payment to the priest must be the *sawolsceatt*, 'soul-payment', that is, the burial-fee.

7 Bocking is located on Stane Street, the Roman road that leads due west from Colchester until it strikes the north–south Roman highway of Ermine Street near

Hertford. Ealdorman Byrhtnoth also held some of his property on or near Stane Street – just west of Colchester – at Lexden and Stanway, as well as at other less specific locations near Tey and Colne.

8   This is my interpretation of the language, by analogy with *be eastan stræte* in the next sentence. The text implies the presence of Stane Street, though the name is not used. Another *stræt*, that is, another Roman road, a north–south route from London, comes up through Chelmsford and Little Waltham and crosses Stane Street near Bocking.

9   According to the *OED* [consulted 30 November 2019], a *gore* is a triangular strip of land lying between larger areas of land.

10   Sudbury is on the Essex-Suffolk border, in the Stour valley, about halfway between Stoke-by-Nayland to the east and Sturmer to the west. St Edmund's at Bedericesworth is the old name for Bury St Edmunds.

11   Sawyer, *Catalogue*, S 939. Whitelock, ed., *Anglo-Saxon Wills*, no. XVI (2); text and discussion also in Brooks, 'Treason in Essex', and in Brooks and Kelly, eds, *Charters of Christ Church Canterbury*, no. 137.

12   Ealdorman Leofsige was ealdorman of Essex after Byrhtnoth. The Chronicle annal, versions CDE, for 1002, reports him undertaking on the king's orders to pay the tribute to make peace (OE *frith*) with the Danes. But a violent dispute arose between Leofsige and the king's High Reeve; the details are lacking: all we are told is that Leofsige killed the reeve, and was exiled for his crime.

13   For the identification of these figures, see the notes in Whitelock, ed., *Anglo-Saxon Wills*, pp. 149–50.

14   Charles Insley, 'Charters and Episcopal Scriptoria in the Anglo-Saxon South-West', *Early Medieval Europe* 7 (1998): 173–97, at 177–84.

Appendix 4 'The will of Leofwine'

1   Sawyer, *Catalogue*, S 1522. Gordon, ed., *Battle of Maldon*, pp. 85–6; *The Crawford Collection of Early Charters and Documents*, eds, A. S. Napier and W. H. Stevenson (Oxford, 1895), no. 9, p. 22.

2   Victor Watts, *The Cambridge Dictionary of English Place-Names* (Cambridge, 2004), p. 485; Reaney, *Place-names of Essex*, p. 22.

3   Richard Fitter, ed., *The Book of British Birds* (London, 1969), pp. 162 and 170.

4   The noun *botl* is mostly confined to charters and place-names, whereas *bold* is mostly a poetic term, for example, *Solomon and Saturn* (138), *Andreas* (103), *Dream of the Rood* (72); it also occurs in personal names.

5   See entries for Stratfield, Stratford, Street and so on in Watts, *The Cambridge Dictionary of English Place-Names*, pp. 584–5.

Select bibliography

Editions of primary works

Abbo of Fleury. *The Passion of St Edmund. Corolla Sancti Eadmundi: The Garland of Saint Edmund King and Martyr*, ed. and trans. Francis Hervey (London, 1907).

Ælfric of Cerne Abbas/Eynsham. *Ælfric's Colloquy*, ed. G. M. Garmonsway (London, 1939; repr. Exeter, 1983).

Æthelweard the Chronicler. *The Chronicle of Æthelweard*, ed. and trans. Alistair Campbell (London, 1962).

Aldhelm. *The Poetic Works*, trans. Michael Lapidge and James Rosier (Cambridge, 1985/2009).

Aldhelm. *The Prose Works*, trans. Michael Lapidge and Michael Herren (Cambridge, 1979/2009).

Alfred the Great. *King Alfred's Old English Prose Translation of the First Fifty Psalms*, ed. Patrick P. O'Neill (Cambridge, MA, 2001).

Alfred the Great. *King Alfred's West Saxon Version of Gregory's Pastoral Care*, ed. Henry Sweet. 2 vols, Early English Text Society, original series, 45 (London, 1871).

Anglo-Saxon Chronicle. *The Anglo-Saxon Chronicles*, trans. Michael J. Swanton (London, 2000).

Anglo-Saxon Chronicle, Version A. *The Anglo-Saxon Chronicle: A Collaborative Edition, Volume 3, Manuscript A*, ed. Janet Bately (Cambridge, 1986).

Anglo-Saxon Chronicle, Version B. *The Anglo-Saxon Chronicle: A Collaborative Edition, Volume 4, Manuscript B*, ed. Simon Taylor (Cambridge, 1983).

Anglo-Saxon Chronicle, Version C. *The Anglo-Saxon Chronicle: A Collaborative Edition, Volume 5, Manuscript C*, ed. Katherine O'Brien O'Keeffe (Cambridge, 2001).

Anglo-Saxon Chronicle, Version D. *The Anglo-Saxon Chronicle: A Collaborative Edition, Volume 6, Manuscript D*, ed. G. P. Cubbin (Cambridge, 1996).

Anglo-Saxon Chronicle, Version E. *The Anglo-Saxon Chronicle: A Collaborative Edition, Manuscript E*, ed. Susan Irvine (Cambridge, 2004).

Anglo-Saxon Wills, ed. and trans. Dorothy Whitelock (Cambridge, 1930).

Anlezark, Daniel, ed. *Old Testament Narratives* (Cambridge, MA, 2011).

Ashdown, Margaret, ed. and trans. *English and Norse Documents Relating to the Reign of Ethelred the Unready* (Cambridge, 1930).

B. *Vita S. Dunstani* [Life of St Dunstan]. *The Earliest Lives of St Dunstan*, ed. and trans. Michael Winterbottom and Michael Lapidge (Oxford, 2012), pp. 1–109.

The Battle of Brunanburh. A Casebook, ed. Michael Livingston (Exeter, 2011).

The Battle of Maldon, ed. E. V. Gordon (London, 1937).

The Battle of Maldon, ed. D. G. Scragg (Manchester, 1981).

The Battle of Maldon: Text and Translation, ed. and trans. Bill Griffiths (Pinner, 1993).

Bayeux Tapestry. *The Bayeux Tapestry*, ed. David M. Wilson (London, 2004).

Bede. *Bede's Ecclesiastical History of the English People*, ed. and trans. Bertram Colgrave and R. A. B. Mynors (Oxford, 1969).

Bede, Old English. *The Old English Version of Bede's Ecclesiastical History of the English People*, ed. T. Miller, Early English Text Society, original series 95–6, 110–11 (London, 1890–8).

Beowulf. *Klaeber's Beowulf and the Fight at Finnsburg*, ed. F. Klaeber, 4th edn, revised by R. D. Fulk, Robert E. Bjork and John D. Niles (Toronto, 2008).

Beowulf, trans. Michael Alexander (Harmondsworth, 1973).

Beowulf, trans. Seamus Heaney (London, 2000).

Beowulf. *Beowulf: A Translation and Commentary, together with Sellic Spell*, trans. J. R. R. Tolkien, ed. Christopher Tolkien (London, 2014).

Birch, Walter de Gray. *Cartularium Saxonicum*, 3 vols (London, 1885–1899).

Bjork, Robert E., ed. *Old English Shorter Poems, Volume II: Wisdom and Lyric* (Cambridge, MA, 2014).

Boethius. *The Old English Boethius: An Edition of the Old English Versions of Boethius's De Consolatione Philosophae*, 2 vols, ed. Malcolm Godden and Susan Irvine (Oxford, 2009).

Boethius, Old English. *The Old English Boethius: With Verse Prologues and Epilogues Associated with King Alfred*, ed. and trans. Susan Irvine, and Malcolm R. Godden (Cambridge, MA and London, 2012).

The Book of Ely. Liber Eliensis: A History of the Isle of Ely, trans. Janet Fairweather (Woodbridge, 2005).

Bradley, S. A. J., trans. *Anglo-Saxon Poetry* (London, 1982).

Braune, W., K. Helm and E. A. Ebbinghaus, eds. *Althochdeutsches Lesebuch*, 17th edn (Tübingen, 1994).

Byrhtferth of Ramsey, *The Life of St Oswald*. In *The Lives of St Oswald and St Ecgwine*, ed. and trans. Michael Lapidge (Oxford, 2009), pp. 1–203.

Charters of Abingdon Abbey, ed. S. E. Kelly, 2 vols (Oxford, 2000–2001).

Charters of Christ Church Canterbury, ed. Nicholas P. Brooks and Susan E. Kelly, 2 vols (Oxford, 2013).

Clayton, Mary, ed. *Old English Poems of Christ and His Saints* (Cambridge, MA, 2013).

Crawford Collection. *The Crawford Collection of Early Charters and Documents*, ed. A. S. Napier and W. H. Stevenson (Oxford, 1895).

Cynewulf. *The Old English Poems of Cynewulf*, ed. Robert E. Bjork (Cambridge, MA and London, 2013).

Domesday: A Complete Translation, ed. Ann Williams and G. H. Martin (London, 2002).

Exeter Book. *The Exeter Anthology of Old English Poetry: An Edition of Exeter Dean and Chapter Manuscript 3501*, ed. Bernard J. Muir, 2nd edn (Exeter, 2000).

Exeter Book, ed. George Philip Krapp and Elliot Van Kirk Dobbie, The Anglo-Saxon Poetic Records 3 (New York, 1936).

Guthlac. *The Old English Prose Life of Guthlac*, ed. P. Gonser, *Das angelsächsische Prosa-Leben des heiligen Guthlac* (Heidelberg, 1909).

Hamer, Richard F. S., ed. and trans. *A Choice of Anglo-Saxon Verse* (London, 2006).

The Heliand: The Saxon Gospel, trans. Ronald G. Murphy (New York, 1992).

Heliand: Text and Commentary, ed. James E. Cathey (Morgantown, 2002).

Heliand, nebst den Bruchstücken der altsächsischen Genesis, ed. Moritz Heyne (Paderborn, 1905).

Jones, Christopher. *Old English Shorter Poems, Volume I: Religious and Didactic* (Cambridge, MA and London, 2013).

Liebermann, Felix, ed. *Die Gesetze der Angelsachsen* (Halle, 1903–16).

Malory, Thomas. *Le Morte Darthur*, ed. Eugene Vinaver, *The Works of Sir Thomas Malory*, revised P. J. C. Field, 3 vols (Oxford, 1990).

McKillop, Menzies. *The Battle of Maldon: A Play for Radio* (London, 1991).

Ohlgren, Thomas, ed. *Anglo-Saxon Textual Illustration. Photographs of Sixteen Manuscripts with Descriptions and Index* (Kalamazoo, 1992).

Oswald, Alice. *Memorial* (London, 2011).

Pope, John C., ed. *Eight Old English Poems*, 3rd edn, revised by R. D. Fulk (New York and London, 2001).

Prudentius. *Psychomachia*, in *The Psychomachia of Prudentius: Text, Commentary and Glossary*, ed. Aaron Pelltari (Oklahoma, 2019).

Ramsey Chronicle. *Chronicon Abbatiae Rameseiensis*, ed. W. D. Macray (London, 1886).

Regius Psalter. Der *altenglische Regius Psalter* [*The Old English Regius Psalter*], ed. Fritz Roeder (Halle, 1904).

Robertson, A. J., ed. and trans. *Anglo-Saxon Charters* (Cambridge, 1939).

Robertson, A. J., ed. and trans. *The Laws of the Kings of England from Edmund to Henry I* (Cambridge, 1925).

St Margaret. The Old English Lives of St. Margaret, ed. Mary Clayton and Hugh Magennis (Cambridge, 1994).

Thorpe, Benjamin, ed. *Diplomatarium Anglicum ævi Saxonici* (London, 1865).

Treharne, Elaine, ed. and trans. *Old and Middle English c.890-c.1450: An Anthology*, 3rd edn (Oxford, 2010).

Utrecht Psalter. *The Utrecht Psalter in Medieval Art: Picturing the Psalms of David*, ed. Koert van der Horst, et al. (Utrecht, 1996).

Vercelli Book, ed. George Phillip Krapp, Anglo-Saxon Poetic Records 2 (New York, 1932).

The Vercelli Homilies and Related Texts, ed. Donald G. Scragg, Early English Text Society, original series 300 (London, 1992).

Whitelock, Dorothy, trans. *English Historical Documents I: c. 500–1042*, 2nd edn (London, 1979).

Wulfstan of Winchester. *The Life of St Æthelwold*, ed. and trans. Michael Lapidge and Michael Winterbottom (Oxford, 1991).

Wulfstan of York. *The Homilies of Wulfstan*, ed. Dorothy Bethurum (Oxford, 1957).

Secondary literature

Anderson, Earl R. '*The Battle of Maldon*: A Reappraisal of Possible Sources, Date and Theme', in P. R Brown, G. R. Crampton and Fred C. Robinson, eds, *Modes of Interpretation in Old English Literature* (Toronto, 1986), pp. 247–72.

Andersson, Theodore. 'The Viking Policy of Ethelred the Unready', *Scandinavian Studies* 59 (1987): 284–95.

Ashe, Laura. *Conquest and Transformation: The Oxford English Literary History, Volume I, 1000–1350* (Oxford, 2017).

Atherton, Mark. *Complete Old English*, 3rd edn (London, 2019).

Atherton, Mark. 'The Image of the Temple in the *Psychomachia* and late Anglo-Saxon literature', *Bulletin of the John Rylands University Library of Manchester* 79 (1997): 263–85.

Atherton, Mark. *The Making of England: A New History of the Anglo-Saxon World* (London, 2017).

Baxter, Stephen. *The Earls of Mercia*, (Oxford, 2007).

Bostock, J. Knight. *A Handbook on Old High German Literature*, 2nd edn (Oxford, 1976).

Bowman, Mary R. 'Refining the Gold: Tolkien, *The Battle of Maldon*, and the Northern Theory of Courage', *Tolkien Studies* 7 (2010): 91–115.

Brooks, Nicholas. 'Treason in Essex in the 990s: The Case of Æthelric of Bocking', in Gale Owen-Crocker and Brian W. Schneider, eds, *Royal Authority in Anglo-Saxon England*, BAR British Series 584 (Oxford, 2013), pp. 17–27.

Brooks, Nicholas. 'Weapons and Armour', in Donald Scragg, ed., *The Battle of Maldon, AD 991* (Oxford, 1991), pp. 208–19.

Brooks, Nicholas and Catherine Cubitt, eds. *Oswald of Worcester: Life and Influence* (Leicester, 1996).

Burrow, J. A. *The Poetry of Praise* (Cambridge, 2008).

Busse, W. G. and R. Holtei. '*The Battle of Maldon*: A Historical, Heroic and Political Poem', *Neophilologus* 65 (1981): 614–21; repr. in Katherine O'Brien O'Keeffe, ed., *Old English Shorter Poems: Basic Readings* (New York, 1994), pp. 185–97.

Bzdyl, D. G., 'Prayer in Old English Narrative', *Medium Ævum* 51 (1982): 135–51.

Cameron, Angus, Ashley Crandell Amos, Antonette diPaolo Healey, eds. *Dictionary of Old English: A to I online* (Toronto, 2018).

Campbell, James. 'England, c.991', in Janet Cooper, ed., *The Battle of Maldon: Fiction and Fact* (London and Rio Grande, 1993), pp. 1–17.

Campbell, Robin. *Byrhtnoth and the Battle of Maldon* (Kibworth Beauchamp, 2016).

Clark, Cecily. 'On Dating *The Battle of Maldon*: Certain Evidence Reviewed', *Nottingham Medieval Studies* 27 (1983): 1–22.

Clark, Cecily. 'The Narrative Mode of *The Anglo-Saxon Chronicle* Before the Conquest', in Peter Clemoes and Kathleen Hughes, eds, *England Before the Conquest: Studies in Primary Sources Presented to Dorothy Whitelock* (Cambridge, 1971), pp. 215–35.

Clark, George. '*The Battle of Maldon*: A Heroic Poem', *Speculum* 43 (1968): 52–71.

Clark, George. 'The Hero of *Maldon*: Vir Pius et Strenuus', *Speculum* 54 (1979): 257–82.

Clarke, Catherine A. M. *Literary Landscapes and the Idea of England, 700–1400* (Cambridge, 2006).

Cooper, Janet, ed. *The Battle of Maldon: Fiction and Fact* (London and Rio Grande, 1993).

Cross, J. E. 'Oswald and Byrhtnoth – A Christian Saint and A Hero who is Christian', *English Studies* 46 (1965): 93–109.

Crystal, David. *The Cambridge Encyclopaedia of the English Language*, 3rd edn (Cambridge, 2019).

Damon, John Edward. 'Advisors for Peace in the Reign of Æthelred Unræd', in Diane Wolfthal, ed., *Peace and Negotiation: Strategies for Coexistence in the Middle Ages and the Renaissance* (Turnhout, 2000), pp. 57–78.

Dance, Richard. '"þær wearð hream ahafen": A Note on Old English Spelling and the Sound of *The Battle of Maldon*', in Hugh Magennis and Jonathan Wilcox, eds, *The Power of Words: Anglo-Saxon Studies Presented to Donald G. Scragg on His Seventieth Birthday* (Morgantown, 2006), pp. 278–317.

Danet, B. and B. Bogoch. 'From Oral Ceremony to Written Document: The Transitional Language of Anglo-Saxon Wills', *Language and Communication* 12 (1992): 95–122.

Davies, Craig. 'Cultural Historicity in *The Battle of Maldon*', *Philological Quarterly* 78 (1999): 151–69.

Doane, A. N. 'Legend, History and Artifice in "The Battle of Maldon"', *Viator* 9 (1978): 39–66.

Dodwell, C. R. *Anglo-Saxon Art* (Manchester, 1982).

Dumitrescu, Irina. *The Experience of Education in Anglo-Saxon Literature* (Cambridge, 2018).

Elliott, Ralph W. V. 'Byrhtnoth and Hildebrand: A Study in Heroic Technique', *Comparative Literature* 14 (1962): 53–70.

Finch, Ronald G. *Heroes in Germany: Ancient and Modern* (Belfast, 1971).

Freeman, Edward A. *The History of the Norman Conquest of England, its Causes and Results*, vol. I (Oxford, 1867).

Frese, Dolores Warwick. 'Poetic Prowess in *Brunanburh* and *Maldon*: Winning, Losing, and Literary Outcome', in P. R. Brown, G. R. Crampton and Fred C. Robinson, eds, *Modes of Interpretation in Old English Literature* (Toronto, 1986), pp. 83–99.

Frye, Northrop. *Anatomy of Criticism: Four Essays* (Princeton, 1957).

Geertz, Clifford. 'Thick Description: Toward an Interpretive Theory of Culture', in his *The Interpretation of Cultures: Selected Essays* (New York, 1973), pp. 3–30.

Gelling, Margaret. *Place-names in the Landscape: The Geographical Roots of Britain's Place-Names* (London, 1984).

Gelling, Margaret and Ann Cole. *The Landscape of Place-names*, new edn (Donington, 2014).

Gillingham, John. 'Chronicles and Coins as Evidence for Levels of Tribute and Taxation in Late Tenth- and Early Eleventh-Century England', *English Historical Review* 105 (1990): 939–50.

Gillingham, John. '"The Most Precious Jewel in the English Crown": Levels of Danegeld and Heregeld in the Early Eleventh Century', *English Historical Review* 104 (1989): 373–84.

Gneuss, Helmut. '*The Battle of Maldon* 89: Byrhtnoth's *ofermod* Once Again', *Studies in Philology* 73 (1976): 117–37; repr. in O'Keeffe, ed., *Basic Readings*, pp. 149–72.

Gneuss, Helmut. 'Die *Battle of Maldon* als historisches und literarisches Zeugnis', *Bayerische Akademie der Wissenschaften, Phil.-Hist. Klasse, Sitzungsberichte* 5 (1976): 3–68.

Gordon, E. V. 'The Date of Æthelred's Treaty with the Vikings: Olaf Tryggvason and the Battle of Maldon', *The Modern Language Review* 32 (1937): 24–32.

Gretsch, Mechthild. *The Intellectual Foundations of the English Benedictine Reform* (Cambridge, 1999).

Griffith, M. S. 'Alliterative Licence and Proper Names in *Maldon*', in M. J. Toswell, ed., *Prosody and Poetics in the Early Middle Ages: Essays in Honour of C.B. Hieatt* (Toronto and London, 1995), pp. 60–79.

Griffith, M. S. 'The Battle of Maldon; the Guile of the Vikings Explained', *Notes and Queries* 63, no. 2 (June 2016): 180–6.

Grybauskas, Peter. 'Dialogic War: From the *Battle of Maldon* to the War of the Ring', *Mythlore: A Journal of J. R. R. Tolkien, C. S. Lewis, Charles Williams, and Mythopoeic Literature* 29, no. 3 (2011): article 5.

Harris, Joseph. 'Love and Death in the *Männerbund*: An Essay with Special Reference to the *Bjarkamál* and *The Battle of Maldon*', in Helen Damico and John Leyerle, eds, *Heroic Poetry in the Anglo-Saxon Period: Studies in Honor of Jess B. Bessinger, Jr.* (Kalamazoo, 1993), pp. 77–114; repr. in Susan E. Deskis and Thomas D. Hill, eds,

'*Speak Useful Words or Say Nothing': Old Norse Studies by Joseph Harris* (Ithaca, 2008), pp. 287–317.

Harris, Stephen. *Race and Ethnicity in Anglo-Saxon England* (New York, 2003).

Hart, Cyril. *The Danelaw* (London, 1992).

Hill, Thomas D. 'History and Heroic Ethic in *Maldon*', *Neophilologus* 54 (1970): 291–6.

Honegger, Thomas. 'The Homecoming of Beorhtnoth: Philology and the Literary Muse', *Tolkien Studies* 4 (2007): 189–99.

Irving Jr., E. B. 'The Heroic Style in *The Battle of Maldon*', *Studies in Philology* 58 (1961): 457–67.

Jayakumar, Sashi. 'Eadwig and Edgar: Politics, Propaganda, Faction', in Donald Scragg, ed., *Edgar, King of the English, 959–975* (Woodbridge, 2008), pp. 83–103.

Kabir, Ananya Jahanara. *Paradise, Death and Doomsday in Anglo-Saxon Literature* (Cambridge, 2001).

Kapelle, William E. *The Norman Conquest of the North: The Region and its Transformation, 1000–1135* (Chapel Hill, 1979).

Karkov, Catherine E. *The Ruler Portraits of Anglo-Saxon England* (Woodbridge, 2004).

Kelly, Susan. 'Anglo-Saxon Lay Society and the Written Word', in R. M. Liuzza, ed., *Old English Literature. Critical Essays* (New Haven and London, 2002), pp. 23–50; originally published in Rosamond McKitterick, ed., *The Uses of Literacy in Early Medieval Europe* (Cambridge, 1990), pp. 39–62.

Kennedy, Alan. 'Law and Litigation in the *Libellus Æthelwoldi Episcopi*', *Anglo-Saxon England* 14 (1995): 131–83.

Keynes, Simon. 'The Declining Reputation of Æthelred the Unready' (1978), rev. and repr. in David Pelteret, ed., *Anglo-Saxon History: Basic Readings* (New York, 2000), pp. 157–90.

Keynes, Simon. 'The Declining Reputation of King Ethelred the Unready', in David Hill, ed., *Ethelred the Unready*, B.A.R. British Series 59 (Oxford, 1978), pp. 227–53.

Keynes, Simon. *The Diplomas of King Ethelred 'the Unready' 978–1016: A Study in their Use as Historical Evidence* (Cambridge, 1980).

Keynes, Simon. 'Ely Abbey, 672–1109', in Peter Meadows and Nigel Ramsay, eds, *A History of Ely Cathedral* (Woodbridge, 2003), pp. 3–58.

Konshuh, Courtney, '*Anræd* in their *Unræd*: The Æthelredian Annals (983–1016) and their Presentation of King and Advisors', *English Studies* 97 (2016): 140–62.

Kuhn, Hans. 'Die Grenzen der germanischen Gefolgschaft', *Zeitschrift der Savigny-Stiftung für Rechtsgeschichte: Germanistische Abteilung* 73 (1956): 1–83.

Laborde, E. D. 'The Site of the Battle of Maldon', *English Historical Review* 40 (1925): 161–73.

Lapidge, Michael, John Blair, Simon Keynes and Donald Scragg, eds. *The Wiley Blackwell Encyclopedia of Anglo-Saxon England*, 2nd edn (Oxford, 2014).

Lavelle, Ryan. *Alfred's Wars: Sources and Interpretations of Anglo-Saxon Warfare in the Viking Age* (Woodbridge, 2010).

Lawson, M. K. 'The Collection of Danegeld and Heregeld in the Reigns of Æthelred II and Cnut', *English Historical Review* 99 (1984): 721–38.

Lawson, M. K. 'Danegeld and Heregeld Once More', *English Historical Review* 105 (1990): 951–61.

Lawson, M. K. '"Those Stories Look True": Levels of Taxation in the Reigns of Æthelred II and Cnut', *English Historical Review* 104 (1989): 385–406.

Locherbie-Cameron, Margaret A. L., 'Ælfwine's Kinsmen and *The Battle of Maldon*', *Notes & Queries*, n.s. 25 (1978): 486–7.

Locherbie-Cameron, Margaret A. L. 'Byrhtnoth and his Family', in D. G. Scragg, ed., *The Battle of Maldon, AD 991* (Oxford, 1991), pp. 253–62.

Locherbie-Cameron, Margaret A. L. 'Byrhtnoth's Noble Companion and his Sister's Son', *Medium Ævum* 57 (1988): 159–71.

Locherbie-Cameron, Margaret A. L. 'The Men Named in the Poem', in D. G. Scragg, ed., *The Battle of Maldon, AD 991* (Oxford, 1991), pp. 238–49.

Loyn, Henry. 'The Hundred in England in the Tenth and Early Eleventh Centuries', in his *Society and Peoples: Studies in the History of England and Wales, c. 600–1200* (London, 1992), pp. 111–34.

Macdonald, Helen. *H is for Hawk* (London, 2014).

Macrae-Gibson, O. D. 'How Historical Is *The Battle of Maldon*?' *Medium Aevum* 39 (1970): 89–107.

Magoun, Francis Peabody Jr. 'The Oral-Formulaic Character of Anglo-Saxon Narrative Poetry', *Speculum* 28 (1953): 446–67.

Maitland, F. W. *Domesday Book and Beyond: Three Essays in the Early History of England*, new edition with foreword by J. C. Holt (Cambridge, 1987).

McBrine, Patrick. *Biblical Epics in Late Antiquity and Anglo-Saxon England: divina in laude voluntas* (Toronto and London, 2017).

Molyneaux, George. *The Formation of the English Kingdom in the Tenth Century* (Oxford, 2015).

Morgan, J. O. *At Maldon* (London, 2013).

Morgan, Philip. 'The Naming of Medieval Battlefields', in D. Dunn, ed., *War and Society in Medieval and Early Modern Britain* (Liverpool, 2000), pp. 34–52.

Neidorf, Leonard. 'II Æthelred and the Politics of The Battle of Maldon', *Journal of English and Germanic Philology* 111, no. 4 (2012): 451–73.

Niles, John D. '*Brunanburh*, *Maldon*, and the Critics', in his *Old English Literature: A Guide to Criticism with Selected Readings* (Oxford, Malden and Chichester, 2016), pp. 142–9.

Niles, John D. '*Maldon* and Mythopoesis', *Mediaevalia* 17 (1994): 89–121; repr. in R. M. Liuzza, ed., *Old English Literature: Critical Essays* (New Haven, 2002), pp. 445–74; repr. with an excursus and response in J. D. Niles, *Old English Heroic Poems and the Social Life of Texts* (Turnhout, 2007), pp. 203–36.

Niles, John D. 'Orality', in his *Old English Literature: A Guide to Criticism with Selected Readings* (Oxford, Malden and Chichester, 2016), pp. 112–35.

North, Richard. *Pagan Words and Christian Meanings* (Amsterdam, 1991).

Oggins, Robin S. *The Kings and their Hawks: Falconry in Medieval England* (New Haven, 2004).

Orchard, Andy. 'Oral Tradition', in Katherine O'Brien O'Keeffe, ed., *Reading Old English Texts* (Cambridge, 1997), pp. 101–23.

Parks, Ward. 'The Traditional Narrator and the "I heard" Formulas in Old English Poetry', *Anglo-Saxon England* 16 (1987): 45–66.

Pascual, Rafael. 'A Possible Emendation in *Beowulf* 1042a', *Notes and Queries* 66, no. 2 (2019): 166–8.

Paz, James. *Nonhuman Voices in Anglo-Saxon Literature and Material Culture* (Manchester, 2017).

Petty, George and Susan Petty. 'A Geological Reconstruction of the Site of the Battle of Maldon', in Janet Cooper, ed., *Battle of Maldon: Fiction and Fact* (London and Rio Grande, 1993), pp. 159–69.

Pewsey, Stephen and Andrew Brooks. *East Saxon Heritage: An Essex Gazetteer* (Stroud, 1993).

Phillips, Helen. 'The Order of Words and Patterns of Opposition in *The Battle of Maldon*', *Neophilologus* 81 (1997): 117–28.

Pinner, Rebecca. *The Cult of St Edmund in Medieval East Anglia* (Woodbridge, 2015).

Ostberg, K., 'The *Ludwigslied* in the Context of Communication between the Continent and Anglo-Saxon England', *German Life and Letters* xxxviii (1985): 395–416.

Owen-Crocker, Gale. *Dress in Anglo-Saxon England*, rev. edn (*Woodbridge*, 2004).

Owen-Crocker, Gale, ed. *King Harold II and the Bayeux Tapestry* (*Woodbridge*, 2005).

Pakis, Valentine. *Perspectives on the Old Saxon Heliand* (Morgantown, 2010).

Parks, Ward. *Verbal Duelling in Heroic Narrative: The Homeric and Old English Traditions*. (Princeton, 1990).

Phillpotts, Bertha. '*The Battle of Maldon*: Some Danish Affinities', *Modern Language Review* 24 (1929): 172–90.

Porck, Thijs. *Old Age in Early Medieval England* (Woodbridge, Boydell, 2019).

Porter, David W. 'The Latin Syllabus in the Anglo-Saxon Monastic Schools', *Neophilologus* 78, no. 3 (1994): 463–82.

Priebsch, Robert. *The Heliand Manuscript, Cotton Caligula A. VII, in the British Museum: A Study* (Oxford, 1925).

Pulsiano, Philip. '"Danish Men's Words Are Worse than Murder": Viking Guile and *The Battle of Maldon*', *Journal of English and Germanic Philology* 96 (1997): 13–25.

Rahtz, Philip. *The Saxon and Medieval Palaces at Cheddar: Excavations 1960–62*, BAR Series 62 (Oxford, 1979).

Reaney, P. H. *The Place-names of Essex* (Cambridge, 1935).

Roach, Levi. *Æthelred the Unready* (New Haven and London, 2016).

Robinson, Fred C. 'Some Aspects of the *Maldon* Poet's Artistry', *Journal of English and Germanic Philology* 75 (1976): 25–40.

Robinson, Fred C. 'Some Aspects of the *Maldon* Poet's Artistry', *Journal of English and Germanic Philology* 75 (1976): 27; repr. in Robinson, *The Tomb of Beowulf and Other Essays on Old English* (Oxford, 1993).

Rogers, H. L. '*The Battle of Maldon*: David Casley's Transcript', *Notes and Queries*, new series, xxxii (1985): 147–55.

Salvador-Bello, Mercedes. 'The Edgar Panegyrics in the *Anglo-Saxon Chronicle*', in Donald Scragg, ed., *Edgar, King of the English, 959–975* (Woodbridge, 2008), pp. 252–72.

Sawyer, Peter. *Anglo-Saxon Charters: An Annotated List and Bibliography* (London, 1968).

Scattergood, John. '*The Battle of Maldon* and History', in John Scattergood, ed., *Literature and Learning in Medieval and Renaissance England: Essays Presented to Fitzroy Pyle* (Dublin, 1984), pp. 11–24.

Schwab, Ute. '*The Battle of Maldon*: A Memorial Poem', in Janet Cooper, ed., *The Battle of Maldon: Fiction and Fact* (London and Rio Grande, 1993), pp. 63–85.

Scragg, Donald, ed. *The Battle of Maldon, AD 991* (Oxford, 1991).

Sharpe, Richard. 'The Use of Writs in the Eleventh Century', *Anglo-Saxon England* 32 (2003): 247–91.

Shippey, Tom. *Old English Verse* (London, 1976).

Shippey, Tom. 'Tolkien and "The Homecoming of Beorhtnoth"', in his *Roots and Branches: Selected Papers on Tolkien* (Zollikofen, 2007), pp. 323–39.

Stafford, Pauline. 'Byrhtnoth and his Family', in Janet Cooper, ed., *The Battle of Maldon: Fiction and Fact* (London, 1993), pp. 225–35.

Stanley, Eric G. 'Old English *ÆR* Conjunction: "rather than"', *Notes & Queries* 39 (1992): 11–13.

Terasawa, Jun. *Old English Metre: An Introduction* (Toronto and London, 2011).

Thomas, Daniel. '*Landes to fela*: Geography, Topography and Place in *The Battle of Maldon*', *English Studies* 98 (2017): 781–801.

Thompson, Victoria [Victoria M. Whitworth]. *Dying and Death in Later Anglo-Saxon England* (Woodbridge, 2004).

Tolkien, J. R. R. 'The Homecoming of Beorhtnoth, Beorhthelm's Son,' in his *Tree and Leaf*, ed. Christopher Tolkien (London, 2001), pp. 121–50. Originally published in *Essays and Studies* n.s. 6 (1953): 1–18.

Tollerton, Linda. *Wills and Will-Making in Anglo-Saxon England* (York, 2011).

Toswell, M. J. *The Anglo-Saxon Psalter* (Turnhout, 2014).

Trilling, Renée. *The Aesthetics of Nostalgia: Historical Representation in Old English Verse* (Buffalo, 2009), pp. 125–74.

Tyler, Elizabeth M. *Old English Poetics: The Aesthetics of the Familiar in Anglo-Saxon England*.

van Deusen, Nancy. *The Place of the Psalms in the Intellectual Culture of the Middle Ages* (Albany, 1999).

Wareham, Andrew. *Lords and Communities in Early Medieval East Anglia* (Woodbridge, 2005).

Watts, Victor. *The Cambridge Dictionary of English Place-Names* (Cambridge, 2004).

Wieland, Gernot R. 'The Origin and Development of the Anglo-Saxon *Psychomachia* Illustrations', *Anglo-Saxon England* 26 (1997): 169–86.

Williams, Ann. 'A Bell-House and a Burh-Geat: the Lordly Residences in England before the Norman Conquest', in C. Harper-Bill and R. Harvey, eds, *Medieval Knighthood* IV (Woodbridge, 1992), pp. 221–40.

Williams, Ann. *The English and the Norman Conquest* (Woodbridge, 1995).

Williams, Ann. '*Princeps Merciorum gentis*: The Family, Career and Connections of Ælfhere, Ealdorman of Mercia, 956–83', *Anglo-Saxon England* 10 (1982): 143–72.

Woolf, Rosemary. 'The Ideal of Men Dying with their Lord in the *Germania* and in *The Battle of Maldon*', *Anglo-Saxon England* 5 (1976): 63–81; repr. in R. Woolf, *Art and Doctrine: Essays on Medieval Literature*, ed. H. O'Donoghue (London and Ronceverte, 1986), pp. 175–96.

Wormald, Patrick. 'Charters, Law and the Settlement of Disputes in Anglo-Saxon England', in Wendy Davies and Paul Fouracre, eds, *The Settlement of Disputes in Early Medieval Europe* (Cambridge, 1986), pp. 149–68; repr. in his *Legal Culture in the Early Medieval West*, pp. 289–311.

Wormald, Patrick. 'Handlist of Anglo-Saxon Lawsuits', *Anglo-Saxon England* 17 (1988): 247–81.

Wormald, Patrick. 'The Strange Affair of the Selsey Bishopric 953–63', in R. Gameson and H. Leyser, eds, *Belief and Culture in the Middle Ages: Studies Presented to Henry Mayr-Harting* (Oxford, 2001), pp. 128–41.

Yorke, Barbara. 'Æthelwold and the Politics of the Tenth Century', in B. Yorke, ed., *Bishop Æthelwold: His Career and Influence* (Woodbridge, 1988), pp. 76–8.

Index

Significant words in Old English are given in bold, while specific modern English words and concepts are in inverted commas. Page references to images are shown in italics. The letter A is followed by Æ, then B, C and so on through the usual order of the alphabet.